MY MOUNTAINS, MY PEOPLE

A note from the publisher

For almost four decades, John Parris' brief and illuminating non-fiction essays comprised his Asheville-Citizen-Times column, "Roaming the Mountains." A selection of Parris' columns was first published as a book by the same name in 1955. *My Mountains, My People* was his second book of collected columns, originally published in 1957. Both volumes quickly became popular in Western North Carolina homes but eventually went out of print. When we discovered these beloved books were no longer available, Two Hoots Press was born.

Parris wrote with the crispness of Hemingway and the grace of Thomas Wolfe. Indeed, he was a war correspondent like Hemingway and a decorated hero for his work with the Belgian underground during World War II.

The book's original publisher, Robert Bunnelle wrote, "Western North Carolina is a many storied country of wondrous mountains and valleys, so rich in beauty, in history and in folklore, that it needs a very special chronicler. Such a chronicler is John Parris, to whom nothing in the mountains of Western North Carolina is an old or jaded story…it is all new and fresh and wonderful."

As Western North Carolina rises to meet the changes and challenges of the 21st century, these stories are more vital than ever. They remain as "fresh and wonderful" as the day they were written. With every word John Parris reminds us that we are stewards of these mountains and their history.

Two Hoots Press is honored to publish this edition of *My Mountains, My People* making John Parris' beloved book available for generations to come.

        Marty Keener Cherrix   Amy Cherrix
        Publisher   Editor

MY MOUNTAINS, MY PEOPLE

By JOHN PARRIS

Bee Balm

*Native Flower Sketches
by Dorothy Luxton Parris*

CITIZEN-TIMES PUBLISHING COMPANY
ASHEVILLE, NORTH CAROLINA

Two Hoots Press
P.O. Box 15496
Asheville, North Carolina, 28813

ISBN 978-0-9975069-1-4

Copyright © 2017 by Two Hoots Press
All rights reserved
Printed and bound in the United States
First Edition, 2017
10 9 8 7 6 5 4 3 2 1

To learn more about our books, visit www.twohootspress.com.

Our books may be purchased in bulk for promotional, educational, or business use.

Please contact Two Hoots Press at twohootspress@gmail.com.

Original copyright, John Parris, 1957

Two Hoots Press

Asheville, North Carolina

DEDICATION

This book is reverently dedicated to
WILLIAM RILEY TALLENT
*My grandfather, The Old Man of a thousand tales
that chronicle the life and times of my mountains and my people.*

Foreword

A WANDERER HOME FROM A WORLD OF BIG NEWS ASSIGNments, John Parris now is a prophet with honor in his own Western North Carolina mountains.

His knowledge of the area and its people, his memory and reverence for their legends and customs, his high sense of responsibility, and his sympathetic and nostalgic style of writing have brought this to pass.

Always a good reporter, always a good craftsman to a degree that won him national acclaim for his news work abroad, he has done a much more difficult thing in achieving a very special place in the hearts of the people at home for his interpretation of Western North Carolina to itself and to others.

About three years ago, it was decided that the Asheville newspapers should be given warmer regional voice. So, John Parris, then recently returned from a tour as United Nations correspondent for The Associated Press, undertook a column called *Roaming the Mountains.*

He wrote of Western North Carolina's mountains and their people, of the bite of sourwood honey, of the crisp, blue smell of hickory smoke, of the voices of the mountain winds—in short, of many homey things.

As a result of hundreds of requests, the best of John Parris' first columns were reproduced in a book published just two years ago. It was called *Roaming the Mountains.* Overnight, it became a best-seller and established something of a record for this type of publication.

Now, on the basis of what John Parris has written since that initial volume, on the basis of renewed requests to give this work a permanant form, too, a new book is in order.

This sequel to *Roaming the Mountains* is called *My Mountains, My People*, a title that speaks for itself. It is a pleasure to publish it.

ROBERT BUNNELLE
Publisher
Asheville Citizen-Times

November 23, 1957

Contents

	Page
Foreword	vii
A Heartbeat of Molded Time	1
A Century of Golden Memories	4
Burning Logs Whisper Secrets	7
Pinchin' Times	10
The Old Grindstone	13
A Mountain Wind Blows a Long, Long Mile	16
Autumn Is Time for Apple Butter	19
Soap-Makin' Art Lives On	22
The Old Ones Know the Signs	25
King of the Square Dancers	29
Rockin' Chairs and Lemon Juleps	32
Granny Donaldson and the Cow Blanket	35
Living Symbols of a Lost Cause	38
Everlastin' Settin' Chairs	41
Encyclopedia of Superstitions	44
The Vittles Is Fittin'	47
Tiffany of the Hills	50
Loafin's Gettin' to Be a Lost Art	54
Greatest Tracker In All the Land	57
The Patient Weaver	60
Good Coffee Ought'a Have a Bite	63
Light-'N'-Hitch	66
Mighty Peart Woman With a Skillet	69
December In the Hills	72
Nothin' Like Battlin' Stick For Noise	74
In Huckleberry Time Courtin's a Pleasure	77
Artist With Ax Handles	80
How Molly Got Her Ear Bobs	83
Maybe the Ground Hog Knows	86
Last of a Shoemakin' Clan	89
Pipe-Maker to the Cherokee	93
Autumn's Rainbows Aglow	96
Lullaby of Buckeye	99
A Mountain Man and His Hound Dog	102
The Gillespie Rifle-Gun	106

	Page
Grandma's Cooking	109
She Shore Loved Her Man	112
Loggin' Days and Loggin' Ways	115
First Indian Republic	119
A Frontier Gypsy	122
Of an Angel and a Giant of a Man	127
Mountain Balladeer Singing Reporter	130
Potlikker and Corn Pone	133
And That's to Say Buncombe	136
Charming Old Lady Makes Fine Moonshine	139
October's a Mountain Prophecy	143
"Pucker Mouth"	146
A Tear For a By-Gone Era	149
Give Me a Good Corn-Cob Pipe	152
Old Chimney Monument to Past	156
Gritted Bread	159
Ballad Singers Becoming Scarce	162
When Anvil-Shootin' Rocked the Hills	165
Frog Rains Mighty Common	168
Never Cuss a Man's Hound Dog	171
June's a Whippoorwill A-Callin'	176
Rustic Imagery Disappearing	178
Old Way of Life Dying	180
No Cause to Be Lonesome	183
Johnny Holsclaw Gets a Ballad	186
Mineral of the Rainbow	190
My Mountain Woman	193
He Rightly Knowed B'ars	196
Tell Weather By Rhododendron's Curl	199
Sword of a Preacher	201
Old-Time Shape-Note Singing Still Lives	204
The Fasola Singers of Dutch Cove	208
November's Full of Hound Music	211
Day of the Rived Shingle	214
Pine Resin Made Finest Chewin'	218
Valley of Rubies	221
Missing Buckeye Causes Crisis	224
Grandma Smoked a Clay Pipe	227
Groun'-Hawg Meat's Good Eatin'	230
Whittlin', Swappin', and Throwin'	233
Now, Talk About Freezin' Weather	236
Handlebar Mustache and Shavin' Mug	239
Always Money in Galaxin'	242
There's He-Holly and She-Holly	246
Ghostly Choir of Roan Mountain	250
Of the Chimes and the Gift of Life	253

MY MOUNTAINS,
MY PEOPLE

A Heartbeat of Molded Time

Cartoogechaye

MEMORY IS A GOLDEN THING.
It's a breath of yesterday, a heartbeat of molded time.

The old ones, sitting in the twilight of their years, treasure it as a sort of Aladdin's Lamp whose magic returns them to their lost youth.

And because they do, the past becomes something more than just a faded, forgotten remnant of time.

It becomes a pageant of people and dreams.

A house emerges on yonder knoll where cows graze.

There is the sharp ring of an anvil, loud talk and louder laughter.

A log church sits back from the winding little dirt road.

A barefoot boy with a dream sits on a stool in the shade of the blacksmith shop and watches hour after hour while the smithy works at his trade.

That's the way the Old Man remembered how it was when he was a boy in the valley of Cartoogechaye.

There always will be room for nostalgia, and maybe for a slight tear it brings to the eye of an old-timer who knew this country "when."

A rainy day, gray and chill, somehow lulls a'body into a mood for recalling old things and old ways and old customs. This seems particularly true if there is a simmering fire and the rain is a steady rain.

It was that kind of a day today.

And the Old Man and his grandson were of a same mood as they talked of many things, the Old Man remembering when churches had an "Amen Corner" and the grandson remembering when a boy with a buck-handled Barlow knife figured he owned the world.

"I recollect," said the Old Man, "when folks used barley as a substitute for green coffee and dried their own apples which were as tough as leather if you tried to eat 'em raw."

Those were days when the churn, the apple-butter pot, and the venerable quilting frames were conspicuous in every mountain household.

Boneset tea was the conventional remedy for a cough, and a cup of this bitter concoction, even if it did not cure, was calculated to make the patient forget all else for a time at least.

"Bitterest thing you ever tasted," said the Old Man.

The Old Man grew up when the rocking chair was an institution.

It's vanishing now, and that's a pity and a shame, for there's something about sitting in a rocking chair that is conducive to good talk and tall talk.

Together the Old Man and his grandson swapped memories, and each recalled the eras they remembered best and the things that appealed most to them.

The grandson wondered if boys still make beanshooters out of river cane or swing on a wild grapevine.

And the Old Man talked about the circuit riding judges and preachers and when crackers were shipped in barrels and folks sat around the cracker barrel at the country store and spun yarns.

They remembered, each to his time, when . . .

Every boy was taught a-what-to-do to make his cowhide shoes winter through.

The tin dipper hung beside the overflowing water trough.

Folks carried match-safes and loaded them with big matches.

Molasses or vinegar or coal-oil were drawn from barrels in the side room of the store.

The barber shop was a gathering place for the men who liked to play checkers.

Little boys made cornstalk fiddles the same way little girls made rag dolls.

Women bought their food at the country store from bins and barrels.

Veils were called bonnet curtains.

Cake-walks and box-suppers were the vogue.

Calico was called muslin and prints were called calico.

Camphor was the steady standby.

Boys collected little metal chewing-tobacco tags.

Packs of cigarettes contained pictures and little boys collected full sets of flags, baseball players and actresses and traded among themselves.

The clock peddler made a couple trips a year.

Folks shaved with straight razors and paid a fancy price for fancy shaving mugs.

Eggs sold at ten cents a dozen and chickens at ten cents apiece.

Passenger trains ran through the mountains twice daily and the whole town turned out to meet the train.

The post office replaced the barber shop and the general store as a gathering place to visit and gossip and swap news.

The hardware store was a magazine of wonders for small boys.

Buggy whips by the dozen either stood in a corner or were racked along the wall at the general store which handled a little bit of everything.

It took six cents to buy a cone of ice cream.

The grandson remembered when folks made little pillows and stuffed them with the aromatic needles of the balsam tree and sold them to visitors.

And the Old Man remembered when covered bridges spanned the rivers and creeks in the mountains.

Together they set the echoes flying from out of the past and stirred the whispers of yesterday on this rainy day.

Holly

A Century of Golden Memories

Sylva

THE YEARS OF NEARLY A CENTURY KNOCK WITH FROSTY fingers upon his heart.

He is the last link to a pioneer past.

And this being his birthday, he could look back down the years with a memory bright as a red thread on a loom and weave a tapestry of mountain life that covers an era from homespun to nylon.

He was born in the Macon County hills the year Dan Emmett wrote "Dixie" and John Brown tried to play God.

That was in 1859, the year when folks were hearing about a man named Lincoln who was rumored to have been sired by a mountain man over in the Smokies.

It was Valentine's Day of '59 and his folks wrote his name into the family Bible. Wrote the name: William Riley Tallent.

He grew up in homespun in a time and place when this was a land of do-it-yourself-or-do-without.

He was two years old when the Civil War started down in Charleston.

And, now almost a hundred years later, he measures his fabulous memory on that conflict that divided a nation.

For he remembers, almost like it was yesterday, the men in tattered gray returning from Chickamauga and Appomattox.

His memory is a wonderful thing, sort of unbelieveable.

And the years have neither dimmed it nor confused it.

His brain is a cunning picture-maker and his faculty for detail of things long vanished is a wonder to behold.

In his time he has seen many faces and bodies, young and then old, so much life, so many patterns of death and birth.

He has known time like the cock of red dawn and time like a tired clock slowing. He has seen the horse and buggy disappear.

He has known the Golden Age, the Naughty Eighties and the Gay Nineties. He has lived through the eras of boom and bust, of want and of plenty.

He has known hoopskirts wide as the front veranda.

He remembers sun-bonneted ladies and black-shawled men.

He remembers cocked-pistol men, white-sheeted men, hoof-beats and terror in the night, and a man dangling from the end of a rope on a bridge at Franklin.

He was with Col. C. J. Harris when the first kaolin mine was opened in Western North Carolina. He was paymaster at the Hog Rock mines near Webster and paid off the men in shiny new dimes.

He saw the first automobile come to the mountains.

He talked to Ford and Edison and Firestone when they came this way in a White Steamer and helped them free their car when it got stuck in the mud below Webster.

He remembers when the whipping post and the branding iron were still the instruments of punishment for law-breakers.

He remembers when folks took down their rifles and shot the railroad train when it first came.

And he remembers the man who sat by with his rifle and said, when the first telephone and telegraph wires were stretched through the section, that it was all right to send messages over them, but he aimed to kill the first man that come traveling over his property on the thin strands.

In his time he lived by the almanac and planted his crops by the sign of the moon. He learned to tell time by the sun's shadow falling through the door on the puncheon floor.

He remembers when mountain folks had to do their trading in Walhalla and Augusta. He remembers the trips with hams and chestnuts and swapping them for salt and coffee and gunpowder.

He knew a time when matches were scarce and fetched a dollar a box and how folks kept twisted paper tapers in a box beside the hearth for lighting their pipes or else used coals from the fire.

He grew up when candles and tallow-dips furnished light.

He has known sweat and back-breaking toil.

Time was when he parched his own coffee and had a coffee-mill to grind it.

He was born in a log cabin and never knew a home other than logs until he was almost thirty.

He got his fun at corn-shuckin's, bean-stringin's, and house-raisin's. He celebrated Christmas with firing anvils and setting off hog-rifles.

He was a grown man before he got his first suit of store-bought clothes. The spinning wheel and loom and quilting bars were as familiar as bread and salt.

He has known winters when the ice was so thick in the streams that horse teams loaded with logs could cross without fear. He has knocked holes in frozen streams so there could be a baptizing.

He grew up when folks made their own shoes. He remembers the traveling dentist, the horse-and-buggy doctor, the drummer.

And now, with a century-less-two-years behind him, his mind is as fresh as a sixteen-year-old, and just as curious of the things about him.

He lives in the present and it's difficult to get him talking of the past.

But when he does, the memories are a floodtide of wonders.

Television and radio have captured his attention.

He would travel to the ends of the earth, and on a moment's notice, if he had the chance.

And, yet, he still holds to the past in words he uses and in the things he does.

He still carries three knives in his pocket. One is for whittling. One is for trading and the third is for "throwin'." Throwin' being a blind swap, sight unseen.

He has seen the last, lost, wild-rabbit of a girl civilized with a mail-order dress and his beloved mountains slashed and torn by saw and bulldozer.

The pioneer-island in the world of his youth has disappeared.

The fiddle-tunes he knew as a boy are only echoes.

He sits by the fire of a winter night and studies the leaping flames. The fire still burns as it did in his youth. The flames still dance ghosts and witches over the low, near ceiling. And perhaps as he sits there he sometimes dreams. Yet, he knows that dreaming men are haunted men. The ghosts of the past never die.

And for him they walk as bold as life through his years.

He hears them in the wind that blows outside and sees them in the flames that dance before him.

But if they worry him, he never lets on.

And for his grandson he brings them to life.

He stirs the sleepy dust of his storehouse of memories so that his grandson may know what it was like when folks wore homespun.

And when he does his eyes snap from their wrinkle-nests.

Somehow, he doesn't seem like an old man when they light up.

But, be that as it may, he's a landmark.

And his years have made him a legend, and a ballad.

Burning Logs Whisper Secrets

Sylva

THE OLD MAN SAT BEFORE THE FIRE LISTENING TO THE hiss and simmer of the burning logs which tell him their secrets on winter nights.

"They're trampin' along like a'body walkin'," he said. "They're sayin' that company's comin'. Never seen it fail when they burn like that.

"I remember when me and your grandma was first married and livin' over in Macon County how we'd be settin' around the fire and the logs would begin to talk. I'd tell her what they was a'sayin'. She'd just laugh at me but in time she come to know that a burnin' log could be counted on to tell a'body things."

For a moment he sucked on his pipe and stared into the leaping flames, his eyes far away in time and in another place. And when finally he spoke there was a hint that the memories of nearly a century were tugging for expression.

"Most folks now-a-days just don't seem to be able to read signs and listen to what goes on about 'em," he said. "They think it's all a lot of foolishness. They put all their faith in thingo'dos like machines and such.

"These new inventions is all right but folks has to go to a lot of bother to find out when it's goin' to rain or snow or be fair weather, when they'd learn a lot quicker and be a heap more right if they'd watch nature around 'em and get to know the signs.

"Why, a heap of folks borrow trouble just because they don't read nature's signs and don't listen to their elders. Then they fuss because somethin' happens to 'em.

"Now, take this fire. A feller can sit by it most of the time and tell when it's goin' to snow or rain or if there's to be peace in the family or a fuss.

"The fire's got a way of kind of sobbin' and that means rain.

And when the logs putter and make a sound like a'body walking through snow, you know snow's a'comin. When the fire roars up the chimney like it wants to get out of the house you can look out for a fuss in the family.

"Same way you can tell the weather by the way chickens act. It's a sure sign of rain when the hens gather on high ground and trim their feathers.

"I remember once when we lived over at Webster it got to gettin' dark about midafternoon one winter and all the chickens came in to roost thinkin' it was night. They huddled up closer than I'd ever seen 'em huddle before and I told all the folks that we was goin' to be in for some mighty rough weather. Pretty soon it started snowin'. Before mornin' the snow was up to the windows of the house. It snowed more than three feet. I reckon it was the biggest snow we ever had in this section.

"Another thing about weather signs is the moon. You watch the moon and you can tell what it's goin' to do. A ring around the moon means dry weather. If a new moon falls on a Saturday you can look out for 20 days of rain and wind.

"My father used to say, and it's a fact, that a wet March makes a bad harvest and a dry and cold March never begs its bread."

Over the days of nearly a century the Old Man has come to collect a lot of superstitious lore which is still prevalent to a great extent here in the mountains.

Many of the signs and beliefs and customs were born in the hills in a time when the region was isolated and a man had to keep a sharp eye out to exist.

But much of the superstitions were fetched into the hills by the first settlers who had the lore drummed into them back in Scotland and England and Ireland where today there is a healthy respect for such.

One belief I grew up with as a boy was that if snow fell so that the flakes crossed each other, slanting out of the sky in two directions to form a pattern of an X, that it would snow the same time the following day.

When I told this to a young newspaperman named E. C. Daniel in Raleigh back in 1937 he wrote a story about it, pointing out that according to an old mountaineer saying when it snowed "cross-legged" folks could expect another snow fall the same time the next day. Later in Moscow for the *New York Times*, he dropped me a post card at Christmas which read:

"It was snowing cross-legged in Moscow today, which according to an old Russian tradition means there will be snow tomorrow."

Somehow I had a feeling that the Russian censor who passed this one went straight from his office when he got off and walked into a bistro, hoisted a glass of vodka, and said, "Well, it's snowing cross-legged, so we can expect more snow tomorrow," thus adding a bit of Carolina mountain lore to the growing list of Russian "firsts" which originated in America.

I remember, too, how my mother used to make me walk softly as a boy—she still does—when she was baking a cake.

"Stay out of the kitchen," she would warn. "If you walk across the floor the cake will fall."

And when she dropped a dish cloth she was quick to say that we could expect company.

Since she is the daughter of my grandfather, she grew up learning the old superstitions and taboos.

"Mama would say," she recalls, "that to drop a fork when laying the table would break your love affair, and that if a girl turned the spout of a kettle toward the chimney or the wall she would be an old maid."

There was another one that went like this: Knife falls, gentleman calls; fork falls, lady calls; spoon falls, baby calls.

My grandmother argued, too, that if you didn't put a pinch of salt in the churn before churning the butter wouldn't come.

And when I happened to bite my tongue while eating, my mother would say: "You bit your tongue because you told a story."

My father impressed one superstition upon me which was a sort of game, and one that I still observe religiously. He said it was unlucky to see a white horse or a white mule unless you spit in your hand and stamped it with your fist. He carried a potato in his pocket as an infallible cure for rheumatism, but I have an idea he didn't put all his faith in it because he carried a buckeye, too.

When I mentioned this to my grandfather, who gets pains in his legs at night after he has retired, he said:

"Somehow, I plumb forgot about that remedy."

And he sent my mother hurrying to the kitchen for a potato.

"I'll have to get somebody to fetch me a buckeye," he said. "With a potato in my pocket and a buckeye I'll get rid of these pains in my legs."

He leaned back in his chair, took another puff at his pipe, and then the doorbell rang.

A neighbor came in and said he had come to see my grandfather.

My grandfather gave me a knowing look.

The logs on the fire simmered and hissed.

On winter nights they tell him their secrets.

Pinchin' Times

Burningtown

THE OLD MAN OF THE MOUNTAINS HAS KNOWN SOME PRETTY pinching times.

He remembers when white sugar was worth its weight in gold and calico was so dear the womenfolks fashioned their sunbonnets, and even their Sunday-go-to-meeting bonnets, out of corn-husks and wheatstraw.

He remembers when folks were forced by the pinch of necessity to use parched rye as a substitute for coffee.

He remembers when hickory ashes, hoarded from the hearth-fire, served as a makeshift for baking soda.

The Old Man has lived through times of boom and bust, times that were tolerable, and times that sorely tried a'body.

But you never would know it to look at him, except for the thin, wrinkled, withered frame that testifies to a life that spans almost a hundred years.

There is nothing of trial or tribulation in the pale blue eyes that laugh gently under eyebrows the color of hoar-frost. There are no scars of worry in the ripely mellowed merry face.

Whatever might have soiled his yesteryears no longer concerns him. For time has a way of casting a halo over the past. And when the Old Man's memory sits at the spinning-wheel, idly twisting the thread, the flow of reminiscence is of happy, gay and merry times.

It is only when the Old Man's grandson raises questions about the seamy side of his life long ago that he will ever reconstruct that part of the past.

And yet, once started, the Old Man will lose himself in the memories of hardship and heartbreak, of poverty and sadness, of less-than-tolerable times and pretty pinching times.

What he calls pretty pinching times were the war years—the

Civil War, that is—and the years of Reconstruction.

Although he was a small boy when the Civil War came, the Old Man remembers the pinch of necessity it inflicted on families like his here in the mountains.

He remembers, too, what older folks recalled, later on, of those hard times and how they coped with them.

"Folks made do with what they could lay their hands on," said the Old Man. "It was either that or starve. And a'body that's hungry will eat sole-leather if that's all there is.

" 'Course, it wasn't nearly as bad as some folks made out. A heap of folks just complained to be complainin'. A lot of it was doin' without somethin' they'd got used to havin' that they'd growed up without.

"When war come on about the first thing to go was white sugar. The Yankee blockade chased it right off the kitchen table. Folks turned to long sweetenin'. That's what we called sorghum molasses. If you let it set out in the open it would dry up and get crusty-like. Sort of like brown sugar when it gets damp and cakes up.

"Wasn't too much fuss about not havin' white sugar, 'cept by some of the womenfolks. They had to have white sugar for their cake-makin'.

"Some folks hereabouts went through the whole war and never was without white sugar. It could be got if you had the price but it come mighty dear. Wasn't many that had that kind of money.

"As a matter of fact, hard money was mighty scarce. Was that way until I was grown and more. Folks done a heap of trade by what you call barter. Or you'd work for a feller and get paid off in corn or meat or whatever he had to offer that you wanted and he had.

"I reckon just about the thing that pinched the hardest was when coffee started gettin' scarce and then just wasn't to be had at all.

"Folks tried to make what they had stretch out by mixin' it with all sorts of stuff. They'd mix a few beans of coffee with parched rye or corn-meal or chestnuts and roast it that way, thinkin' it would taste just like real coffee.

"It didn't work, not by a jugfull. It was the awfullest tastin' stuff a'body ever tried to swallow. Wasn't fit to feed the hogs.

"Finally, when there wasn't no coffee to be had, folks settled on makin' it out of parched rye sweetened with sorghum molasses. Called it rye-coffee."

The Old Man shook his head and screwed up his face at the memory.

"All the womenfolks wore bonnets back then," he said. "A few owned store-bought bonnets. But most of the womenfolks made their own. 'Specially their ever'day bonnets. Sunbonnets we called 'em. Why, your mama's still got one that belonged to your grandma. Wore it back when they had the celebration a few years ago and ever'body dressed up old-timey.

"Well, as I was sayin', when I was a'comin' on all the womenfolks wore bonnets and made 'em theirselves. What with the war and ever'thin', it got so there wasn't no fine dress goods to be had at the store. Wasn't no calico or silk and the likes.

"Somebody—I never did hear tell just who it was—figured out how to make bonnets out of corn-shucks and wheat-straw. Made 'em out of oats-straw and rye-straw, too.

"They took the shucks or the straw and wove it together like you would cloth and made the prettiest bonnets you ever saw. Made 'em by hand.

"Then the menfolks got to wearin' hats made out of the same stuff. That was when wool got scarce. One of Pa's brothers made hats. They was the finest hats you ever laid your eyes on. Wool hats, that is.

"Well, for a time there when he couldn't get no wool he had to turn to makin' 'em up out of straw. He didn't take to it much. And soon as times got straightened out he went back to makin' 'em out of wool."

The Old Man paused. He stared off into space and into time.

"You might," he said, "call them pinchin' times."

The Old Grindstone

Burningtown

THE OLD GRINDSTONE LIES ABANDONED BACK OF THE sagging old log barn.

Time and rain and the earth have stained it and begun to weave a coverlet of moss over it.

For the Old Man, standing there in the fading afternoon, the old grindstone turned a whirl of memories in his head.

It was a relic of his past, symbol of an era in the mountains when everything came the hard way.

"You hardly ever see a grindstone any more," he said. "Folks don't have a need for 'em. Farmin' ain't like it used to be. Machines do all the work now.

"But when I was a'comin' on, a'body couldn't get along without a grindstone. Back then folks on a farm had to do their own sharpenin' of their tools.

"Why, there wasn't a farm that didn't have a grindstone. Most of 'em had two or three. All the stores carried 'em and there was fellers that come around and sold 'em."

The Old Man paused. He stared at the old grindstone a moment. And then he smiled and nodded his head, as a man will when sorting out long-hoarded memories.

"Me and my brother used to run the grindstone," he said. "Took two to operate it. One had to turn it while the other done the honin'. We was always arguin' which one would do the turnin' and which one would get to hold the blade against the grindstone.

"My brother wanted to be the one to do the blade-holdin' so he could boast to Pa how good he was at sharpenin' tools and makin' 'em do their work.

"But when it come to puttin' an edge on a cuttin' tool it just seemed like I had a proper knack for it. And Pa knew it. He made it plain that was my job. It didn't set well with my brother.

"I've put many a edge to that grindstone a'layin' there. Folks all around fetched tools for me to sharpen. They was ones that was too lazy to do their own sharpenin', or else didn't have nobody to help 'em."

The Old Man recalled that the first grindstones were turned by hand. After he got married and left home and had a farm of his own, foot-pedal grindstones made their appearance.

"One feller could operate one of them," he said. "But they cost a heap of money if you bought one at the store. I made my own. Saw a store-bought one and just went home and made one like it."

The Old Man's grandson remembered when he was a boy how he used to visit his grandfather and spend hours all by himself peddling such a grindstone.

"Some folks here in the mountains made their own grindstones," said the Old Man. "They'd hunt out a proper piece of stone and make their own. But most folks bought the stones already fashioned."

In the Old Man's day, country stores in the mountains always had grindstones in stock.

The first ones were imported from England. Later they came from Nova Scotia. The first ones made in America were quarried in Ohio.

By 1840 small grindstone-making mills sprung up all across the land, particularly in the East.

With the advent of these mills, the grindstone peddler made his appearance on the American scene.

He became a familiar figure along the country roads with his horse-drawn wagon groaning under the weight of grindstones.

The grindstone peddler simply sold the stone and let the farmer make his own "grinding horse."

"We made our grinding horse out of a forked tree trunk," the Old Man recalled. "Or else we hewed a couple timbers and bolted 'em together with wooden shafts and fit the grindstone between 'em.

"You had to keep a tin of water around to splash on the wheel as it turned. I remember when I was barely high enough to a grinding horse how I'd beg Pa to let me put water on the grindstone."

The grindstone peddler gave way to the grindstone-man who went about the country with his grindstone and sharpened tools for a price right on the spot.

The grindstone-man concentrated mostly on knives and scissors.

He was particularly popular with the womenfolks, for he brought news and gossip and gave them something to talk about and remember.

"Why, I remember how we children used to look forward to the coming of the knife-and-scissors sharpener," said the Old Man's daughter. "Once a year he would come by the house and see if we needed any knives or scissors sharpened. It was always in the spring.

"The one that used to visit our house came in a wagon. Besides sharpening knives and scissors, he had things to sell. He had knives and scissors and needles and dress goods and tin-ware.

"He had bells on his horses and you could hear them jingling as he came down the road. And when he got close to the house he would call out, 'Want your scissors sharpened?' We children would hear him and run to the window and peep out. And then he would call out again and beat on a tin pan until Mama went to the door.

"Mama would invite him in and he would drive his wagon into the yard and get out his grindstone and set up under a tree in the yard or on the porch and go to work.

"It wasn't until he had finished that he would bring out the things he had to sell. That's the time we children liked best. For usually he had something among his wares that would catch our eyes, like gilt finger-rings or bracelets or clasps or cards of pearl buttons.

"But that was a long time ago."

The Old Man nodded.

"Yes," he said, "that was a long time ago."

And he looked down at the old grindstone, abandoned to time and weather and the seasons.

"Folks have got no use for 'em any more," he said. "Like a lot of the old things."

And as he turned and walked off past the sagging old log barn, his grandson bent down and tugged the old grindstone loose from the earth that held it.

A Mountain Wind Blows a Long, Long Mile

Balsam

THE FIRST COLD WINDS OF WINTER BLOWING OFF THE HIGH Balsams blow a long, long mile—and wherever you are they find you.

They blow half way around the world and beyond.

For they are the winds of home touching the strings to the heart.

And you can no more get away from them than you can run from God.

To know that this is so, you must come to know their hum and sob of a winter day and of a winter night and then be cast upon some far-away shore.

And no matter where you go or how long you stay away, the ear remembers and the heart turns homeward to the mountains when they begin blowing off the high Balsams.

Wherever you are they find you.

They hummed and sobbed this day of thanksgiving, crying for something that has no answer—like something never seen but only felt and this something touching the strings to the heart.

They went blowing to the ends of the earth.

They went seeking those far from home with whom there is an affinity quite beyond the ken of any folk that never has seen the hills look blue, or heard a midnight serenade from a pack of hounds or the thunder of grouse exploding underfoot and rocketing into a thicket, or felt the sting of wind-blown snow while crouching in a bear stand among the laurel-covered heights.

This November day being what it is, the winds of home blowing off the high Balsams blew a long, long mile.

They touched the heartstrings of a boy in Japan, another on Okinawa, one in Europe, another in the Pacific.

Each knew that the first cold winds of winter were blowing off the Balsams and seeking each of them.

They could look at the calendar and know.

And in looking at the date, the memory of the hum and sob of the winds off Balsam became, as it must for all who live and grow up under these towering peaks, a sound alive and real and forever haunting.

In Tokyo, the winds whispered to Colonel Harold Tidmarsh of Whittier and Major John Buchanan of Sylva.

They crooned to a boy in air force blue on Okinawa, William Hooper of Sylva.

They whistled about the U.S.S. *Breckenbridge* ploughing through the Pacific with Marine Pfc. Louis Eckstein of Bryson City.

Somewhere over Europe, in an air force weather squadron plane, Richard Wilson of Sylva studied his weather instruments and gauged the wind. It was a homing wind, a good wind. And he knew that it was blowing a long, long mile.

And in the Philippines, if your name is Bill Miller, the winds blowing off the Balsams half-a-world-away are as sharp and haunting as the image of some woman long beloved and never forgotten.

The years and fate, teamed with war and crisis, have made of him an exile from these mountains of his upbringing but here is his heart and his longing.

From the home of his mother in Waynesville he developed an affinity with the high Balsams whose winds filled his head with tone poems.

Later as a fledgling newspaperman in Sylva, the winds blowing off the Balsams sharpened his prose and forever bound his heart to the mountains.

When finally he left, albeit with misgivings, he went because the career he had chosen called and because he was young he had to go.

Then came the Korean War and he was called into service, cutting short a fabulous name he was beginning to make with a worldwide news service.

He slugged it out in the snow and mud of the Korean hills and in the precious rare moments from the killing and bloodletting his thoughts turned to home and the high Balsams and the winds that always were in his ears.

When the war was over, he stayed on as a correspondent for United Press. He covered the armistice negotiations at Panmunjon. Then to Tokyo and from there to Formosa as director of United Press news operations.

Always there was the promise of a visit home. But always something came up and the Balsams were as far away as ever. Then he was transferred to Manila as Philippines manager.

A few days ago, Bill Miller looked at the calendar on his desk and his thoughts turned to home and the Balsams. And then he turned to his typewriter.

"I've just been reading ROAMING THE MOUNTAINS again," he wrote. "I must say that I find one terrible personal fault with your book. It makes me so lonesome for those mountains. And now with autumn and fall—the prettiest of all times there, and the most lonely—it really gives me an emotional jolt to leaf through your book."

Any hope of a visit home, he said, seemed pretty remote. Maybe a year, maybe two.

"I hope to see you before many more autumns," he said. "I miss those mountains so much sometimes. You know, sometimes I believe the ones who just stay there in the coves and valleys—spend their lives there and die there—are the wise ones.

"Perhaps the fools are the ones who wander down into the hot, flat country and take ships and planes a thousand miles away. You can't escape it. The first, cold winds of winter blowing off Balsam blow a long, long mile—and wherever you are they find you."

The first winds of winter were blowing off the Balsams today and they were blowing a long, long mile.

They were the winds of home touching the strings to the heart.

And a'body could no more get away from them than a'body can run from God.

For wherever you are they find you.

Just ask anybody who has ever lived and grown up with their hum and sob in his ears.

They blow a long, long mile—and wherever you are they find you.

Autumn Is Time For Apple Butter

Lower Savannah

THE AUTUMN WIND WAS IN HER SNOW-WHITE HAIR THAT day. She stirred a great black iron pot over a hickory-fed fire.

The smell of the wood smoke blended with the spicy smell of apples cooking.

Grandma was making apple butter.

Into the autumn ritual had gone long hours spent in peeling and preparing the choicest apples from Grandpa's trees that went creeping up the hillside back of the house.

Grandma stirred the boiling apples with a long wooden paddle. Grandpa had made it for her. He had whittled it and shaped it out of a piece of hickory with his pocketknife. Grandma said that Grandpa could make anything he set his mind to.

"He's right smart with his hands," she would say. "Nobody makes a better churn. He's always whittlin' somethin'. Makes a nice butter-mold, too."

While Grandma was stirring away at the boiling, bubbling apples, stirring round and round, Grandpa sat whittling under the big oak. Every now and then he would lay aside his work and tend to the fire.

Grandpa looked after the fire and Grandma looked after the stirring. Between them they turned out a rich and tasty product that was considered well worth the effort.

Apple-butter-making was an all-day job in boiling alone.

A'body had to stick right with it. The fire had to be kept going and the apples had to be stirred every single minute. If a'body didn't stand right there over the iron pot and stir daylong the apples would burn and the apple butter would be ruined.

"A heap of folks ruin their apple butter by not watchin' after it like they should," Grandma used to caution her daughter-in-law. "It's not for a lazy-body or a weakly person. Why, I can take a taste of apple butter and tell right away whether it was cooked slow or fast and just how much stirrin' was done. There's nothin' worse than scorched apple butter."

Grandma was no weakling. Neither was she lazy. Nobody had ever pampered her when she was growing up. She had always been used to working. And she helped Grandpa build a home and she had three sons without a doctor. Grandpa tried to slow her down but Grandma wouldn't listen to him. She told him to stick to his fields and his whittling and she'd take care of the things a woman was born to do.

Grandpa was a little man and Grandma was a big woman. Not fat and waddling. She was tall, sort of tall like the mountains. Bigboned and tall and strong. And when she died, she just tidied up the house and walked to the bed and went to sleep. Maybe she figured that Grandpa would be lonesome for her. He had died the week before.

No, Grandma was no weakling. She was right peart at eighty. She was eighty that autumn she stood over the great black iron pot and stirred the boiling apples, the wind in her snow-white hair.

She stood there that autumn day and stirred the great iron pot over the hickory-fed fire. She had been up since break of day.

Grandpa had laid the fire under the big iron pot and touched a match to it while the dew was still on the grass. He had carried the tub of peeled and pared apples out to the fire there just above the spring-house. And he had fetched a jug of cider freshly made.

Grandma poured the cider in the big iron pot and then Grandpa dumped in the peeled and pared apples. Grandpa said it was enough that Grandma had to stand by and keep stirring the apples when they came to a boil and started bubbling and making little popping sounds. Grandpa loved Grandma.

By the time the sun was peeping over the ridge, Grandma was working away with her hickory paddle, the one Grandpa had made for her. Beside her, on a little bench Grandpa had made, sat a sack of sugar and a tin of spice.

As the apples came to a boil, Grandma stopped stirring long enough to pour the sugar and the spice into the pot. The cider had been poured in long ago. Slowly, she stirred the bubbling apples. The wood smoke got in her eyes but she kept right on stirring. As the day wore on the apple butter boiled and bubbled. It jumped up like soap bubbles and popped, and kept right on bubbling and popping. The apple butter got redder and stickier and the stirring got harder. Grandpa kept putting wood on the fire.

Now and then Grandma looked up and around her.

Her eyes took in the things about her—the ash-hopper for running the lye to make soap, the beegums sawed from hollow logs, Grandpa's cider press, the battlin'-block where she hammered the wash with a battlin'-stick.

She looked at Grandpa sitting under the big oak, his back against the bole of the tree. She saw him pause at his whittling, try the edge of his knife on his thumb and then strop it lightly on his palm. Grandma smiled and then looked back to the boiling, bubbling apples. They were now a mass of thickening butter.

And as Grandma stirred the great pot, the wind pressed the boughs of the giant oak, shaking the withered leaves.

Grandpa laid aside his knife and got to his feet. He looked off toward the west. The sun was going down, big and red in the blue haze hugging the far-off peaks.

He rubbed his leg, the right one. The one that carried the Minnie ball back from Chickamauga. The one he had cut into one spring while plowing and took out the Minnie ball that now lay on the mantle over the fireplace inside the house.

Grandpa picked up a couple of short hickory sticks and came over to where Grandma was stirring the apple butter. He started to mend the fire.

Grandma said, "It's done." And Grandpa put down the sticks.

"You can move the pot off the fire," Grandma said. "It's so thick you can most cut it with a knife."

Grandma stopped her stirring. She straightened up. She lifted the hickory paddle and gave it a couple good shakes. She held it in one hand and put a finger to it. She raked some of the apples butter onto her finger and stuck her finger in her mouth.

Grandpa watched her as she tasted it and smacked her lips.

"It'll do," she said. "Right tasty. Not a bit burnt."

Then Grandma laid the paddle down on the bench.

Grandpa bent over and lifted the pot off the dying fire with some pot-hooks. He rested a moment, then picked up the pot again and started off toward the house with it.

Grandma stretched a moment. She rubbed her hands. Then she moved off behind Grandpa.

Another autumn had come and she had made another batch of apple buttter.

When the apple butter cooled it would be hard and she would put it in cans and put the cans on the shelf in the kitchen.

She walked slowly toward the house.

The autumn wind was in her snow-white hair.

Soap-Makin' Art Lives On

Whittier

THE OLD ASH HOPPER HAS BEEN RELEGATED TO AN ANTIQUE of memory but soap-makin' still survives as a household art among mountain women.

And hog-killin' time is soap-makin' time in the hills.

The two go together like hog and hominy, and mountain women look forward from one hog-killin' season to another because they mean a new batch of soap.

When the hogs have been killed and the meat put away, then the womenfolks start making soap enough to do the family a whole year.

Of all the arts and customs handed down from one generation to another, soap-makin' has survived the longest.

And for the most part, the process has changed little since the first homemade soap was concocted out of goat's tallow and wood ashes in Italy more than 600 years ago.

The advent of commercial lye a half century ago sounded the deathknell of the old ash hopper and the use of hickory ashes.

But it didn't stop homemade soap-makin', and soap commercials have done little to woo mountain women to the store-bought variety.

If you bother to stop and inquire at mountain homes from the Blue Ridge to the Smokies, you'll find that soap-makin' is a thing still practiced on a scale that almost is unbelievable.

And a mountain woman will be quick to tell you that she is partial to homemade soap because "it seems to last longer and you can't beat it for suds and cleanin' powers, though some say it'll eat up a'body's hands, which ain't truthful."

When my mother was a girl, the ash hopper still held a prominent place back of the house, and my grandfather was mighty particular about the ashes he dumped into it to make lye.

"A feller had to use hickory ashes," he recalled, "and you had to clean out your fireplace and burn your hickory so there wouldn't be nothin' but the pure hickory ash. Some folks used oak, but hickory was the best. Everybody mostly used hickory ashes."

Recently we discovered that Mrs. Katie Gibbs here at Whittier still makes her own soap for washing clothes and dishes. She is 69 and she is mighty partial to the homemade variety.

"I've made soap the real old way," she said. "That is, with lye from the ash hopper. But for years I have used commercial lye. Not much difference in the lye. Only thing is, you can make soap faster with it. Otherwise, the making is the same as it was with my mother and her mother before her.

"Back when I was a girl everybody had an ash hopper. It usually set back of the house. And from time to time you took hickory ashes from the fireplace and put them into the hopper.

"Then when you got ready to make soap you poured water on top of the ashes and let it soak through. You had a container that caught the drippings that soaked through. That was your lye liquid.

"Soap was made by cooking lye water with grease from cracklin's.

"It would take about a half day for the water to soak through the ashes in the hopper. Sometimes you'd stick your finger under the hopper and taste the drippings. It was mighty bitter.

"You took your cracklin's and meat skins and other bits and pieces of hog meat and put them in an iron pot and poured the lye drippings over them and boiled them until they were rendered.

"While it boiled you stirred it with a stick. It was a sassafras stick. That was the only kind folks used. Some folks said it was used because it gave the soap a good smell. But that wasn't the reason at all. Sassafras was used because the bark would get stringy and fall off the stick and that would tell you that the soap had boiled enough.

"Folks always made their soap on a waning moon. It wouldn't boil over if you made it then. But to get back to the sassafras stick. As I say, when the soap got the right strength it would eat the bark right off the stick. And you knew the soap was right to put away.

"It was made so thick that you could dip it out with a cup or a gourd. Lots of folks had a gourd that they called a soap-gourd and never used it for anything else except to dip up soap.

"The soap was sometimes stored in jars but more often you had a soap trough which set in the corner of the house outside.

The soap trough was made out of a poplar log. It was cut in the spring when the sap was up. That was so the bark would slip whole off the log. Then the log was scooped out, sort of like the Indians made canoes. They would hold 10 or 12 gallons. The bark was used as a sort of lid or cover and was put over the trough when it was filled with soap. That was to protect it from the rain and the snow.

"You couldn't make hard soap back then. It was soft and was called soft soap. Only when commercial lye came in was soap made hard enough that you could cut it up in blocks and pack it away. I've heard, however, that if you put salt in with ash lye it would cause the soap to harden till it could be cut with a knife, but I never did try that.

"The way I make soap now is with commercial lye, and I make it right on my stove back there in the kitchen. It doesn't take long at all, not like it did when you had to use hickory ashes and boil it in an iron pot outside.

"I make my soap out of clean and nice grease. I mix up my lye in water and start it to boiling. You have to stir it fast when you use commercial lye. You have to get up and move. If you don't it will get hard before you know and you can't take it up. It gets hard enough to dip up in about five minutes after it starts to boiling.

"My husband usually makes me a box about six feet long and about six inches wide and three inches deep. I pour out my soap in that and let it mold and then cut it up into cakes about six inches long and three or four inches wide. Makes a nice cake of soap.

"When I've got it all cut into blocks I pack it in some of this new kind of paper. It keeps it nice and moist, not too moist, but it don't get hard. A year from now it'll be just like it was the day I made it."

Mrs. Gibbs said back in the old days when hickory ash lye was used, that folks said the drippings was strong enough to use when they were stout enough to float an egg.

"I'm right partial to homemade soap," she said. "It will sure do the work. And I reckon I'll go right on making it as long as I need it."

There are other mountain women who feel the same way that she does.

The old ash hopper may have been relegated to an antique of memory but soap-makin' still survives as a household art here in the mountains.

The Old Ones Know the Signs

Luck

THE OLD ONES ALONG SPRING CREEK PAY CLOSE ATTENTION to the signs.

Theirs is a wisdom born of living close to nature.

The sun and the moon and the stars guide their planning.

The katydid warns them of frost. The fire on their hearth prepares them for snow. The spider foretells a bad winter.

The old ones know all the signs.

Theirs is a heritage as old as the hills.

It is a thing that comes to those who live long and make use of their eyes and ears and who, through years of experience and repetition of happenings, confirm certain beliefs that others call superstition.

This heritage is not confined just to the folks along Spring Creek which winds out of the Madison County hills past Troublesome Gap and Trust and Luck.

It belongs to all the old ones, and even some of the young ones, throughout the mountains. From the high coves of the Blue Ridge in Watauga to the rolling valleys of the Nantahalas in Cherokee.

Somehow it is sort of like an unfinished coverlet on a loom. A piece of homespun picking up the threads of the philosophy of the mountain folks.

Woven into it are many threads of superstition handed down, even as mountain ballads and mountain speech, from father to son, mother to daughter, generation after generation.

The old ones are familiar with the pattern.

To know the pattern is to know what your father and grandfather and great-grandfather did or believed.

And to identify the threads of superstition is to be able to glimpse a bit of colorful whimsicality or some homespun virtue never recorded on the pages of legitimate history.

For superstitions are older than recorded history.

As my grandfather says, if folks would pay more attention to the signs they'd live a lot better.

He is 97 and he has lived right well.

Like the old ones along Spring Creek, he gives a heap of thought to the weather. Especially now that fall is here and winter is not far off.

Which is by way of paying attention to the old ones who are paying close attention to the signs.

"It's time to look sharp," said the Old Man. "Time to notice things more'n usual. Like examinin' the fur of the rabbit and the squirrel and the possum. Now if they've got a pretty thick coat, then that's a sure sign winter'll be colder than usual."

The Old Man, and all members of his clan, will give particular notice as to how the cat acts when it comes in by the fire.

"You can count on a cold snap," said the Old Man, "if the cat sits with her back to the fire."

Each year the old ones tune their hearing for the first cry of the katydid. And once it is heard they begin marking off the days on the calendar.

"You can count with a certainty that the first frost will come three months after the first katydid is heard," said the Old Man. "Never fails."

Now if the first killing frost comes late, a'body can count on a mild winter. But watch out if it comes early. Then you'd better see that the wood's stacked high.

The old ones who know pay especial attention to spiders. If there are more spiders in the house than usual, a severe winter is promised.

Then there are the "Ruling Days." They form a sort of almanac for the old ones.

"Watch the first twelve days of January," said the Old Man, "and you've got what the weather'll be like for the whole year."

Like if it rains on New Year's Day, most of the month of January will be rainy. If it snows on the second day of the New Year, February will be a snowy month. A blustery third day means a blustery March, and so on right through the twelve days, each representing a month.

A circle around the moon means rain and a circle around the sun promises fair weather.

It's a certain prediction of snow if the fire on the hearth makes a noise like walking on snow or tramping snow.

A heavy crop of mast is the sign of a severe winter.

Hang a blacksnake head down and rain will come within 48 hours.

Friday is the day to trim toenails and fingernails. Keeps away toothache.

Just finding a four-leaf clover is considered lucky in itself.

But the Old Man has a right smart piece of advice picked up from his grandmother who used to tell all the single girls in the community:

Place the four-leaf clover in the left shoe and walk on and you will meet your intended husband.

Which falls into the same category as seeing a white horse.

Now when a girl sees a white horse she should moisten the index finger of her right hand, touch her left palm, and then strike her palm with her right fist in order to seal the stamp. When she stamps 100 white horses thus, she will meet her future husband.

In making a fire, the builder should name it for a lover. If the fire burns readily from only one match, the lover is true.

The Old Man doesn't vouch for this but he's heard tell that a young girl can prove her sweetheart is true if she can hold on to a burning match until it has burned completely to the end.

Mountain women who make their own soap—and there are plenty of them still around—look to the moon to tell them when to make it.

Only when it's made in the light of the moon will the soap be firm and white.

For luck and a good smell, the soap must be stirred with a sassafras paddle.

Timber cut in the dark of the moon lasts much longer than that cut during the light of the moon.

All plants that produce fruit above ground should be planted during the light of the moon. Those that produce underground should be planted in the dark of the moon.

Never look at a new moon for the first time through the trees. It's bad luck. But a new moon seen for the first time over the left shoulder is good luck.

Many a man who has laughed at superstition has had cause to regret it if he went contrary to the moon-sign when putting shingles on his roof.

They've got to be nailed down when the moon is on the wane. Put them on during any other phase of the moon and they'll warp upward at the edges.

Next time you're on the way to make a trade, take heed if a covey of quail thunders out of the brush. It's a sign the day's not right for trading. Could be you'll end up with only a saddle.

Ever hear a hen crow? The Old Man never has either but he's got a word of warning passed on to him when he was a boy.

"The old folks used to say if you heard a hen crow you'd better kill her right then and there," he said. "Else the family was in for a heap of bad luck."

But if a rooster crows in the doorway, look out for a visitor.

To keep hawks from bothering the chickens, take a pebble from the spring and put it in the ashes of the fireplace.

"There's nothin' as lonesome as an owl a-hootin' in the night," said the Old Man. "They can keep a-body awake all night unless you know what to do.

"Your grandma could stop an owl from hootin'. She'd put an iron in the fire. Right away the owl quit hootin'. Many's the night she got out of bed to put an iron in the fire."

Such are the threads of superstition woven into the mountain way of life.

And before you laugh at them or attribute them to the religion of feeble minds, think on this:

Many superstitions go hand in hand with economy, convenience, preparedness, kindness to animals, wisdom, and the working of natural laws.

And if these odd beliefs had not been beneficial to some degree, or contained grains of common sense, then it is certain they would have been forgotten generations ago.

That is why the old ones along Spring Creek, and the old ones of all the earth, pay close attention to the signs.

King of the Square Dancers

Maggie Valley

THE FIDDLES WERE CRYING AND FEET WERE SHUFFLING. The man in the bright plaid shirt was chanting a strange sing-song rhythm.

There was lightning in his heels and a patter in his voice.

Sam Queen was putting on a show.

He is the dancingest man in all the land.

They call him the "King of the Square Dancers."

He has done more to popularize square dancing than almost any man alive.

He comes from a square dancing clan in a square dancing land.

He began square dancing when he was hoe-handle high. He began calling dances—"Now swing your partner and do-se-do" —about the time he learned how to handle a straight razor.

He danced away a fortune before he learned that square dancing was anything more than fun.

The crowning point of his career was a command performance for a king and his queen—the late King George VI and the present Queen Mother Elizabeth.

In almost 50 years of dancing, Sam figures he has shuffled, stomped and do-se-doed a distance equal to the moon and back. He's burned up enough shoe leather to keep a tannery going.

And he is still dancing, still shuffling and stomping and do-se-doing, and calling the patterns in that lilting voice that is known far and wide.

"Reckon I'll be dancing and calling when Gabriel blows his horn," Sam said recently. "It seems to run in the family."

His grandmother was still clogging at the age of 96.

"She could clog so smooth as if she had a bucket of water on her head," Sam recalled. "She sure could cut that pigeon wing and ride a short loper."

Square dancing, properly executed, is one of the most graceful dance patterns in the world.

"My father," said Sam, "was a big man but a graceful man on the dance floor. He stood six feet two inches with his boots off and weighed 240 pounds. He was as light as a feather on his feet."

When Sam was a boy here in the valley just about everybody danced.

"It was the only social habit they had where everybody could join in," he explained. "Of course, the women had their quilting bees and their bean stringings, and the men their log-rollings and barn raisings. But the square dances were a get-together for everybody, and everybody joined in the hoe-down.

"Then, as now, many square dances were got together on the spur of the moment. They started whenever couples and a fiddle happened to get together There was scarcely a family in the gap that wouldn't move the bed out of the cabin for a dance."

Often the shindig would last all night long. There's a story that when John Sevier returned to the Watauga highlands from the Indian campaign of 1788 his friends gathered and they danced a whole week.

One type of dance in pioneer days was known as a bran dance. Modern usage in an attempt to recall bygone days has mouthed this into "barn dance." Bran or sawdust was spread over the floor of a cabin to make it smooth and slick.

Then as the years rolled by and the big barns went up with their floored lofts the dancers really began to have barn dances but they still used bran on the floor.

Sam is in demand as "caller" and organizer of square dances not only here in the mountains but as far away as New York.

His Soco Gap dance team, recruited from the coves and ridges of the rugged Soco country, is one of the most famous in all the land. It is a permanent but ever-changing group, as the old-timers retire from participation.

Due to Sam Queen's persistence in keeping the old alive, square dancing has all but killed round or ballroom dancing in the mountains and it is even making strong headway in the North, particularly in the university and college towns and the resorts.

Summer visitors to the mountains become immediate converts. And every town in the mountains has its weekly square dance during the summer.

Asheville, through its annual Folk Festival, has become the square dance capital of the nation.

Although this is a land of square dancers, Sam Queen probably has executed more square dance figures than any man in the Southern Appalachians.

The people he has taught to execute these lively, exciting steps are legion.

"Square dancing is easy," Sam explained. "If you can move your feet, you can have fun. For beginners I call simple figures. And pretty soon they'll be doing Bird-In-The-Cage or any figure you want to call."

Sam knows a headful of the old rhyming or singing calls that go to not only delight the visitor but put a zing in the dance.

When the fiddle is crying and feet are shuffling and the rafters are ringing, Sam is liable to sing out:

>"*Elbow Joe and Bootblack John*
>*Kick a double shuffle and keep a hookin' on,*
>*Watch your partner. Watch her close*
>*When you meet you can double the dose,*
>*You swing Sal and I'll swing Kate*
>*And swing her again like swingin' on the gate,*
>*Then do-se-do and a little more do,*
>*Now swing her again and on you go.*"

Mountain Magnolia

Rockin' Chairs and Lemon Juleps

Flat Rock

THIS WAS ONCE THE ROCKING CHAIR CAPITAL OF THE South and the only place in the mountains where a man could mix himself a julep with home-grown lemons.

Henry Tudor Farmer, a shrewd man with a heap of gumption, had a lock on both.

He created the Flat Rock rocker, the South's answer to the Boston rocker—a right peart answer, too—and then hauled off and invented the lemon-julep, a drink that could have been our secret weapon in the Civil War if there had been a way of getting it up North.

Be that as it may, a lot of Yankees came this way after the conflict and sipped Squire Farmer's lemon-julep and decided to stay.

Nobody ever has figured out whether it was the lemon-julep or the rocking chair, or both, that decided them on buying a piece of property in these parts and settling in.

But this is a story about a rocking chair and a lemon-julep, not about Yankees, so let's get back to Squire Farmer who, among other things, built the first summer hotel for tourists and vacationists in Henderson County and the mountains.

Never a man to miss a beat on tom-toms, golden harp or sourwood fiddle to keep the name of his hostelry before the carriage trade, he parlayed the two into a crackerjack commercial that kept the Farmer Hotel jam-packed for 30 years.

Squire Farmer figured, and rightly so, that between a rocking chair and a lemon-julep there was nothing more comforting to a man.

And he was a man who believed in seeing that his guests were comfortable, which meant that they came for a week and stayed out the summer.

He did it with a rocking chair and with the lemons he grew down along the south fence.

Nobody knows where he got the lemon trees or how he come to plant them.

And nobody knows how they come to grow here in the mountains.

But grow they did, and produce they did, and they are still growing and still producing.

But there's something sad about it all.

The squire is dead, been dead since 1883, but the hotel he built back around 1850 is still standing and is still catering to folks, albeit they've changed the name to Woodfields Inn.

A few of the visitors who stop here now are told about the lemon trees and the lemons that come to ripening in July but few of them attempt to mix a lemon-julep.

Yet they sit on the overhanging gallery of the old hostelry and rock of an evening in rocking chairs which are poor copies of Squire Farmer's famous Flat Rock rocker.

The rocking chairs are lined up along the gallery like dragoons and they number into the twenties.

And of all of them there is only one—just one, mind you—of the original Flat Rock rockers turned out by Squire Farmer.

The guest who happens to occupy this rocker, even though ignorant in the lore of rockers, can't help but recognizing immediately that it is different from all the others.

This one—the Flat Rock rocker—doesn't creep.

It's made of walnut and walnut rockers just don't creep. There is a quality in walnut that causes it to cling to the floor. It will stay in place no matter how vigorous the rocking.

A contractor by trade, Squire Farmer apparently figured that he might as well furnish the homes he built here, too.

So, long before he built the Farmer Hotel he set up a furniture factory and wood working plant on Earle's Creek, on the present road leading from Flat Rock post office to the depot.

For years he made chairs, beds, tables, wardrobes, cases for grandfather clocks and other pieces. Much of the furnishings that went into the Farmer Hotel came from his factory. And some of the furnishings in Woodfields Inn today are those he turned out.

Though its origin can not now be traced, the pattern Squire Farmer used for making rocking chairs resulted in comfortable, sturdy and distinctive types, mostly made of black walnut.

He furnished the Farmer Hotel with these chairs, and they became quite popular with all the Low Country families in Western

North Carolina and it wasn't long until their fame spread throughout the South.

Orders began to pour in to Squire Farmer from all over for his distinctive type of rocking chair, which made the Boston rocker seem like a torture chamber.

For a while the Flat Rock rocker threatened to move into the North and replace the Boston rocker.

But this happened about the time the squire closed down his factory, wherein before the Civil War he used slaves to mold the chairs and after the South started clawing its way back out of devastation he used whatever help he could get, and retired to his swing on the long veranda of his hostelry and smoked cigars.

The factory just closed down and the building fell into ruin.

Nobody seemed to have a hankering for making rocking chairs.

And so the Flat Rock rocker, which really was an American institution, faded into the limbo of memories.

Long after the squire died somebody tried to reproduce them, but they couldn't match the squire's pattern, and they, too, went out of business.

And as far as we know, the only original Flat Rock rocker still in existence, still capable of rocking a-body, is right here on the gallery of Woodfields Inn, and Mrs. Joseph Clemons, the present owner, sort of watches over it like it was made of gold.

It's really a shame that the thing Squire Farmer created has been allowed to disappear.

Like the lemon-julep, which somebody should bring back.

After all, the lemon trees are still here.

But then, maybe it's just as well.

Folks now-a-days haven't got much time for rocking of an evening and lemon-julep somehow is a little out of fashion.

Even so, folks coming this way these days ought to be told that this was once the rocking chair capital of the South and the only place in the mountains where a man could mix himself a julep with home-grown lemons.

As it stands right now, I'm all ready to help rescue that vanishing American institution, the rocking chair.

But it's got to be a Flat Rock rocker.

Granny Donaldson and the Cow Blanket

Marble

GRANNY DONALDSON NEVER HAS BEEN TO ITALY, BUT she and the peasant women of the Po Valley are linked together by a rare folk art that was old when Columbus was a weaver's helper.

Out of the genius of their hands and their imaginations they fashion quaint tapestries of a sort whose symbolic figures proclaim the spirit of life.

They are among the most unusual tapestries in all the world and there is something about them that suggests a kinship to the pictographs of ancient Egypt.

There were created originally to deck the backs of Italian cows on certain festivals, a custom practiced still in Italy and one that probably grew out of the cow cult among the Greco-Roman peoples almost two thousand years ago.

But Granny Donaldson never had heard of the cow blanket with its decorations of crocheted flowers and animals when, in a moment of strange inspiration, she conceived and made the first one back in 1920.

"I can't rightly tell you how I come to make the first one," she said. "Nobody taught me or showed me. I never got the idea from anybody and I never copied one for the good reason I'd never seen one, much less heard tell of one."

She slowly shook her head, this mountain woman of 86 who can't quite understand all the stir she has created in folk art circles whose critics have described her creations as reflecting a delightfully refreshing spirit.

"Of course," she said, "you'll hear all kinds of stories about how I got started makin' what they've come to call cow-blankets but which I never have give a name except crocheted pieces. Maybe you've already heard 'em.

"Law me, such stories. Like how I seen one of them cow-blankets fetched over from Italy and run straight home to copy it. They said I was in such a hurry to get to my crochet needles I never bothered to take the path but went a-hurryin' right across the field.

"Or how I made one for my cow named Bessie and hung it on her and kept her tied out where everybody could see her a-wearin' it.

"Ain't none of 'em true. I never had a cow when I set out to make these pieces. And I never owned one named Bessie. Even if I'd had a cow wasn't nothin' to my mind that called for fittin' a blanket to her, especially one all crocheted with flowers and animals. Folks would have thought I was plumb crazy.

"But them stories got around. Spread like wild-fire, they did. Folks from away would stop by and want to see Bessie and her cow-blanket. Some of 'em acted like they was real put out when I told 'em there wasn't no cow and no cow-blanket. Reckon they thought I wasn't being sociable."

For a moment she rocked in her chair there by the fire in the living room of her daughter's home, her thin hands smoothing the folds of her dress.

"Now, I'll tell you how it was I come to make what they all call a cow-blanket," she said. "I was livin' over on Brasstown Creek. A neighbor-woman stopped by to feed her baby. When she left she forgot the baby's blanket, and that started it.

"Well, I noticed the blanket, a little thing it was, and I picked it up and sat there in the chair with it. First thing you know, I was a-rockin' and a-thinkin' and all at once it come to me that it'd be right pretty if I crocheted some chickens and cows and birds and mules and flowers and fixed 'em on the blanket.

"So I got out my needles and some wool thread and started. I made 'em as I went along. Didn't have no pattern or nothin' to go by. Just imagined 'em. About the time I got it all finished Miss Louise Pittman come by. She's connected with the Southern Highlanders Handicraft Guild. I'd been doin' some scarves and things for her. Well, she saw that blanket and she wanted it right away. Took a fit over it, she did.

"Miss Pittman put me to work makin' 'em. That was a long time ago, about 35 years. Since then I've made hundreds and they tell me they've gone all over the world. I can still make the figures, but since I've got so old I can't do no good in sewin' 'em on. My daughter here helps me now. She sews 'em on.

"I never have made no two alike, but on each one you'll find a man and a lady and a boy and girl. And a flower pot, too. Then there'll be different animals scattered over it. And I put a tree on it, too. It's the Tree of Life. They tell me all the cow-blankets in Italy have got a Tree of Life on 'em, too. But I was puttin' trees on mine before I heard tell them Italian women used it."

Granny Donaldson has been using her hands to make things all her life. As a girl she learned to weave and spin and card, but she never cared too much for weaving.

"Crochetin' was what I liked best," she said, "and that's what I settled down to doin' with a purpose. A-body can sit and crochet and talk and not be bothered."

Since 1933 she has lived here with a daughter, Mrs. C. T. Winkler, who also makes cow-blankets. And strangely enough, the only one hanging on the wall of the living room was made by Mrs. Winkler.

"We don't have one of mama's," she said. "Don't know why. Guess as fast as she makes them we turn them over to one of the craft shops and never have got around to keeping one back for ourselves."

Granny Donaldson smiled. "What's that?" she said. "Did I ever use bone needles? Of course, I have. But I don't like 'em. Don't like these plastic needles, either. Give me steel needles every time.

"My son-in-law there once made me a crochet needle out of hickory. It was bigger than the steel needles. About eight inches long. I used it to make rugs, crocheted rugs. I've still got it, and it's still a good needle."

The blankets Granny Donaldson makes really are not blankets. They are small squares about 24 inches each way and are decorative pieces to hang on a wall, not deck the back of a cow. They are a combination of crocheting and applique. The figures are made separately and sewn on a background of homespun or linen.

Strange as it may seem, the art she created has had few imitators.

For 35 years she has had the field almost to herself here in the mountains, albeit the demand is greater than her capacity for production.

"Don't rightly know," she said, "why more folks haven't picked it up. I wouldn't have minded a bit."

So if you see one of these quaint tapestries, you can be almost certain without asking that it's one created by Granny Donadlson.

And you will be reminded that she thought it up all by herself.

For you must remember that she has never been to Italy.

Yet, this is something that she and the peasant women of the Po Valley have in common.

For they are linked together by a rare folk art that was old when Columbus was a weaver's helper.

Living Symbols of a Lost Cause

Beech Gap

THE THUNDER ROLLED ASSEMBLY TO THE CLOUDS.
And because the pilgrim's mind was turned to another time, the drum-beat conjured up thoughts of old battles and of a lost cause and of the men who fought and lost.

Maybe the balsam trees, massed along the mountain slope like a bivouac of soldiers, heard the sound and recognized something familiar, for each is a living symbol of a man in Confederate gray.

There are 125,000 of them growing here, one for each North Carolinian who served in the Confederacy.

Set out more than a dozen years ago by the state division of the United Daughters of the Confederacy, the balsams stand as sort of a memorial forest here in the high reaches of Haywood County.

And come Saturday, a bronze marker will be unveiled so that posterity can know that the balsams that troop along this section of the Blue Ridge Parkway and down the slope toward Shining Rock Mountain are a monument to the state's Confederate soldiers.

This is a quiet spot, nestling in the cathedral silence of Pisgah and the Pigeon, far from the battlefields where the men the trees represent struggled in a conflict that started in the stars and ended in the gutter.

There's never been a blast of grape or canister or rifle fire here, but sometimes the clouds hover and the fog swirls in like smoke over a battlefield.

In the mind's-eye, the forest of balsam somehow takes on a reality and each tree becomes a soldier.

Perhaps someday someone will tag each tree with the name of each of the state's Confederates.

And thinking thus, the pilgrim looks out across the acres of balsam and wonders which might bear the tag engraved with the name of his grandfather who fought at Chickamauga and came home limping and ragged with a minnie ball in his thigh.

And which would bear the name of Captain James Iredell Waddell, commander of the C.S.S. *Shenandoah* which fired the last shot in the Civil War off in the Arctic Ocean on June 22, 1865, and whose Confederate flag was the last to come down.

Three of the trees represent the Singleton brothers of Haywood County—John, Anderson and Columbus—who were known as the "Three Musketeers" and were mustered out at Appomattox.

Look upon the trees and remember that these were the men of the South, the ragged, bloody South, soldiers that Napoleon and Caesar would have given their right arm for.

These were Tar Heels who were first at Bethel, farthest at Gettysburg and Chickamauga, and last at Appomattox.

They represented one-fifth of all Southern soldiers, albeit North Carolina had only about one-ninth of southern population.

They represented a number larger than the state's voting population.

More than 40,000 of them died in action, about one-fourth of all the Confederates killed in action.

They fought and bled and died in a conflict that was a rich man's war and a poor man's fight.

But they took up arms believing in their cause. They never did know they were licked, not until they died or came straggling home when it was all over.

They believed in miracles—the water into wine, a handful of fish for a multitude, the blind man who saw again, and the crucified One who rose.

But the miracle for which they prayed never came.

Look at the balsams and put a name to the trees.

The tall one there, the one standing high and straight could be Zebulon B. Vance who organized the second company to leave Buncombe County—the "Rough and Ready Grays."

Maybe the one nearby is Captain W. W. McDowell who organized the first company that left Asheville for the front.

The generals are few. And the state has boasted, with pride, that she furnished more privates and fewer generals to the Confederacy than any of her sisters.

And as you stand here and the wind whispers in the balsams there is a sort of melody. Perhaps they are singing "Lorena," the most beautiful song of the Civil War.

Then you remember the stories of how it was at Antietem. It was there that the 3rd North Carolina lost 90 per cent of its men.

Or you think of Gettysburg where Company F of the 6th North Carolina was losing 100 per cent.

These were men who fought in a war that produced iron-clads and breech-loading guns, balloons and submarines, trenches and hand grenades.

Maybe one of them was the first to cry the Rebel Yell, which was heard first at First Manassas or Bull Run and repeated in hundreds of charges throughout the war.

It could have been a fox hunter from the Carolina hills who shouted it first, for the Rebel Yell was a hunter's cry, let loose when his dog jumped a fox.

Remember these men. Trace them through the battles. They fought in the bloodiest the world has ever known. Many died. Some lived to tell their grand-children how it was at Missionary Ridge and Chickamauga and Gettysburg.

Some saw their likeness molded into bronze and placed on the town square or before the courthouse.

Many lived to attend reunions and raise their voices, never admitting that they were licked.

The balsams stand here as a monument to them, living monuments that somehow seem to come alive.

They come alive especially, or so it seems, when the thunder rolls assembly to the clouds.

Deer's Tongue

Everlastin' Settin' Chairs

Alarka

THE OLD MAN IS ONE OF THE LAST OF THE OLD-TIME CHAIR-makers of the mountains.

He has been making settin' chairs since he was nine.

And come June he will be 87 years old but you never would know it to look at him or if you tried to match him hefting an axe.

For John Elaxander Davis is as hard and tough and seasoned as the hickory from which he fashions his ever-lasting chairs.

"The chairs I make," he said, "are made to last a'body a lifetime. Make 'em out of red hickory. Bottom 'em with white oak splits.

"My father taught me to make chairs when I was a boy. Made my first one when I was nine years old. Been makin' 'em ever since."

We were sitting before a smouldering fire in the front room of his big two-story house here on Alarka. A copy of the *Ladies Birthday Almanac* hung from a peg beside the fireplace. Two oil lamps, an owl etched into each glass shade, sat on a corner table at the foot of one of the two big bedsteads.

"This here chair I'm a settin' in," he said, "I made some fifty years ago. You won't find a better settin' chair in all the country. It'll be here when I'm gone. And if folks take care of it, it'll outlive them, too. It's that kind of a chair. You'll never find a store-bought chair to equal it.

"Why, I reckon there's chairs here in these mountains that's over a hundred years old. Chairs made by folks like me who've passed on but their chairs are still around.

"Now, I want to tell you there's an art to chairmakin'. Just everybody don't know how it's done. If a feller wants to make a chair to last a life-time he's got to make it right. Can't go turnin' it out just any old way. You have to work careful with it. You've got to select the proper wood and you've got to cut it at the right time. Then you've got to be mighty careful in shapin' it up."

Davis grew up in the Smokies when this was a wilderness and a man felt right crowded if he had a neighbor closer than five miles.

He came along at a time when this was a land of do-it-yourself or do-without.

"I had to do it myself," he said. "There won't no stores where a'body could go fetch things like now-a-days. A man had to do his own clearin' and grubbin' and buildin'. Had to cut his own logs for his house. Made his own chairs and stools and tables and benches and bedsteads.

"Shucks, I grew up with a pocketknife and an axe and a drawing-knife. Them was as necessary as a rifle. Made my own barrels, too. Still do. They're better'n any you can get at the store. Just as watertight as you please. Won't warp and crack.

"But gettin' back to chairs. I always was partial to makin' chairs. Seemed to pleasure me a lot to make somethin' like that so a'body would be comfort-like.

"Of course, there's all kinds of chairs. Straight-backed and curved, and high chairs for babies and rockers for the old folks. I never put much stock in makin' anything but settin' chairs. Don't like rocking chairs. Ain't healthy. They get a man down in the back and ruin his will to get out and work.

"Me, I've got to be a'doin' things. Can't sit around the fire and think. If I ain't a'makin' chairs, I'm up there on the mountainside a'cuttin' timber. Can't work as fast as I used to, but I still manage to get a heap of timber out.

"I was out up there yesterday a'cuttin' pine. I'd chop a few minutes, stop and get my breath, and then go at it again. Reckon I got over-heated. Come down with a little cold last night and it's in my chest, makes it hard for me to talk."

His wife, America, said maybe he ought to grease his throat with a bit of pneumonia salve.

The old man said there wasn't much use. But she argued a spell and he wanted to know where the pneumonia salve was.

"Why, right there where's it's always been," she said.

"Well, I shore can't see it," he said. "Reckon my eyes is all clouded with cold, too."

Mrs. Davis reached up on the mantel and took down the salve.

"It's as big as a churn jar," she said, "and you can't see it."

The old man rubbed some of the salve on his throat and then said he reckoned he ought to have a "choker" to put in his mouth, which Mrs. Davis explained was his way of saying cough-drop.

"You sure ought to see him weave splits together when he's bottomin' a chair," she said, "It's a sight to see. He does it like no machine ever done it. Weaves 'em tight and true, pretty as you please."

The old man grinned.

"Now, 'Merika," he said, "no use you goin' on like that. You'll make this feller think nobody can make chair bottoms but me. Of course, there ain't many around now. But if a feller takes pride in his work he'll turn out a good chair bottom just like he'll turn out a good chair. Both of 'em have got to be made with the idea that they're goin' to last a life-time and more.

"Time was when I'd bottom two chairs for a quarter. And I'd get a dollar for a chair. But them was back when times was hard and money was scarce."

Be that as it may, the old man turned out enough chairs and barrels and what-not to put three sons through college at the same time.

"Education's a fine thing," he said. "I never had none but I was shore my children got one. And I ain't never had no regrets. I'm proud the way things turned out."

The old man leaned back in his chair. For a moment he closed his eyes and smiled.

"My chairmakin's been a God-send," he said. "Kept us goin' all these years, what with my farmin' and raising cattle and sheep and hogs. Reckon I've made a powerful lot of chairs. Wouldn't have no idea how many. And I'll keep right on makin' 'em as long as I can use a pocketknife and a drawin' knife."

Encyclopedia of Superstitions

Cartoogechaye

THE OLD MAN IS AN ENCYCLOPEDIA OF SUPERSTITIONS. He carries a buckeye to ward off rheumatism and totes around a pinch of salt in his coat pocket—the left one—for good luck.
 He is a careful man and he has a keen eye for all the signs, albeit he is just three years shy of a hundred.
 Sometimes he will talk willingly about his beliefs and about good luck charms and superstitions. But these are rare occasions.
 "Some things," he will say, "a-body oughtn't to talk about. Bring you bad luck if you do."
 But when he does break over, he lights up his pipe, grins a bit and tells you that a-body's got to know the signs and go by 'em if he expects to get along.
 "Now, take the jay bird," he says. "That's a bird that's been known to be a sign of bad luck as long as I can remember. When I was a boy the old folks told me the jay once sold himself to the devil for a grain of corn. Ever since then the entire jay bird tribe has been paying off the debt by carrying sticks and sand to the devil every Saturday.
 "I don't want nothin' to do with a jay bird. It's a bird of the devil. Nothin' but trouble. They start comin' in just as soon as spring things start to growin' and start their devilment."
 Other old timers consider that the jay bird is a reporter for the devil and that he makes regular trips to hell carrying a list of the sins of the people.
 Others say the jay makes visits to hell only on Fridays to take kindling, a drop of water or a grain of sand to the devil. Some say this grain of sand is part of a ransom for the souls waiting there who cannot be released until all sand visible on the surface of the earth has been carried below.
 Back when the Old Man was working he paid more attention

to signs. And there are folks today in the mountains who believe in them and swear by them.

For instance, Good Friday is always sure to find a lot of mountain farmers planting beans and other vegetables. Each succeeding crop after the first is in is also planted on a Friday.

But no other work of any kind was ever started by mountain folks on Friday. For such work begun then was sure to meet with bad luck. One belief was that a person who started a certain work on a Friday would never live to complete it.

Naturally, this observance sometimes created a great deal of inconvenience in planning.

Saturday also never was chosen as the starting time for any task that could not be finished during the day. For to carry it over into another week was to risk its never being done.

Mountain folks long have looked to the moon for guidance in planting, harvesting and other activities.

The lunar seasons, or "secret times," more than any other of the traditional customs, signs or superstitions have survived and are still being observed religiously by many a mountain family.

Crops are made or blasted according to whether they are planted in the proper time of the moon.

Light of moon must be chosen for planting all things that bear fruits above ground, while all that produce underground must be planted in the dark of the moon.

"If a feller splits his rails except in the dark of the moon," the Old Man explained, "he's sure in for a passel of trouble. You've got to split rails and shingles and boards when the moon is dark to keep 'em from warpin' and splittin' on you.

"Now if you want fence rails to keep from rottin' they've got to be laid or built when the moon is light. Boards and shingles should be put on when the horn of the new moon points down. Then they won't cup on you."

"A time for cutting trees so that the stumps and sprouts die and rot is August when the moon is dark. And white hard soap can be made only when the moon is light and just coming into full."

When it came to predicting the weather, the old timers were pretty fair prophets.

They argued that if the first day of June was fair and clear no rain would fall for 15 days. Rain on the first dog day meant rain for 40 days to come.

Rain falling when the sun was shining was a sign that witches were dancing and that rain would fall again next day.

Being a farm boy when he was growing up, the Old Man recalls his folks were forever being plagued with hawks.

"We kept a flint rock warm in the fireplace," he said, "to keep hawks from carrying off the young chickens. It worked, too.

"And another thing. If you've got a dog that you want to watch your house and let you know when things ain't right, just cut some hair from the end of his tail and bury it under the doorstep. He'll never fail to warn you when things ain't right.

"We never would take the ashes out of the fireplace on a Friday. If you did then you could expect something to be stolen from the house before the next Friday.

"Eggs should be gathered before dark. Carryin' 'em in after the sun's down or burnin' their shells in the fireplace causes the hens to quit layin'."

The Old Man puffed on his pipe a moment.

"They used to say when I was a boy that a baby mustn't be allowed to see itself in a mirror before it was six months old or else it would be in danger of dying before another six months was up. But if it did live to grow up it would be a two-faced person, never could believe a thing it said."

Yes, the Old Man is an encyclopedia of superstition.

And come Friday, he'll be particularly careful and watchful.

For besides being Friday, it also is the thirteenth.

But, then, the Old Man does tote a pinch of salt in his pocket—the left one—and that makes him immune.

The Vittles Is Fittin'

Burnsville

FOR MORE THAN A HUNDRED YEARS THE WRAY FAMILY has been setting a mighty fine table.

Folks with a penchant for putting a name to things call it fabulous.

There's really nothing like it in all the land.

Why, it's enough to make a man's eyes pop right out of his head.

A stranger wandering into the dining room of the Nu-Wray Inn is likely to gulp a couple times at the sight spread out before him and wonder if life will ever be the same again.

Presiding over this groaning table of culinary achievements is Mrs. Julia Wray, a mountain woman of 86 whose magic with the skillet has been bewitching folks since she was big enough to swing a pot over the fire.

She is white-haired and as cute as a button, hale and hearty and chipper as a school girl, albeit she fusses because she has to use a cane.

"Miss Julia" is really an institution. She's done more to make outlanders appreciate good mountain cooking than anybody from Watauga to Cherokee.

Her recipes are famous. Gourmets collect them.

When you get right down to it she is an extraordinarily good cook, although she does little herself these days.

But she rules her kitchen with a firm hand and a quick mind, passing on her know-how to those who work for her.

Yes, she's an extraordinarily good cook—something that folks have known since the horse and buggy days.

No one ever has been known to go hungry at Miss Julia's table.

As a matter of fact, a man could founder himself at her table.

Her family began setting a groaning table back in the days before young women wanted to be so thin they wouldn't cast a shadow at high noon.

The men folks, too, paid no mind to calories back then. They come along when a man was eager to build up a prosperous paunch upon which he could wear a heavy gold watch chain and charm.

The quickest way in the world to give up dieting is to sit down to Miss Julia's table.

There was a feller who used to come by every month or so who was on a diet of eggs. He had been warned by his doctor that he had to stick to it if he wanted to stay alive.

"This was a travelling man," said Miss Julia. "All he was supposed to eat at a meal was five or six eggs and some milk. Well, he'd come here and order his eggs and milk and eat them and then pitch into the other things on the table. He figured if he ate his diet first he could then eat what was before him. He just couldn't refuse my food."

Hal Boyle, who spins a column for the Associated Press and who has a tough time pushing back from the table, told Miss Julia he could sympathize with the traveling man.

A lot of other folks can, too.

Miss Julia's inn is a place of charm. It is authentically old.

The lobby comes right out of the 1890's. And the music room is an echo of the past when Grandma sat by in her rocking chair while her daughters did their courting.

What with the dining room and its fabulous table, folks drive here from all over the country to relax and view the mountains and eat three meals a day that would have had Henry The Eighth hanging on the ropes.

The guests rock on the long porch—there are 17 rocking chairs—before mealtime awaiting the sound of the old dinner bell. And once it tolls, the rush toward the dining room is on.

The food is all on the table.

This is called country style or family style.

This means that piled up platters keep coming in and you eat until you're full to the neck and you're fit to bust.

Nobody pays attention if you loosen your belt a couple notches. Everybody does it.

Guests are able to choose from this unbelievable assortment:

Chicken fried to a crisp brown in fat rendered from smoked ham, platters of sliced baked ham—country ham, that is—and baked chicken and dressing, plump lima beans, snap beans, corn on the cob, cream gravy, potatoes smothered in melted cheese, cole slaw, honey, grape and apple jelly, apple butter and apple sauce, plates of cornbread and baskets of hot biscuits.

For dessert there is homemade cake, usually chocolate layer.

Dinner is at noon. Breakfast comes along at 7:30 a.m. when the table groans under the weight of platters of fried country ham and red-eye gravy, eggs, hot biscuits, apples, jelly and honey. Supper is a duplication of dinner.

Folks who toss caution out the window and eat right hearty at Miss Julia's table pleasure her no end.

"I like to see people come in and eat with a will," she said. "I've got no patience with those who come in, take a look and turn up their noses.

"It's a pleasure to have folks who bring good appetites with them. I like to see folks eat industriously, taking second helpings."

Through all the years Miss Julia has remained true to her heritage. She has refused to have any truck with store-bought food.

She grows her own vegetables, smokes and cures her own hams.

She makes all her own preserves, jams, jellies, relishes and pickle.

Even in these days of high food costs, Miss Julia has managed to keep the price of her meals down. Breakfast is $1.50, the noon meal $2 and the evening meal $2.50, and you can eat all you want.

But back 75 years ago a man could get supper and breakfast and a night's lodging for a dollar.

"And even then," she said, "some folks kicked at the price."

But there is one thing for sure now-a-days: the dishwashers at Nu-Wray have more "take-up" dishes to wash than dinner plates.

For Miss Julia serves up homespun delicacies a'body just can't turn down.

But then, the Wray family has been setting a mighty fine table for more than a hundred years.

Tiffany of the Hills

Hawk

THEY CALL HIM THE TIFFANY OF THE HILLS. He's a wiry little mountain man of 51 with an Aladdin touch for digging precious stones from his native earth and turning them into gems of rare and sparkling beauty.

For half his years a good-sized chunk of the world has worn new ruts into the country road that leads to his humble doorstep at the head of narrow Cane Creek Valley where Lightwood Mountain and the Mine Fork Rough crowd up to Hawk Mountain.

His name is Roby Buchanan and his trademark is "Gems by Roby."

He is a remarkable man, the epitome of the Horatio Alger story.

A self-taught gem-cutter who learned his highly skilled trade through trial and error, he is recognized throughout the land as a master craftsman as well as a man blessed with a rare gift for finding beauty buried deep in the heart of rocks.

"But I'm not trying to run Tiffany or anybody else out of business," he explained. "What I'm doing is entirely different from what Tiffany is doing. I work only with precious stones found in these mountains. You know, they're the gem showcase of the world."

Roby was sitting on a stool in his unpainted weathered old shop as he talked. Tucked away among alder bushes, it once was a mill house that ground out corn meal for the folks here in the hills of Mitchell County.

"I reckon I've been interested in pretty stones all my life," he said. "When I was a boy I used to mess around the mines picking up pretty stones. I wanted to build me up a large representative collection of the gems of the mountains.

"I knew I could find all the stones I wanted but getting them cut and polished was expensive, so I got to thinking about learning to do it myself. I was about 19 then and my father was running the grist mill here. Well, he got sick and I had to take over the mill. Between grinding out corn for the neighbors I started piddling with cutting stones.

"First stone-cutting I did I tried to hold the stone in my hand and cut it. You can guess what happened. I didn't do much cutting. I tried to get a book on it and found there wasn't one.

"Well, I sat myself down and wrote about 50 letters to stone-cutters all over the country, asking them how it was done. They wrote back that cutting was a trade in itself. They said if I couldn't master it myself I'd better get into something else."

So Roby buckled down to the job of teaching himself. He worked out his own method and his own machinery. The machinery was crude but it worked.

"I made myself a gem wheel and geared it up to the mill. Fixed me a lever that I could pull so the water power could leap from the grindstones over to a contraption that turned a diamond saw.

"Three or four months after I got my rig working I made my first sale. Cut and polished a garnet and got $20 for it. I thought I had done something. A dollar would go further back then."

But Roby ruined a lot of stones. It was trial and error. And then he didn't have much time for his hobby. Seemed like folks were forever waiting for a bushel of corn meal. Folks could wait for a "pretty" stone, but a mountain man had to have his meal right then.

This went on for two or three years and then Cane Creek went on a rampage and washed away the old millrace and the wheel.

Roby didn't replace them.

He bought an electric motor for his cutting and polishing.

It marked the end of a miller and the beginning of a lapidary.

"I never ground any more meal," Roby said. "I started working at cutting and polishing stones with a purpose then. That became my business. But I cut, faced and polished my pretties for a good ten years before anybody got around to paying much attention to what I was doing."

He paused, looked around his shop for a moment at the piles of boulders studded with their precious colors.

"Tourist folks over at Linville and Burnsville and Bakersville started coming in and talking with me and leaving orders for a native emerald, a ruby, a topaz, a zircon, or aquamarine," he said. "From then on I've kept mighty busy. Turn out about five or six hundred stones a year."

The building where Roby works never was intended for anything more than a shelter for the corn mill, but that's where he started out and that's where he plies his trade.

He first takes the rough stones and cuts them into blocks on a diamond saw. Then the perfect blocks are ground into rough shapes on a carborundum wheel. Next the gem is placed in a holder, which applies the stone to the grinder for the facets.

"The more facets," he said, "the more brilliance there is in a stone. I've put as many as 900 facets on one stone but the average is only about one to two hundred given a stone."

For years Roby sold the stones uncut, but now he sells them set.

"I do the cutting and polishing," he explained. "My daughter-in-law Margerethe who's a skilled goldsmith does the designing and my boy James does the metal work and mounting.

"We make rings, pins, brooches—everything in the world in the way of jewelry. And it's all done by hand. The stuff we make is sold in jewelry stores all over, but mostly in North Carolina. Once I made up a cluster of emeralds and rubies into a brooch that a jeweler sold for $2,300."

As Roby talked, I happened to glance to the wall back of him and a penciled poster caught my eye. It read:

"We lick rocks
"We buy rocks
"We sell rocks
"But we don't throw rocks."

Roby himself collects 90 per cent of the better stones that he fashions into rare and beautiful ornaments.

He explained that rubies found in Western North Carolina have more silk in them than those found in foreign countries.

"Rubies in these mountains are rare," he said. "But you find them and when you do you've got a collector's item."

Through the years Roby has collected aquamarines, garnets, landscape agates that look like Japanese brush paintings, smoky topaz, moonstones, sunstones, rutilated quartz, rose quartz, amethysts.

What is his favorite of all native mountain stones?

"The aquamarine," he said. "It takes my eye first."

But he's partial to the rhodolite garnet, too.

"It's a mighty important gem-stone," he said. "And it's found nowhere else in the world. Now the nearest thing we have to an emerald is hiddenite. Once its been cut and polished you can't tell it from an emerald unless you study it closely under a glass, and then it's hard to differentiate.

"This here," he said, picking up a piece of rough stone, "is cynite. It's the nearest thing there is to a blue sapphire. It's found over in the Balsam Gap section of Buncombe County on the Blue Ridge Parkway. It has two hardnesses. It won't scratch one way and will the other and that makes it the hardest of all stones to cut. Only recently did I find a piece of it in gem quality and I've been looking for it for 30 years. It's a scarce stone and will bring a high price in the market."

How does it rate in value with other stones.

"I'd say it'll rate in price with the better quality aquamarine," he said.

Dusk was coming on. Roby got off his stool and began putting away a collection of rings and pins and brooches that lay sparkling out of cotton pads on his work bench.

Looking at them, it was easy to understand why they call him the Tiffany of the Hills.

Hearts A 'Bustin' With Love

Loafin's Gettin' to Be a Lost Art

Loafer's Glory

LOAFERS ARE ABOUT AS SCARCE HERE AS HEN'S TEETH. "Folks just don't seem to have no time for loafin' any more," said Charlie Burleson. "Why, it's got so they're in such a hurry to get some place they hardly take the time to say howdy,"

Charlie reckons he's about the only real honest-to-goodness loafer left in Loafer's Glory.

"Somebody's got to uphold the glory of our heritage," he said, "and I guess I'm as well fixed for the job as anybody. I don't strike a lick of work if I can help it. I'm retired. But it gets pretty lonesome when a feller has to do his loafin' all by hisself."

Now don't get the idea that Charlie is a lazy man. He isn't.

And if you think that loafing is a lazy man's occupation, Charlie will set you straight real quick.

"There's a time for loafin' and a time for work," he said. "Folks who work are the only folks who know how to loaf. Don't reckon you ever saw a lazy feller a sittin' around whittlin' or playin' checkers or spinnin' yarns.

"Loafin' is a sort of unwindin' when the crops are in and the plowin' and the hoein's been done. Saturday is loafin' day, and so's a rainy day. But you've got to have folks to loaf with."

For a moment there was a sort of wistful look in his blue eyes, and he seemed to be rummaging through his past when a man took a pride in loafing.

"Time was," he said, "when Loafer's Glory really had a glory. That was back in the days when folks made a business out of loafin'. But for the past ten or fifteen years this loafin' business has been a'slippin'.

"Why folks come a'ridin' through here now and never know they've passed through Loafer's Glory. We used to have a sign up down the road there sayin' Loafer's Glory but it either rotted and fell down or somebody tore it down and never put it back."

Charlie looked off to where the old country store used to stand, there above the bridge over Cane Creek.

"Loafer's Glory never was a big place," he said. "Just a bend in the road and thirty acres. Same as it is today. But it was a right peart community back sixty years ago when I come along.

"There was a few more people back then than there is now. But ever since my grandfather named this Loafer's Glory the population hasn't changed much. There's about five families now and a handful of loafers. Most of us are gettin' along in years and I reckon when we're gone the loafin' will go too. The young folks don't seem to take to it."

However, Charlie isn't giving up all together.

He's putting his faith in young Fred Garland who operates the general store here and who is right proud of Loafer's Glory.

"Fred's doing his best to get folks back to loafin'," he said. "He's fixin' it so a man can loaf summer and winter, just like folks hereabouts used to do when the country store was a real loafin' place.

"When my grandfather was coming on this was really Loafer's Glory. He was a farmer. Jonathan Burleson was his name. He knew how to loaf.

"My grandfather was the one that named this Loafer's Glory. Folks would gather at the country store operated by Nathan Deyton and Joe Wilson. On Saturdays and of evenings they'd sit around the store and play checkers or horseshoes and whittle and spin yarns.

"You know how a person will give something a name and how it'll stick. Well, that's how this place got to be Loafer's Glory. My grandfather hauled off one day and said this was Loafer's Glory. The name stuck. That was more than seventy years ago. It's been Loafer's Glory ever since. It used to be on all the road maps, but for some reason they took it off."

Hal Boyle, the Associated Press columnist, and I had come into Mitchell County searching for Loafer's Glory and a man who knew the story of this loafer's haven.

We found the man in Charlie Burleson who happened to wander into Fred Garland's store about the same time we did.

"Charlie and I are going to make this the Loafer's Glory it once was," said Fred, who is forty and who was born and raised in these mountains. "First thing I did when I got out of the service was to start thinking how good it would be to get back to the mountains to live, and then I got to thinking about Loafer's

Glory and figured that was the place for me.

"Well, I settled in here and built myself a store. It's going to be just like the old country store. I'm getting me a couple benches from one of the churches they're tearing down and I'm putting those benches right out in front of the store so folks can have a place to sit and whittle and do some loafin'. I'm going to furnish the whittling sticks.

"Sure, I stock whittling knives. Out of them right now but I've got a supply coming in any day now. Want to get folks back to whittling. That's almost a lost art. But whittling and loafing go together like ham and eggs."

Charlie cocked an eye at Fred and said he reckon he'd have to buy him a knife now that Fred was fixing to furnish whittlin' sticks.

"I've got a pocketknife," Charlie said, "but it's too little for whittlin'."

As a matter of fact, Charlie never has been much of a whittler.

"Just never seemed to figure it into my loafin'," he said. "I liked checkers and liked to sit around the stove and yarn. Now my father was a master whittler. He was 86 when he died back in 1947. When he died, Loafer's Glory lost its last whittler. But I reckon it's not too late for me to take it up, now that Fred's making all his plans for bringing back real loafin' to Loafer's Glory."

Greatest Tracker in All the Land
Big Tom

THIS SOMBER, BALSAM-DRAPED PEAK TOWERING AMONG the Blue Ridge sentinels stands as a monument to one of the greatest trackers that ever followed a trail.

It was named for Big Tom Wilson, a giant of a mountain man who carved out an empire with axe and rifle-gun in the most rugged land east of the Rockies.

His hunting life made him a peer of Boone and Crockett and established him in folk history as the greatest bear-hunter ever to stalk the big blacks in the wild Appalachians.

As a tracker, he followed trails through the rhododendron hells and laurel slicks that baffled hounds.

This fabulous knack for reading signs, which has become a lost art among mountain men, made him a living legend while still in his prime and tagged him with superlatives long before he set the outside world buzzing with his name back in 1857.

But the thing he did a hundred years ago this coming July nailed down for all time the claim his neighbors made for him as the greatest tracker in all the land.

For it was Big Tom Wilson who followed a 10-day-old trail through miles of rugged wilderness to find the body of Explorer Elisha Mitchell, the man that discovered the highest peak in all Eastern American and for whom it was named.

But that is another story. Right now, we want to talk about Big Tom Wilson the bearhunter, Big Tom Wilson the man, and Big Tom Wilson's mountain empire.

For there are many things you must know about him and the land before you can appreciate the story of how he discovered the body of Elisha Mitchell here in the Yancey County highlands.

From the beginning, the Wilsons were destined to become the bear-huntin'est family in all the land.

Ned Wilson came into these parts first, came with axe and rifle. He came seeking wing-room and a place where a man could live off the land, where game was plentiful and a'body could spit without hitting a neighbor.

As patriarch of the clan, Ned Wilson settled on Cane Creek shortly after the American Revolution and started a family whose name even now is synonomous with bear-hunting and bear-hunters.

Big Tom was his son.

There are some who say Big Tom was born with a rifle-gun in his hand and set up a squall three days later to go bear-huntin' with his pappy.

Be that as it may, there was the blood of the hunter in his veins and he took to the woods with as keen an eye as a man ever squinted at a bear.

He stood six-feet-two in his stocking feet. He was spare and bearded, shrewd and quick-witted. His muscles were as tough and stringy as the vines of the wild muscadine.

His empire stretched as far as the eye could see.

It was bear land. Wild and rugged, draped with the black of balsam and spruce, thick with rhododendron and laurel, nursed by fast-flowing streams that rippled with trout.

A hundred years later it would still be a bear-hunters' paradise, a 17,000-acre preserve for his grandsons and great-grandsons stretching out the line and holding tight to the distinction as the bear-huntin'est family in all the land.

As the mountain area opened up and folks from afar came to visit and to hunt, Big Tom became a guide and picked up some cash money to help support the ten children born to him and his wife Niagara Ray.

All the while, Big Tom was killing bear and learning to read signs that furnished him meat every time he took to the hills with his gun. Before he came to the day he laid aside his rifle-gun, he had 113 big blacks to his credit.

Bear-huntin' in this wild region was slavish work and a man had to know the country if he expected to come out alive.

Folks were always getting lost in the rugged reaches. Once a man got lost in the rhododendron hells for nine days before he finally found his way out. But Big Tom had the kind of eyesight and the wilderness savvy that always brought him back home.

He was such a skilled woodsman and hunter that he would leave home alone with only a handful of corn meal and his rifle. He would stay out a week, living off the game, making corn pones from the meal and water, caching his kills and returning with horses later to pick them up.

Back during Big Tom's reign, hunters came from afar in wagons or on horseback to do their bear-hunting. These hunters, then as now, stayed with the Wilsons. And when Big Tom's house overflowed, they camped nearby. Sometimes for weeks.

Once Big Tom was out in the woods without his rifle-gun or even his dogs. He treed a couple bear cubs. They became frightened and started climbing down. But Big Tom wasn't about to let 'em out of the tree. He grabbed some pine knots and struck a light to them and began waving the pine torches at the bear cubs.

Figuring he would be disgraced by allowing them to get away, he yelled: "Stop! This is Big Tom a'talkin' to ye!"

The cubs scampered back up the tree.

Back in 1870, Charles Dudley Warner of Boston came down this way and, having heard of Big Tom, decided his journey wouldn't be complete without a visit with the famous hillsman. So he spent some time in Big Tom's house.

In his diary, Warner wrote that Big Tom "weighed in the scale more than Mount Mitchell" and described him as "one of the most characteristic productions of the country."

Once Big Tom came down from his mile-high cabin to attend a banquet in Asheville of the Southern Society of New York.

They had gathered to honor the old man and the speakers, one after the other, tried to out-do themselves in extolling his deeds and qualities. Eventually, Big Tom was asked to say a few words.

He rose to his feet, looked out over the banquet hall and said: "I'm glad I seed you, because if I hadn't seed you I wouldn't have knowed you."

Long before Big Tom died, folks throughout the mountains had come to call this 6,558-foot peak "Big Tom."

But it was not until 1946 that it was officially designated "Big Tom" and so named on the maps. Government maps until then had merely referred to it as "the north fork of the Black Brothers."

Just to the south of this peak is Mount Mitchell, rising a mere 77 feet taller than the mountain named for Big Tom Wilson.

Few folks ever have explored the peak called Big Tom. It is difficult to reach. But it is a magnificent mountain, covered with a virgin balsam forest.

And it stands among the Blue Ridge sentinels as a fitting monument to a mountain man who walked tall in life and continues to walk tall in death.

For Big Tom Wilson was one of the greatest of a fabulous breed of mountain men who carved their names on the land.

The Patient Weaver

Valle Crucis

IN THE COMING ON OF A WINTER GLOAMING THE DAY RAN away swift as a weaver's shuttle.

A whimpering wind whistled down from the high peaks of the Blue Ridge and scampered through the Valley of the Cross.

It tore at the wild vines traipsing over the cabin and pushed through the crack under the wooden-hinged door and into the walled room of hand-hewn logs.

It eddied about the dead ashes of a long dead hearthfire and stirred up old ghosts and old memories.

In the fading light the gaunt frames of the two ancient looms etched dark shadows on the walls and on the puncheon floor.

And suddenly, somehow, the silent old cabin seemed to come alive. Maybe it was only the wind and the shifting shadows. Or perhaps it was only a memory, bright and alive, touching the eye and the imagination, creating the illusion of a little old lady a'settin' at the weaver's bench and trampin' the treadles of her loom.

She might have been your great-grandmother or mine, hands a-flyin' about so spry, weaving a ballad to the rhythm struck by the hum of the shuttle and the dull thud of the loom batten beating up the web.

But, this being the Valley of the Cross, it was only fitting a-body's thoughts should be on the little old lady they called the master weaver of the mountains.

After all this was her weaving house. This was where she beat out harmonies in form and color until the end of her days, weaving more webs than she could count.

Her name was Josephine Mast.

She has been dead for twenty years and her loom has gathered dust, the shuttle stilled, but the tools of her art have been preserved in the hand-hewn log weaver's cabin that was grooved together back in 1812.

And her name is woven forever into the homespun tapestry of mountain history. For it was her hands and from her loom that cloth was woven for the draperies in the Mountain Room of the White House during President Wilson's administration.

She began weaving in an era when storebought cloth was unknown in the mountains or so dear abody couldn't afford it.

It was a time when women sat to their looms and tramped the treadles and threw the shuttle to weave linsey for petticoats for their womankind and jeans for the menfolks.

Josephine Mast was noted for the fabrics her loom turned out, especially her linsey-woolsey.

Hers was truly a homespun family and the wealth of homespun fabrics she turned out was amazing. She was a weaver of unusual skill and patience. She learned early to put her thoughts on a thing and not let 'em squander all over creation.

As a girl she had heard the old ones say many a time that a slack-twisted person never could make a success as a weaver, especially of coverlets.

Around the fire, the old ones spoke a lot of wisdom and they talked with the experience and knowledge of their years.

Abody just couldn't be devilled with a lot of botherments if they was aiming to do a piece of weaving. That's what the old ones cautioned.

Josephine Mast learned that patience and perseverance were the first necessities of a master weaver.

The old ones said the exercise at a loom strengthened the fibers of the soul. And they were quick to point out that a'body could look all over creation and never find a girl weak or flabby of character whose mother was a weaver.

Josephine Mast carded and spun, and wove coverlets, rugs, and other textiles. When she grew up, folks in the mountains depended on the output of their home looms to supply their needs.

In winter the men wore shirts of bright colored linsey and the women and girls were clad in linsey dresses.

Linsey-woolsey was a cloth woven of woolen thread on a linen warp.

A skillful weaver of coverlets took the wool as it came from the backs of sheep.

Plain weaving fetched a dollar for every eight yards. Weaving of a coverlet brought a dollar for every four yards.

The difference in price was in the work.

A weaver didn't have to know drafts or patterns for plain weaving. But to do a coverlet, a weaver was called upon to work out a draft or pattern of the design that would show up in the finished piece like it was stamped on.

Some of the mountain weavers—a rare few like Josephine Mast—could sit right down to the loom with nothing but a pattern in their mind and draw it in and tromp it the same as if they had a draft all written out and a'standing there before their eyes.

In a homespun family of those days, sheets, towels, blankets, coverlets, counterpanes, petticoats, dresses, shirts and britches were made right in the house. It took a heap of wool to do a family back then, what with all the menfolks went through in a year, and for blankets and a petticoat apiece for the womenfolks.

Many a man is still around throughout the mountains who grew up wearing jeans britches.

Down in Waynesville, retired Judge Felix E. Alley recalled that he didn't have a storebought suit until he was sixteen years old.

"For the greater part of the first sixteen years of my life," he recalled, "I was a house-ridden invalid, and it was part of my occupation during this period to help pick the wool, card the bats and warp the chain, preparatory to weaving of the cloth.

"Hundreds of days and nights until midnight I have listened to the hum of the flying shuttle, the banging of the drumming batten, and the whir of the spinning wheel.

"I was the youngest of five brothers. By the time clothes had been made for my father and these older brothers, the jeans was about all gone. So my clothes were usually made of scraps left over from the other suits.

"I never had a full suit of clothes made of the same kind of cloth until I was sixteen years of age. Then I got my first storebought suit. I have had many a coat and many a pair of trousers made of scraps of jeans of five different colors—gray, blue, brown, black, and tan."

Like many another dedicated mountain weaver, Josephine Mast always figured weaving was the prettiest work she ever did.

There was something about settin' and trampin' the treadles and watching the pretty blossoms come out and smile at her in the coverlet that started a song in her heart and in her soul.

She used to say when she was weaving she never had any botherments. It was a time when nothing could fret her or devil her.

Josephine Mast is gone but the memory of her is as alive and bright as the wisp of red cloud-lace in the coming on of a winter gloaming when the day runs away swift as a weaver's shuttle.

Good Coffee Ought'a Have a Bite

Burningtown

SHED A TEAR FOR THE PAST!
The old coffee mill that hung on Grandma's kitchen wall has disappeared.

The home-made oven Grandpa used to parch his own coffee in has been torn down and carted off.

The country store up at the crossroads no longer handles the big tow sacks of green coffee beans.

The fire-blackened old tin coffee pot has been replaced by the percolator.

And the art of brewing coffee is almost lost.

"Folks now-a-days," said the Old Man, "just don't know what a good cup of coffee is. Real tastin' coffee's a scarce thing. Most of the stuff a'body drinks ain't fit to put in your mouth. It ain't got no body to it and it don't taste like coffee used to, least not like the kind your grandma cooked."

The Old Man considers himself an authority on coffee. And well he should. He's been sipping it black and scalding-hot for most of his 97 years.

"I reckon," he said, "I've parched and ground as much coffee as any man in these mountains. Folks used to say I had a right good hand for parchin' coffee. Just wasn't ever'body that could parch it. Some parched it too much and others never parched it enough. Like making molasses. You've got to know when it's right for takin' off the fire."

Somebody had told the Old Man they'd seen by the papers where folks were getting partial to soluble or instant coffee and that regular coffee was losing ground.

"I had some of the quick coffee once," he said. "Couldn't even smell it. Had a right bitter taste. Worse than green persimmons. Why, it was the nearest nothin' I ever put to my mouth.

"But like I've been a'sayin' ever since green coffee went off the market, a'body just don't know what sippin' coffee is unless it's been parched and ground right at home and then cooked in a tin coffee pot.

"I don't put no store by them newfangled percolators and things run by electricity. Besides, folks don't seem to take any pride in makin' coffee any more. Just dump it in the pot and go on about their business. If it cooks, it cooks and they let it sit there.

"For real sippin' coffee, you've got to start with the green bean. Back when I was a boy we had to go all the way to South Carolina to get our coffee. We'd get two or three bushels at a time and bring it home and parch it.

"I had me a parchin' oven I made myself. Got me some rocks and built me a sort of furnace. Fixed me a sheet of tin in it and put my coffee on it and built me a good hickory fire underneath. You could smell that coffee a'parchin' all over the country.

"All the folks back then parched their own coffee. It shore was a tantalizin' smell when you was ridin' around the country and a batch of coffee was parchin.' Made a feller want to hurry on home and get himself a cup.

"Like I said, you've got to start with the green bean. Then you parch it real good. Parch it till it gets brown like a chestnut. Then you get down your coffee mill or coffee grinder and grind just for your wants.

"That way you've always got fresh coffee. Just grind enough at a time for a pot full. Back in them days we never had ways like they've got now for keepin' it fresh and we just ground from one meal to the next.

"Ever now and then I get a good cup of coffee. But it's only them times when some of us go up in the Smokies on a picnic. I always make 'em take along a tin bucket to make coffee in. When it's a-cookin' it smells like coffee and when you taste it, it tastes like coffee should taste.

"Now I like my coffee boiling hot and strong. Most folks make it so weak it's like drinkin' colored water. And then don't drink it hot. The hotter it is the better. Scalding, that's what it should be.

"Why, I drink it with the steam a-boilin' off of it. Sometimes folks look at me like I ain't got good sense. Once a feller said didn't I know if I stuck my finger in it that hot that I'd blister it. I told him I reckon maybe I might, that I'd never tried it, but that I'd been drinkin' it that way since I was hoe-handle high and besides it would kill any germs in my stomach."

The Old Man laughed.

"Some folks are funny," he said. "Don't know nothin' about what a'body can take and can't. Of course, I pour out my coffee in my saucer and blow it a little."

Suddenly, there was a sort of mischievous sparkle in his eyes.

"Did I ever tell you about the time me and my brother went into Franklin to get some green coffee? No, I reckon I didn't."

"Now, some folks won't believe what happened. But it's a true story. It happened, for I was there.

"Well, we'd been to Franklin and got a poke of green coffee and was a-comin' on back home in the wagon. It was in the afternoon and the sun was a-comin' down like fire.

"We was a-ridin' along and I got to smellin' coffee a-parchin.' Oh, it was the finest smell you ever got on the wind. We was about a mile from the nearest farmhouse and I told my brother somebody was really parchin' coffee.

"We kept a-goin' on and the smell of that parchin' coffee kept gettin' stronger and stronger. I suddenly looked down and then I busted out a-laughin'.

"You know what had happened? Well, I'll tell you. I had that sack of coffee a-settin' in a tin pan and the pan was in my lap. Well, that sun had got so hot it had got that pan hot right through that coffee and that paper poke and had started parchin' that coffee."

The Old Man grinned, waiting for his grandson to protest.

"Now that's a fact," said the Old Man. "You don't have to believe it. But it happened, and I'm a-tellin' you."

The twinkle still was in his eyes.

And then it was gone and he stared off into the hills.

I thought there was a tear in his eyes.

A tear for the past, when the coffee mill hung on the wall and a'body parched their own coffee.

Light-'N'-Hitch

Webster

GRANDMA GREW UP IN THE 'LIGHT-AND-LOOK-AT-YOUR-saddle era.

Back then times were neighborly and folks were friendly as peas in a pod.

What most folks nowadays call "hospitality" was so much a part of Grandma's nature that she had no name for it.

Actually, it was a way of life. Common as corn pone and molasses. As unstudied as a "howdy." The latch-string hung outside and folks managed their time for a sight of visiting.

Grandma always said it was a mighty poor house that never had company come a-callin'.

Grandma wasn't much for traipsin' around herself. But she sure loved a house full of company, be it kith or kin.

She figured the world was coming to an end when a Sunday passed without somebody dropping in unexpectedly for dinner and a settin' spell.

Such occasions were rare. They upset Grandma and filled her head with all sorts of omnious thoughts. They were calamities. She was certain sickness, or worse, had struck the families of her sons and daughters, and all her neighbors.

Come Monday morning and Grandma would put on her best calico and her sunbonnet, tell Grandpa to hitch up the wagon, and set out on a round of visits to kith and kin.

Always she would discover it was company come a-callin', not sickness or some calamity, that had kept her kith and kin at home.

Satisfied, Grandma would head back home after her round of calls with an apron-pocket full of promises, which essentially were the same: "God willin', and the creek not too high, we'll be there next Sunday."

Yes, Grandma loved a house full of company. It was the same

with most of Grandma's contemporaries here in the mountains.

That was before hospitality became a marketable commodity. Before folks started advertising it, making up songs about it, and boasting about it all over creation. In Grandma's day, folks didn't sell it. They didn't brag about it, They didn't emblazon it on the doormats.

For that reason, hospitality hereabouts was as real and as quiet as spring rain. It was genuine, pure, unadulterated. Like the kind of corn whiskey that used to flow out of the coves before blockaders lost their patience and started trying to compete with store-bought whiskey.

In the old days, even a stranger was welcome. Folks took him in mainly because there was no other place for him to go. Wayside inns were few and far between.

"Light and look at your saddle," or "Light and hitch," was a stock greeting, followed after a spell by: "Won't you stay the night? You're welcome to the best we've got, such as 'tis."

Back shortly after the turn of the century when Horace Kephart was exploring the Great Smokies and gathering material for a book called *Our Southern Highlanders*, he got lost in the wilds around Huggins' Hell late one afternoon.

Eventually, he ran onto a stream. Fighting his way through thicket and darkness, he stumbled at last upon a mountain cabin where he asked for lodging and was taken in.

The man of the house left on an errand a few minutes later. Kephart was starved but the woman of the house made no move toward the kitchen. It was well into the night before the man returned, carrying a little poke of corn meal. Soon there was hot bread, three or four slices of fatback, and black coffee.

It developed that when Kephart arrived there was barely meal for the family's supper and breakfast. Kephart's host had to shell some corn, go to a tub-mill far down the creek, wait while it was ground out a few spoonfuls to the minute and bring the meal back.

Next morning when Kephart offered pay for his meals and lodging, his host waved it aside. "I ain't never took money from company," he said, "and this ain't no time to begin."

However, Kephart slipped some silver into the hand of the eldest child, explaining it wasn't pay but a present. The girl was speechless and the parents didn't know how to thank him for her.

"Stay on, stranger," the girl said, finally. "Pore folks has a pore way, but you're welcome to what we got."

To many a family far back in the hills in that age of lonely isolation the coming of an unknown traveler was an event that set the whole neighborhood gossiping.

But it was the same down in the valleys, too. A stranger was a new face, a new voice, and something to break the monotony.

Besides, it wasn't any trouble to throw another chicken in the skillet and slice another ham. No trouble at all to bake another pone of bread, put another plate on the table.

Nowadays housewives go into a tizzy when company drops in unexpectedly at dinner-time on a Sunday.

But in Grandma's day womenfolks welcomed unexpected company with a passion and tried themselves with setting up a groaning table piled high with food quicker than a dozen winks of the eye.

All Grandma had to do was step outside and flag down a chicken and wring its neck and beat up a new batch of biscuits and fetch another jar of milk from the springhouse.

Back then this was a land of smoke-houses and sweet-potato patches, fried pies and dried fruit, chickens scratching in the yard and milk cooling in the springhouse, a crock of kraut in the cellar and a freshly-poured jug of molasses in the pantry.

No matter how many relatives or neighbors poured in after church on Sunday, Grandma never got the least bit fussed. She fed 'em all and fed 'em well, albeit in shifts, with the grownups served first and the children last.

Knowing the druthers of her grandchildren, she saw to it that they got something besides the wing or neck. As a matter of fact, there was many a time when Grandpa couldn't find a chicken liver or a gizzard for the life of him, and he was mighty fond of both. He would speak up and reckon the chickens didn't have livers and gizzards any more, teasing Grandma and knowing all the while she had held them back for the children.

Grandma reckoned it was a pretty skimpy gathering if less than fifteen or twenty, including the children, showed up for Sunday dinner. She was happiest when the house was bulging at the seams with company. Grandpa used to say if Grandma could have her way she would keep it like that all the time.

"Well, now," Grandma would say, "that's what a home's for. It does me good to have folks come and stay."

When a day of visiting with her came to a close and the goodbyes were being said, Grandma would always end up saying:

"Well, come again, and fix to stay a week."

In her day, folks didn't need an invite. If they could come a-visitin', they just hitched up the team, loaded up the family and come on.

After all, it was the 'light-and-look-at-your-saddle era.

And Grandma loved it.

Mighty Peart Woman With a Skillet

Burningtown

MY GREAT-GRANDMOTHER WAS A MIGHTY PEART WOMAN with a skillet.

She wasn't a fancy cook. She didn't pretend to be.

She took simple things, homegrown or wild things, and made them taste like nothing a-body ever put in their mouth.

She was blessed with a knack for pleasuring the palate.

At least that's the way the Old Man remembers her cooking.

"You don't find her kind of cookin' any more," he said. "It was the kind of cookin' a-body could founder on mighty easy."

The Old Man has tasted a heap of victuals in his time. He's put his feet under more tables than Barley had oats.

His tastes run to plain food, albeit he's no stranger to caviar or crepe suzettes.

He's a hog-and-hominy man, a corn-pone-and-pot-likker man.

He's a man nudging a hundred who favors the kind of victuals my great-grandmother served up when he was a boy.

"They just don't grow 'em like her any more," said the Old Man. "Not nowadays."

He shook his head. Shook it slowly. There was a wistful look in his eyes.

"She was a mighty good cook," said the Old Man. "Nobody ever had a harsh word for her cookin'. Never a complaint. Nobody was ever known to get up from her table hungry.

"She cooked a lots of things. They was mighty tasty, too. She wasn't scrimpy about her cookin'. Always had enough and then some on the table. She never made no half-dos. She didn't cook a lot of knick-knacks like womenfolks do nowadays.

"No, sir, she wasn't one for knick-knacks. She set a table with substantial victuals. Beef and hog meat and fried chicken and big hominy.

"Back in them days folks started the day out with a big breakfast. None of this juice-and-an-egg-and-piece-of-toast skimpin'. Why, a-body wouldn't of lasted an hour out in the fields on the kind of breakfasts folks eat nowadays.

"When I was comin' along our table had just as much on it at breakfast as dinner, which was a heap. The kind of victuals that stuck with a-body.

"Why, it wasn't uncommon to set down to a first meal of backbones and ribs, sweet potatoes, fried chicken, hominy, corn pone, molasses and apple pie.

"Your great-grandma cooked on an open fire in the fireplace. Folks back in them days took their time doin' their cookin'. None of this slappin' a piece of meat in the skillet and bouncin' it out like it was somethin' alive and runnin'.

"Ma always was one for long cookin' over slow fires. That way things cooked done and tasty. No sooner was breakfast over than she put her beans on the fire for dinner. The beans you get nowdays hardly get warm. Might as well eat 'em raw for all the taste they've got. Same way with boiled cabbage. Ain't fit to eat unless they've been boiled four or five hours.

"If a-body wants to eat beans and cabbage raw, well, then they ought to eat 'em like they come out of the patch. But if they're to be cooked they've got to have time to cook done. There ain't no in between.

"Another thing. To give boiled beans or boiled cabbage or boiled potatoes taste you've got to boil 'em with a piece of fatback. They ain't got no taste if they're not fixed that way. Might as well eat a piece of rawhide as to eat beans that ain't cooked with fatback for all the taste they've got."

The Old Man paused. He tapped the hearth with his cane.

"I've eat many a pone of bread baked right there on that hearth," he said. "That's where Ma done her cookin'. Baked her bread in an iron skillet. She'd grease the skillet by rubbin' a piece of fatback over it while it was heatin' up. Then she'd pour in the batter. Made the finest corn pone you ever tasted. We had ash cake, too. That's bakin' it in ashes.

"In the fall when we butchered our hogs we'd have cracklin' bread. In the early summer when the corn first ripened we'd start havin' gritted bread. Now that's somethin' to make your mouth water. You take fresh corn and rub it over a piece of tin that's been holed with a nail, rubbin' the ear of corn on the rough side, and make a meal that's milky-like. Sweetest, tastiest thing you ever tasted.

"Now when it come to makin' pies and sweet cakes there wasn't nobody that could beat your great-grandma. When the fruit was ripe she'd make fresh pies and spice 'em up. Winter-time she'd make her pies out of dried fruit.

"The cakes she baked was the finest eatin' a-body would want. They was about six or seven inches thick and big as a half bushel. And just as light as a feather and as yellow as a gold watch.

"Sunday dinner was what you might call a feast. There was always eight or ten besides the regular household. Neighbors would come a'visitin', you know, or some of the kinfolks. We always killed a beef or two every fall and there'd be meat a'plenty. We'd saw up bones and Ma would cook 'em in a big pot.

"We'd always have sweet potatoes. We had big ones we called Spanish potatoes. They was as long as your arm and as big as a chair post. Have to break 'em in two to put 'em in the pot. Steamed 'em. You don't have that kind of potatoes nowadays.

"Gettin' back to makin' pies before I forget it. Your great-grandma made apple pies that looked like a half moon or a new moon. She had a vessel that had a ridge in it. She'd bake part of the pie in one side and part in the other. Called 'em moon pies.

"We used to have big corn shuckin's. The whole settlement would come in. We'd have a big dinner and then a big supper. The supper would be after nightfall. We had a whole lot of darkies and they'd sing the corn song. I don't recollect just how it went, but it was the finest thing I ever heard.

"Them darkies would start singin' it when supper was ready. Four or five of 'em would pick up the man of the house and tote him around the house two or three times with ever'body followin' along and singin'. Then they'd set him up at the table and comb his hair before folks got to eat."

Back when he was a boy, the Old Man said, folks were always gathering for a corn shuckin' or a butcherin'-day or a dance or a frolic.

No matter what the occasion there always was food.

"Folks in the settlement," said the Old Man, "sort of favored our house because of Ma's cookin'. They all said nobody could cook like her."

The Old Man paused. He shook his head. Shook it slowly.

"No, sir," he said, "they just don't grow 'em like her any more."

And then he smiled and there was a sparkle in his eyes.

"Yes, sir," he nodded, "she was mighty peart with a skillet."

December in the Hills

Burningtown

IN THE CAROLINA HIGHLANDS, DECEMBER IS AN OLD MAN with memories and a young man with dreams.

It is an old woman with snow in her hair and a young girl with stars in her eyes.

It's winter talk by the fireside, and fiddle tunes and ballad singing.

It's a country road with lantern light throwing golden splashes on the snow at night.

It's a wild and ugly witch called the wind, galloping across the Blue Ridge and the Great Smokies, the Balsams and the Nantahalas.

It's home-coming cattle swinging into the lane and bringing wistful-like spells with their quaint, comforting, wandering bells.

It's snow flakes the size of a dime spinning crazily and clinging softly to old shingled roofs.

It's a little church in the pines glowing with candlelight and happy voices singing once more old songs of Holy Night.

It's a shepherd on a lonely hilltop in Watauga and sheep etched against a raspberry sky in Macon.

December is a time when the stars come close and the night winds are winds of song.

It is a time when potato soup and bean soup come into their own and provide a soul-and-body satisfying meal.

It's a time when a hearthfire is a cheery companion, a deep and abiding comfort.

It's when winter's icy knuckles are at the door.

It's when a house, be it cabin or mansion, reveals its true character and abody gets to know the meaning of a home.

December is laughter and full hearts and the glad hubbub of company coming.

It's mountain women gathering pine cones and galax and holly and weaving them into many-splendored things to garland Christmas mantels.

It's the whisper of a blizzard and the snow and the wind playing hide and seek along the fence rows and across the meadows and among the fir-clad hills and about the barn.

It's clouds all ragged and wispy and weird.

It's a grandmother baking fruit cakes and mince-meat pies and a grandfather saving up eggs for a nog.

It's a little boy with a new sled praying for snow when there is no snow.

It's a bonfire beside a lake at Highlands and folks skating in the frosty night.

It's a boy with skiis fashioned from barrel staves and polished with beeswax having as much fun at Indian Gap as those gliding over the snow on expensive storebought skiis.

December is the sharp ring of the woodsman's axe harvesting a crop of Christmas trees on Roan Mountain for a ride to the Eastern markets.

It's shooting mistletoe out of a tall oak and mistletoe hanging over the door.

It's apples in the bin, pickled peaches on the shelf.

It's cider in the jug and kraut in the earthen crock.

It's the magic of awakening to a mountain world white with snow.

It's swirling snowflakes and the old ones reckoning that "the Old Woman's picking her geese."

It's a corn-shuckin' and a candy-pull.

It's old tunes with new words.

It's a newly finished quilt, its patchwork gay and each small quilting stitch precisely right.

It's a mountain farmer with tobacco money jingling in his pocket.

It's the old ones telling the young ones the shepherd's tale.

It's stars winking in the night in the sky over God's pastures and a new lamb crying below in the valley.

It's church chimes floating across the highlands and the voices of carolers in the night.

December is an old man sitting beside a hearth with a steady flame and a full wood-box.

It's an old man who never has lost his childlike faith.

An old man whose hopes renew each year that he may hear the angel song when Christmas lights burn blue.

Nothin' Like Battlin' Stick For Noise

Whittier

THERE'S MANY A NOSTALGIC SONG ABOUT THE SIMPLE homely things of farm life.

The old oaken bucket, the one-horse shay and bringing in the sheaves still live and are as close as yesterday because of a song.

But the tunesters have missed a good thing in passing up the "battling-stick" and the "battling-block."

We've got a notion some tunester could do himself a real rock-and-roll tune if he set the song of the "battling-stick" to music.

It would be novel, to say the least, but I wouldn't want to be around when it hit the juke boxes.

For noise, there was nothing like a "battling-stick" in the hands of a mountain woman "battling" clothes on wash day.

Old-timers will tell you this "battling" could be heard fully a quarter of a mile away.

Up to 50 years ago and later, the "battling-stick" was as much a part of a mountain woman's household tools as needle and thread.

Just as the finger needle gave way to the sewing-machine, the "battling-stick" passed out of use with the advent of the scrubbing-board and the washing-machine.

But my mother remembers when washing was a chore and when clothes had to be mighty tough to survive the rigors of "battling." So does Mrs. Katie Gibbs who was born and raised up the road from here on Conley's Creek.

"Folks now days wouldn't know what to do with a 'battling-stick' if one was put in their hands," said Mrs. Gibbs. "But back when I was a girl a 'battling-stick' was mighty important and womenfolks knew how to handle it.

"There was nothing easy in those days when it come to turning out a washing. It was hard, back-breaking work. Now all a-body's got to do is put their clothes in a machine and be about something else.

"I'll tell you how it was then. All the washing was done out of doors. Every family had an iron wash pot, a 'battling-stick', and a 'battling-block'.

"You boiled your clothes in the pot. It took a lot of trips from the spring with a bucket to fill up the pot. There wasn't any blueing back then like we have now to make clothes white. But we had things that would make do."

She paused, her eyes brightening at a memory that brought a chuckle to her lips.

"My, my," she said. "The things we had to do with back then. When you tell folks about them now they hardly believe you. Why for blueing, we used peach tree bark and peach tree leaves.

"We'd go to the peach trees and get bark and put it in a flour sack. Then we'd put the sack in the boiling pot along with the clothes. In the summer we'd use peach tree leaves. You never saw clothes so white or smell so good.

"With the water boiling and the fire going good, the clothes were well smeared with soft soap, the kind we made ourselves, and then thoroughly boiled in the big kettle, which was swung under a tripod.

"Then they were laid on the 'battling-block'. It was a big log that had been split in two and the flat side smoothed down. And that's where the 'battling-stick' came in. It was a sort of paddle and made out of poplar.

"With the 'battling-stick' you beat the dirt out of the clothes. It was hard, steady pounding. And it's a wonder we didn't beat our clothes to pieces. But cloth was good and strong in those days, a lot of it woven by hand and it could take a hard pounding.

"Now, after the clothes had been 'battled', they were put into hot water and smeared with soap again. Then the women rubbed them between their knuckles. Another boiling and rinsing completed the program.

"A-body could sort of take a deep breath then and know the worst was over. Once the clothes were rinsed they were hung out to dry. Some folks had clothes lines and others hung them out to dry on the rail fence or on bushes.

"If you really wanted to have the whitest, purtiest clothes, the time for that was in the winter. It was a chore washing on a cold day but it was the best time to wash. When it was cold like that you let your clothes freeze overnight. Just left them hanging out there till the next morning. They'd be stiff but they'd sure be white.

"There wasn't any store-bought starch then. We made our own.

Took some flour and mixed it with water till it got pasty-like. Then we put the dripping through a thin cloth into boiling water.

"For ironing, flatirons were used. Everybody had five or six flatirons back then. Kept them sitting on the hearth or on the mantel. When you got ready to use them you'd line them all up with the flat side facing the fire. You put them real close to the fire and got them hot that way.

"Sometimes you would put salt on the iron to keep it slick and smooth. Most folks used beeswax. When you used beeswax you'd take a cloth and spread it out and shave off pieces of it with a knife onto the cloth."

My mother said the old folks argued that using beeswax on the iron put a gloss on the clothes.

She recalled that her mother always kept her irons right on the hearth. When they wasn't being used for ironing, and if it was winter, they would be heated and wrapped in clothes and taken to bed as footwarmers.

Besides washing clothes, Mrs. Gibbs said she and her sisters were responsible for cleaning the wool after the sheep were sheared.

"Papa let us have his tanning troughs to use after he had tanned the sheep skins," she said. "We'd fill the troughs with water and put soap in it and then get in there in our bare feet and tromp the wool to get it clean.

"It took three or four days to clean the wool. Had to run water through time and again. When the wool was cleaned we would spread it out on the roof of the barn to dry out. It looked like the roof was covered with snow.

"But cleaning wool wasn't half as hard as washing clothes. Doing the wool was fun, but washing was a chore. Especially when it come to battling' the clothes with a 'battling-stick'."

All of which is a far cry from the washing-machine age.

That's why we think somebody ought to write a song about the "battling-stick" and the "battling-block."

In Huckleberry Time Courtin's a Pleasure

Whiteside Mountain

WHEN IT'S HUCKLEBERRY TIME IN THE HILLS, COURTIN'S a pleasure.

That's what the Old Man says, and he ought to know.

In his time, he's done quite a bit of sparkin' and, for all his 97 years, he's still got an eye for a pretty girl.

"Back when I was comin' up." said the Old Man, "a young feller with marryin' in his head could tell pretty well what sort of wife a girl would make when huckleberry time rolled around.

"A feller could mighty well learn a heap about a girl on a huckleberryin'. If she picked a bushel you knew right away she'd keep things a-hummin' around the house. And if she could bake a huckleberry pie that was tasty you knew she was a good hand at fixin' vittles.

"Of course, a right smart of folks never looked at it that way. They just went huckleberryin' for a lark. Never had marryin' in their head at all. Just went along to have some fun and be with the other young folks.

"Mind you, huckleberry outin's back then wasn't just two folks gettin' off together to be alone. No, sir. They was sort of get-togethers like young folks have always been doing. Whole bunch would get together and go out huckleberryin' and have a real time. Stay out all day.

"We always had chaperones, and it was mighty risky business tryin' to sneak a buss from a girl. If a feller managed it, it was a good idea to make a show of lettin' the chaperones see you eatin' a handful of huckleberries. Else you might have to explain some of that juice on your face."

The Old Man grinned. Maybe at a recollection.

Of course, huckleberryin' wasn't all courtin' by a long shot.

Folks swarmed to the huckleberry balds, the high tops where they grow in profusion, during July and August and picked the juicy berries for pies and for winter eating.

This was one of the favorite spots.

You see, Whiteside Mountain has been known as a huckleberry heaven since time out of memory.

And right now the huckleberries are glistening on the mountain, each berry a tiny wine bottle full of refreshment.

Folks who never knew that huckleberryin' and courtin' went together are beginning to come up here these August days just to wander about and eat them on the spot.

Warren Alexander, the 71-year-old Apostle of Whiteside, said this is the best year for huckleberries he can remember.

As a boy, Warren picked many a bushel of huckleberries.

"Folks now-a-days," he said, "don't seem to know too much about huckleberries. They don't get out and pick 'em, like we did. Maybe they want somebody else to pick 'em for 'em.

"But a feller that goes out and picks his own will somehow have a better pie than the feller that buys his from the store. Don't know why it is, but that's the way it seems.

"And unless you've put a tooth to a hot huckleberry pie, you don't know what eatin' is. My wife can shore make a real huckleberry pie.

"When I was a boy folks never knew much about cannin' fruits and things. But we had huckleberries right through the winter. Reckon you don't know how we kept 'em.

"Why, we dried 'em. Dried 'em just like you would apples and peaches. Picked 'em and then laid 'em out on a cloth in the sun. When they got dried out all the juice was gone into the skin and you sort of had just the hulls all withered up, sort of like the way raisins look. Then you put 'em in a jar and capped it and put it on the shelf and used what you wanted from time to time when you got a-hankerin' for a huckleberry pie.

"Dried huckleberries make a fine pie. Of course, you don't have as much juice but you've got the taste, and that's what really counts after all.

"I've seen the time when we've had ten or twenty, maybe thirty jars of dried huckleberries."

He shook his head at the memory

"Now-a-days," said Warren, "folks don't pick 'em and they just go to waste on the mountain tops. And that's a shame. Just look at all the bushes. Folks can come up here and pick 'em and eat all they want. Ain't no price tag on them bushes. Reckon folks are sort of lazy. Maybe like me. I got tired of workin' a few years ago.

"But gettin' back to huckleberry pie. Now I'll tell you what real eatin' was when I was a boy. There wasn't nothin' like settin' down to a table of turkey and roastin' ears and huckleberry puddin' or pie.

" 'Course, turkey's hard to come by now. All the wild ones are gone. But up until the '20's there was wild turkeys hereabouts for the shootin'.

"Them wild turkeys made good eatin', too. They fed on huckleberries. Reckon about the only game birds left to feed on huckleberries are grouse, and we've got 'em down there in the valley."

Warren bent down and picked a handful of berries from a bush and popped them into his mouth.

"You know," he said, "I've been so busy here lately this is the first time in two months I've been on the mountain. But what with these berries a-beggin' to go into a pie I reckon I'll have to get back up here tomorrow and gather me about a bushel."

Warren agreed with the Old Man that the young folks could have a right pleasurable time up here picking huckleberries and looking at the scenery.

The Old Man figured maybe he might like to do a bit of huckleberryin', too.

"That is," he said, a twinkle in his eyes, "if I can find me a pretty girl."

As he said, when it's huckleberry time in the hills, courtin's a pleasure.

Artist With Ax Handles

Sapphire

HE CLOSED THE JACKKNIFE CAREFULLY, TUCKING IT DEEP in the pocket of his blue jeans as if his fingers loved it.

Then he ran a calloused hand over the satiny finish of the new ax helve he had fashioned from a piece of white hickory.

"It's as slick as a buck's horn," he said. "There ain't a catface or a snerl in it. Why, it'll outlive two ax heads, if a-body don't use it as a pryin' bar."

He handed it to the boy, and the boy let his fingers run along the shaft as the man had done.

"Henry sure can make 'em," the boy said. "I reckon there's nobody can beat Henry when it comes to makin' ax handles. You can make 'em better'n a factory, can't you, Henry?"

Henry Alexander, who plies a trade as old as the first ax, pulled at his white mustache and grinned.

"My nephew talks proud," he said. "Real proud."

And well the boy should be proud, for Henry Alexander is a rare man who practices a rare art.

He has been making ax helves for 40 years. He has been a woodsman and a logger since he was big enough to swing an ax. He is 64, red of face, a plump little man with an elfish twinkle in his blue eyes.

"Not many folks make ax helves any more," Henry said. "Most of 'em buy turned or store-bought helves. They sit around and loaf and won't make 'em. They buy 'em and they buy 'em. A store-bought helve won't last much longer than it takes to fit it to the ax."

In the old days everybody made their own ax helves and ground their own axes.

"But folks kind of got lazy when money got to comin' sort of easy," Henry said. "And it was a heap easier to go to the store and buy a so-called ax helve than to spend a couple weeks shaping one out of hickory.

"You couldn't give me a store-bought helve. Why, the men that makes 'em in the factories don't know nothin' about wood or grain or catfaces or snerls. A piece of wood is just a piece of wood to them.

"I was over to Brevard here a while back," he said. "And was rummaging around in a store and the man says let me sell you an ax handle. I said mister, you ain't got a helve I'd have.

"Well, that feller looked kinda taken aback for a moment and then he said, 'I'll bet you ain't got an ax handle.' I said, mister, I've got one that's already wore out two axes and is a workin' on a third.

"You know what I told him? I said, mister, as long as saplings grow and I can see to whittle I'll make mine."

Henry said that good ax helve wood is getting scarce in the mountains.

"Time was when a man could step outside his door and spot a good white hickory," he said. "But no more. Seems like white hickory is gettin' scarcer and scarcer."

Hickory has always served the mountaineer well. It not only made the new helve to his ax, it made a ramrod for his gun.

"Hickory is tough but flexible," Henry said, "and will resist a shock. White hickory has more strength in bending and has more crushing strength. It won't snap like other woods when you swing an ax into a tree or a log."

The first pioneers used ash but then somebody discovered hickory.

The curved hickory handle of the single-bitted ax is of American origin.

This single-bitted ax is sometimes called a "pole ax" because one side is flat and can be used as a driving tool.

The double-bitted ax always takes a straight handle.

This is the ax of the logger.

Henry has both.

The American ax, as European obervers called it, evolved, like the American man, out of Old World models, in the century of George Washington.

The old axes, for Old World woods, were light and brittle by comparison, round in the helve, and they wobbled in the stroke from poor balance.

The American ax, rebuilt by Moravians of the North Carolina frontier, was a tempered weapon that was used in thinning out the wilderness.

"A soft pine wedge will hold better than a hard one in fitting a handle to an ax," Henry explained. "The soft wedge catches hard and holds."

When he goes out looking for a white hickory to make a few ax handles, Henry searches until he finds a tree about six to eight inches through.

"You get about four handles to a cut," he said. "In working up your handles you first use an ax to work out the shape. Then you finish up with a knife, thinning it down and smoothing it. Your knife's got to be sharp as a razor. And you've got to have a good knife. Fact is, they don't make good knives any more, not like they did 20 to 30 years ago.

"You always work with the grain of the wood. The grain's got to run toward the ax head. That's where you get your strength in your handle and it keeps it from breaking.

"Now these store-bought handles," Henry said, "they've got the grain running crossways and they'll break if you look at 'em. Besides, they're full of worm holes and catfaces, and snerls.

"What's that? Why a catface is where a limb comes out of the tree and has been sawed off. A snerl is a knotty place on the timber."

The boy said, "See these notches on the handle. Tell him, Henry."

"Put 'em there so I wouldn't have to fool with a measuring rule when I'm getting wood," Henry said. "That's a 16-inch mark, which I call the stove-wood mark. That other one's the two-foot mark which is for measuring any length of timber I need to cut."

Henry ran his hand over the new hickory helve.

"I'm goin' to give this one to the boy," he said. "He needs an ax of his own."

And the boy's eyes danced and he was rich beyond words.

"That's the finest handle you ever made, Henry," the boy said. "I bet it's the best ax handle in all the world."

How Molly Got Her Ear-Bobs

Webster

INTO THE ROOM CAME A VOICE FROM OUT OF THE PAST TO weave a tapestry of magic memories.

It was a voice that went back a hundred years and beyond.

"I can tell you how it was in '61 and before," said the voice, "and I can tell you about the agony a girl went through when she had her ears pierced."

And you closed your eyes and in your mind you saw her and it was like she was there in the room.

The years rolled away and you remembered that day when Mary Jane Hall Fisher—the "Cousin Molly" of your childhood—waited for death and talked about the life and times she had known.

And now her voice was living again, captured on a spool of thin wire.

"I was born in '51," she said, "had my ears pierced when I was eight, and got married in '66. My father was David Hall and my mother was Rachel Wilson Hall.

"I married Captain J. Webb Fisher. I was only ten years old when he went off to war and I remember how I was there that day when all the boys went away. Webb made a big fuss over me but I never had no idea then that I would marry him.

"During the war years I did all kinds of work. I spun on the big wheel and I hoed corn, hoed until I got so tired I just lay down on the ground and cried.

"When Webb come back from the war we became sweethearts. I was going to school and he wanted me to quit and get married. I told him I'd marry him if he'd give me three more years. I wanted that much more schooling.

"But about that time old man Hicks who taught the school got mad and quit and we didn't have a school. So Webb said there wasn't nothing to keep us from getting married.

"We set the day we was going to get married. Webb was going to ask for me and we was going to step off and get married, not have a fancy wedding.

"I didn't want a wedding with a lot of folks. Back in those days people would go to a wedding even if they wasn't invited.

"But my folks would not hear to us going off and being married all alone. So we was married on the porch of my father's home. There was 82 there for the wedding.

"I bucked up when mama suggested a certain preacher marry us. I didn't like him and I wasn't going to be married by him. Now, I loved Wes Enloe and his wife and I said I wanted him to marry us. You see, he was a justice of the peace and could marry folks.

"I got my way. Joe Sensible and Uncle Dick Wilson and Bert Allen were the groomsmen. Mandy Cannon, Kate Allen and Webb's sister were the bridesmaids. Mag Love and my Aunt Mary were the candle-bearers.

"We was married at night. We was married on the porch. The girls stood up next to the wall and the boys stood at the edge of the porch and Wes Enloe stood at one end. That made a sort of road between them and me and Webb come out of the house and marched between them until we stood before Wes Enloe.

"The candle-bearers stood by Wes Enloe. That was all the light we had back in those days. The bridesmaids and me were all dressed in white and the candle-bearers dressed in black silk.

"They had that silk before the war commenced. You couldn't get much silk when I was married. Everybody wore homespun then, but I did have a nice dress to be married in.

"My daddy went to Franklin to get the goods. You couldn't get goods here then. It was some kind of cotton material. I don't remember just what kind. It had a low neck and short sleeves and the sleeves was tucked. My shoes were cloth, laced at the ankles. They had leather soles and heels, and the vamps and quarters was cotton.

"Of course, in my time I wore button shoes. But they were the hatefulest things I ever wore. The buttons would break. Give me a lace shoe every time.

"I was just 15 when I was married. Only a child in age, a woman in size.

"When Wes Enloe pronounced us husband and wife, he turned and went to the table where a big supper had been set, and we all followed. We sure did have something to eat. It wasn't society like now but it was good old substantial food.

"Mama had cooked up backbones and chicken and dumplin's. And there was a cake in the center of the table, all trimmed and iced.

"It was a pound cake and it had a hole in the center. It was the only sort the old folks baked and it was good, too.

"Well, after me and Webb was married and was celebrating with everybody, he told me he had me a pair of shoes and a dress all ready to make. He had gone to Asheville to get them. I don't think I ever had a prettier pair of shoes. They were fawn color. And he had me enough calico to make a dress."

Of course, she said, she wore ear-rings.

"All girls wanted ear-rings back then. They were the kind you had to have holes punched in your ears to wear. Papa punched holes in my ears before I was eight o'clock. Laws-a-mercy," she laughed. "Eight years old. He was foolish about me.

"Mama didn't believe in ear-rings. She said it was a sin to wear them. She said it was enough to wear a breast pin, because it was necessary. But she said finger-rings and ear-rings were a sin and she wouldn't have them. And she never wore a bustle or hoops, either.

"Papa put holes in my ears with a needle and run a silk string through the hole. I had to turn the strings until my ears got well to keep the string from growing up in my ears.

"Mama had to bathe my ears with alum water and turn the string. She got impatient with me, and I'd take on and she would say, 'You would have, so just grin and endure it'.

"This went on until I was ten years old and I had the holes in my ears but no ear-rings. There wasn't a jeweler here then.

"Mama had some money of her own. It was gold. And once when Papa went to Franklin for something she give him the money and I said, 'Now you can get my ear-bobs'.

"When he come back he give Mama her money and I said where was my ear-bobs and he said he didn't get them. I said I was going to pull out the strings and let the holes in my ears grow up. I said I wasn't going to wear those old strings any longer.

"About that time I happened to look up as he fussed with his pocketbook and I saw he had my ear-bobs. Then he gave them to me and I put them on."

The voice rolled on, vibrant with memories. And sometimes there was laughter in it and sometimes there were tears.

It was a voice from out of the past weaving a tapestry of magic memories.

Maybe the Ground Hog Knows

Hog Rock

THE ALMANAC SAYS TOMORROW IS GROUND-HOG DAY.
But there's many an old time mountain man who will argue that the almanac is wrong.

My grandfather is one. And backing him up is a passel of old timers scattered throughout the mountains from the Blue Ridge to the Smokies.

"Somebody's got their dates all mixed up," said my grandfather. "Why, any of the old folks'll tell you Ground-Hog Day's still nigh on to two weeks off.

"Shucks, tomorrow ain't no more Ground-Hog Day than it's my birthday. And my birthday ain't till the fourteenth of the month, that's when Ground-Hog Day is. I was born on Ground-Hog Day. It's come to be Valentine's Day, too.

"No, sir, tomorrow ain't Ground-Hog Day. My pa and his pa and all the old folks reckoned the fourteenth as the right day and there weren't no argument hereabouts in their time as to when it come.

"But it's got so folks set out purpose-like to change things that don't need changin'. Seems like they ain't satisfied with what comes down to 'em.

"It ain't no wonder folks now days get all mixed up about the weather. They don't pay no mind to the signs any more. A-body's got to give some attention to the moon and the clouds. Folks don't study 'em any more. Got so they put all their dependence in thingumabobs and dojiggers to tell 'em if it'll snow or rain or be sunshiny."

The Old Man paused to light his pipe. The car jolted over the dirt track that wound through the Hog Rock community beyond Webster and the river. To the Old Man the landscape was familiar. Long ago he had worked in the mines here and he knew the hills as a place where the ground hog hibernated.

"Now, you can't beat a ground hog for tellin' you where winter'll hand around for a spell or snap off," he said. "But like I say, tomorrow ain't the day to set by a ground hog hole and see if he comes out.

"A-body's got to spot him a ground hog hole before the time and then be there a-waitin' on the morning of the right day. If you'll come over here on the fourteenth you'll see a ground hog.

"Ain't no particular time of day for him to come out. But you've got to be a-waitin'. Might come out first thing in the mornin' or he might wait till up in the afternoon. The fourteenth is the day to do your watchin', not tomorrow."

Be that as it may, the Old Man agrees that the ground hog can't be beat as a weather forecaster.

"Some folks'll do their weather predictin' on what it's like tomorrow and others'll wait till the fourteenth," he said. "Unless the weather's the same on both days there's goin' to be a lot of argument.

"Now the whole thing centers around the ground hog. If he comes up for air, looks around and sees his shadow, he'll run back into his hole and wait forty days and forty nights for winter to go away.

"But if he finds the climate to his likin' and don't see no shadow, then he'll look around for something' green to eat, and that means an early spring."

The ground hog is a grizzled reddish-brown old codger whose folks became weather prophets centuries ago in Germany and England.

Scientists call him Professor Marmota Monax, a name hung on him back in Germany, but to the mountain man he is just plain Mr. Ground Hog.

Mountain folks to the contrary, he has been for centuries associated with Candlemas Day which falls on February 2.

Candlemas Day is the Feast of the Purification of the Blessed Virgin, observed by Roman, Greek and Anglican churches.

It is a day generally accepted when the weather is a most important affair, for on that date depends good or bad luck for sowing and planting according to the omens.

To those who oppose the old time mountain man's theory, if the ground hog comes out of his hole on February 2 and sees his shadow, he will go back in and stay six more weeks.

So if the day is sunny, winter will continue and the result will be bad crops.

If it is cloudy, the ground hog will see no shadow, and the reverse will be true.

These notions still prevail on the Continent and in England and are nowhere more popular than in the United States.

In Missouri, Ground-Hog Day was officially established as Feb. 2 by Act of the Missouri Legislature.

However, in Arkansas and in Missouri and elsewhere, a hot controversy arose between individuals and in the press disputing this date.

Old timers there as well as here in our mountains cling to Feb. 14 as the proper time for sowing and planting. To them, this date is Ground-Hog Day and not the usually accepted Feb. 2.

And nothing is going to make them change their belief.

"Why, somebody just set down the wrong date," said my grandfather. "Just like folks changed the date of Christmas.

"Them that wants to can consider tomorrow Ground-Hog Day can go right ahead but they'll be wrong if they put any store in the signs.

"Just like some folks never bother to study the moon when they clear new land in the winter for plantin'. Some'll go ahead and burn their brush with no thought of the moon.

"But everbody that study's the moon knows if you burn your brush on the dark of the moon you'll have a good corn crop. If you burn it on the light of the moon the ground'll moss over and turn as red as a fox's tail and never will bring nothin'.

"Same with plantin' corn. Plant it on the dark of the moon and it ears good and don't grow high. But plant it on the light of the moon and it grows high and don't make nothin' but little ears."

And so it goes.

Like the almanac says, tomorrow is Ground-Hog Day but there's many an old time mountain man who will argue that the almanac is wrong.

And my grandfather will hold out for Feb. 14, for it's his birthday, too.

Last of a Shoemakin' Clan

Cove Creek

THE HOMEMADE TANBARK MILL IS TOTTERING INTO RUIN and the old man has laid aside his pegging-awl and hammer.

The machine age has finally forced him out of business.

But time was when folks called him the master shoemaker of the hills and swore that a pair of his shoes would last a'body a lifetime.

Now at 88, hale and hearty, all that Milas Messer has left are the tools of his trade and his memories.

He is the last of a shoemakin' clan, a special breed that kept the feet of the nation shod for two centuries.

His father and his grandfather were shoemakers, mountain men who knew how to tan leather, fashion a last, whittle wooden shoe pegs, and turn out a shoe that wouldn't leak or wear out.

He inherited their secrets and their special know-how, and for almost 50 years he turned this knowledge into a thing of industry and love.

"I raised eleven children," he said, "and I made shoes for all of 'em. When my youngest boy come along and started to school he used to come home and fret because the other children got a new pair of shoes ever two or three months. Them that got shoes so often wore store-bought shoes and I made his. They wouldn't wear out. They was made to last."

As he talked the wind whistled off the Cataloochee Divide and hammered at the windows, and the gentle tapping was like the tapping of a shoe-hammer driving away at maple shoe-pegs.

"I started makin' shoes when I was about twenty," he said. "Made 'em for the family and for the neighbors. Folks put so much by my shoes that they'd come walkin' for miles around to get me to make 'em a pair.

"I tanned my own leather. Tanned it with oak bark. Had me

a bark mill and ground up my own bark for tannin'. Still got the bark mill. It's up there back of the house. Ain't used it in a long time. It's going to pieces.

"But when I kept it a'goin' it was one of the finest bark mills there was. Made it myself. Don't reckon you've ever seen one, huh? It's a big contraption. It was operated with a horse.

"You might say it's like a cider-press or a cane-mill. Horse turned it. You fed the bark in and the teeth—there was three rows of 'em made out of wood—chewed up the bark.

"Once you got your bark chewed up, you put it in a trough of water. What you called a tannin' trough. You put ashes or lime into the trough to dilute the water.

"Before you put the skins in to tan you kept 'em salted and folded together a few days till all the blood had been drawn out. When green hides was to be tanned right away they was first fleshed. To flesh 'em you put 'em on the fleshing block and scraped 'em with a fleshin' knife—one havin' a rounded edge.

"This block was a log. The upper surface was rounded. The lower end rested on the ground. The upper end was supported by pegs and reached to a man's waist.

"When the hides was dried before bein' tanned, they was hung lengthwise on poles, with the fleshside uppermost, and left under shelter till dry and hard.

"You removed the hair from green and dry hides alike. Done it by soakin' 'em in the tan-trough. Used a solution of lime or wood ashes till the hair would slip—that is, come off easy-like."

He didn't know that the process he was describing was first used by the ancient Egyptians—that is, the tanning—and that it was not until 1790 that the hair was removed from skins when tanned.

"After the skins had soaked a while," he said, "they was placed on the fleshin' bench and broken or made pliable. Used a breakin'-knife for this.

"Then they went into the tan-trough for the real tannin' process. The bottom of the trough was lined with a layer of bark, and another layer of bark placed above the upper fold of the side. This was done till the trough was filled. Then water was poured in and the mass allowed to remain two months.

"It was a long process. After two months time the water and bark was renewed, changed at the end of two more months. Two months longer completed the tannin', makin' six months in all.

"This was called the cold-ooze process. Folks got to usin' the hot-ooze method, but it ain't good. It cooks and injuries the leather. That's why leather was so much better back in them days

"Well, when I'd got my hides tanned I was ready to begin makin' shoes. Done my shoemakin' right here in the house. Had all my tools right at hand all the time. Sometimes I'd work at it daytime and there was times I'd work at night by the lamp or light from the fire.

"I'd get several pair of shoes out of one hide. Made my own lasts, too. I'd make a pattern of a feller's foot and then take a piece of poplar and start carvin' out a last.

"You know, feet are all different. Course they got different sizes and widths in storebought shoes now, but to really fit a'body you got to make a last for each foot. That way you get a good fit and a'body won't never have no trouble with their feet.

"I'd put the soles on with wooden pegs. Made the pegs out of birch or maple. Can't beat maple for shoe pegs. They go in easy but you can't get 'em out. They'll stick forever. Once you've got 'em in the sole and get the leather damp they'll swell up and stick better'n molasses. They'll break off before they'll come out. Wooden pegs are better than sprigs. What's that? Sprigs? Why, tacks.

"I used whang leather to sew the uppers together. Made my whang leather out of groundhog skins. Tanned it and then cut it into strips. Used thick thread, too. Had to wax it.

"Gettin' back to lasts. I reckon the loft is full of 'em. Never did throw any of 'em away. Never knew when I might need 'em again. Sometimes I figure I'll get out my tools and make a pair of shoes, but then I don't. Seems like it's easier to go to the store and buy a pair. Course they don't wear as good and as long.

"All the shoes I made was all leather. Even made a leather insole that fitted into the shoe. You used good leather for the insoles.

"What's that? When did I make my last pair of shoes. Well, let me see. Must have been about four or five years ago. Made 'em for one of the family.

"No, I never got too much for makin' a pair of shoes. Most of the time I got three dollars. Not much money today but it was a lot back then. Now a feller has to pay ten or twelve dollars fer a pair of store-bought shoes. And I hear they're gettin' as much as twenty and thirty dollars for 'em and them not hand-made.

"A feller come up here last summer. He was away from here. Said he'd like mighty well if I'd agree to make him a pair of shoes. He never said what he'd give me, cause I told him I wasn't makin' no more shoes. But I heard tell later that folks pay fifty and a hundred dollars for a pair of handmade shoes now-a-days."

For a moment he was silent. He stared into the fire and shook his head.

"Times have changed," he said, and shook his head again.

Then he straightened in his chair and moved his feet on the floor.

He was wearing a pair of store-bought shoes.

He caught me looking at them and grinned.

"Store-bought," he said, grinning. "Don't even make any for myself any more."

And we remembered that the homemade tanbark mill back of the house is tottering into ruin and that the old man has laid aside his pegging-awl and hammer.

Bee Balm

Pipe-Maker to the Cherokee

Cherokee

MOSE OWL IS PIPE-MAKER TO THE CHEROKEE.
He practices an art that was old when history was new.

His people were carving pipes out of bone and stone and smoking tobacco a thousand years before Alfred Dunhill ever fashioned a briar in London.

An elaborately decorated ku-nu-nuwah, which is to say pipe, caught the fancy of Hernando DeSoto when he came this way in 1540.

"Time was," said Mose Owl, "when my people had great respect for the pipe. A sort of reverence. It was never smoked for pleasure. They used it in their rituals. That is all gone now. Most of the old things have been put away. Or forgotten."

To the old Indian, this is a pity and a shame.

"Only a few of us are left who know how to make the old pipes," he said. "You can count them on one hand. And I guess I am the only one that takes the time to make them now. There's hardly ever any use for them any more. I make them because I like to. I like to use my hands. And my hands work best at making pipes."

There was something proud in his word. Nothing boastful. Only pride. A pride of craftsmanship in an ancient art that is disappearing like the leaves now fading from the trees.

For a moment he looked down at his hands. Thin hands wherein pulsed a magic. Hands that had carefully carved out many a stone pipe. Hands that know the feel of a pocketknife and how to use it.

"Somehow," he said, "when I make a pipe I feel I put something of me into it. I can't explain it. I start with a piece of stone. A rough piece and before long as it takes shape it gets to feeling like it is alive.

"A lot of work goes into a pipe. The kind I make. It's long and slow. Has to be if you get it just right. You can't hurry a pipe. If you do, then it's not much of a pipe. Takes me most of a week to make one.

"Of course, a plain pipe don't take too long. But a plain pipe is just a pipe. Anybody can make a plain pipe. My pipes are not plain. I carve figures on them. Mostly animals. All the old pipes had animals on them.

"Each tribe and each clan back in the old days had their own designs. That was so they could be recognized easily by friends or enemies. Sort of like a badge.

"Most of the pipes I make have animals on them. A frog or a bear or a fox. Sometimes a bird. They stand out. I don't cut the figure into the pipe. And some of them are whole animals. Like a bullfrog. I just carve a bullfrog and then work the bowl out of his back and bore a hole all the way through for the stem."

Mose was standing by a case of ancient pipes in the Museum of the Cherokee Indian. He works for the Cherokee Historical Association as a guide and lecturer. The old pipes in the case are his love. When he isn't lecturing, Mose works on a pipe of his own making.

And somehow, when you look at the old pipes that have come out of a mound and then look at the ones he has made, you have a feeling Mose is hoping that someday his pipes will be in a museum, too.

"I've been making pipes ever since I was a boy," he said. "Been making them over 50 years. Been improving all the time, too. Guess I have made so many I could make one with my eyes closed or in the dark. I know the feel.

"Since I have been working here at the museum I've made a study of all the old pipes. Just a part of the collection is on display. I study them all the time. And I look at the pictures in the books on Indian pipes.

"Back in the olden times, pipes were made out of all sorts of material. Pottery, wood, bone, metal and stone. The most common used was soapstone. It's easy to handle.

"There were all sizes of pipes. Some were little tiny things, weighing barely an ounce. Others were big and weighed several pounds. The big ones were used just on special occasions. Like at a treaty-signing or a big gathering of chiefs in council.

"The Cherokee had a great peace pipe in the old days. It was carved out of white stone. It had seven stem-holes. That was so seven men could sit around and smoke from it at once at the peace councils. Seven always has been a sacred number among the Cherokee. You find seven cropping up in almost everything.

"The large cloud-blowers usually were made of stone. I made one once. One of the seven-stemmed ones. Sometimes they use it in a special ceremony up at Oconaluftee Village. When some of the tribesmen a few years ago retraced the Trail of Tears they carried it with them to Oklahoma and smoked it out there with some of the western Cherokee."

Mose called attention to one of the pipes in the case.

"That one," he said, "is the tomahawk or hatchet pipe. It's made of metal. The Spanish brought them in first. Then the English and the French brought them in and give them to the Indians.

"You don't come by the tomahawk pipe much. Only a few of them have ever been found. Some of them were pretty. Inlaid with silver. A design worked out in silver."

Mose picked up a pipe he had been working on.

"This one is to be a bear," he said. "Been working on it about a week. Be another week before I finish it. Then I'll fit a proper stem to it. A straight stem. Though in the old days there was all sorts of stems.

"Some made their stems straight, others curved or twisted, round or flat, long or short. Depended on how they was to be used. All mine have straight stems. A long stem goes with a big pipe and a short stem with a small one.

"Sometimes I put decorations on my pipe stems. Cover some of them in leather and tie a feather to it. Time was when beads, hair, porcupine quills and feathers were used.

"You can always tell one of my pipes. I put my mark on the bottom of it. Carve my name in Cherokee on it. Carve it in the true letters that Sequoyah invented."

Mose picked up his knife and the piece of stone.

Carefully, he whittled away at the stone.

A thousand years ago, Mose Owl would have been using the hard sharp tine of a deer antler for a knife.

Autumn's Rainbows Aglow

Rainbow Springs

THE TAPESTRIES OF AUTUMN GLOWED LIKE RAINBOWS ON the mountains of the Noonday Sun.

"Look," said the hillsman. "Look at that if you want to see the hand of the Almighty in all its glory. Look at the light on that water. Look at the color of them hills.

"There ain't no picture-paintin' artist ever got them colors put down right. There ain't none ever will."

Along the back country road, rows of buckeye and oak and poplar and maple stretched like a palisade to the sky.

"They're right pretty and right useful," said the hillsman. "They growed up with the country and the country growed up with 'em.

"Mark 'em with your eye and call 'em by name. Ever' one of 'em fit in some place. Behind all that pretty they've got a history that's worth knowin' about.

"There ain't a one of 'em that don't stand for somethin' that helped a-body get along when this country was a-growin' up. They was the Almighty's gift to folks that come a-settlin'. Made cabins and gunstocks and cradles and wagon wheels and fence rails. Even furnished medicines and dyes for cloth.

"Folks don't give 'em much mind no more, 'cept to come lookin' at 'em in the fall of the year when they're all pretty and a-shoutin' with color like nothin' on earth.

"Seems like if folks had a knowin' of what uses they'd been put to they'd get a right smart more pleasure out of lookin' at 'em. They'd see a heap more'n just a red maple or a yellow hickory. Be sort of like the trees was a-talkin' back to 'em."

The hillsman looked off toward the mountain called Angel where the buckeye and oak and poplar and black gum and sassafras dripped with gold and blazed against the Indian summer sky of the blue October day.

"That's buckeye up yonder," he said. "The one with the clear yellow leaves. Sort of glows. Drops seeds that look like a deer's eye. Back in the old days folks made cradles out of buckeye to rock their children in. Lots of folks carry buckeyes in their pockets to keep off the rheumetism.

"Now just above the road there—that's sassafras. It takes on all sorts of colors. Sometimes it'll be yellow or orange. Or red like a fire, real bright. The old folks made sassafras tea. Some of 'em still do. I never cared for it myself. But there's them that puts a heap of stock in it. And when it come to makin' homemade soap, a sassafras stick was always used to stir it. No other kind would do. Soap would ruin unless you used a sassafras stick for stirrin'.

"Course, you know all about sourwood. That's it over there with them dark red leaves that sort of reminds you of grape wine. Folks used to brew the leaves. Made a powerful tonic. Bees feed off it. That's how you get sourwood honey. There ain't nothin' to equal sourwood honey."

The hillsman swung his gaze back toward the mountain of the Angel where the hickories stood like tattered old sentinels.

They dripped a soft dull gold and there was a sort of luminous beauty about them as the sun shone through them.

"You can't beat hickory for fire-wood," said the hillsman. "Makes a hot fire. An even heat. Best there is for smokin' hams. Course you use green hickory for that. Can't beat it either for ax handles. Makes good fence rails, too. And ramrods for guns.

"Back in the old days folks made brooms out of hickory. Used a small hickory sapling. Stripped it up eight or ten inches, tied it with tow string and made the pole above the strips into a handle.

"Them's oaks all through yonder. White oaks and red oaks. Them with the winy color are white oaks. Them that's brown or bright orange are red oaks.

"Oak's mighty stout. Can make might near anythin' out of oak. When folks had to get out with an ax and make their necessities they used oak. Barns, mills, cabins. Rived their barrel staves out of oak. Used the bark in tanning skins."

The hillsman paused, squinted into the sun.

"That's a beech over there," he said. "You can tell easy. Leaves lay together sort of like sprays. Plumb clear yellow. They say it was a beech old Dan'l Boone carved his name on that time he killed a bear."

Then the hillsman pointed out the tulip poplar and the pawpaw and the wild cherry.

The poplars stood straight and tall, a rich, rejoicing gold.

"The Indians," he said, "made canoes out of poplar."

Down in the cove, within the sound of the mountain stream, the wild cherry flaunted a crown of fiery red.

"Some folks call it inountain Mahogany," said the hillsman. "It makes a pretty cabMet wood."

He pointed to a pawpaw.

"Don't see so many of 'em any more," he said. "Not like you used to. Leaves are sort of butter yellow. Real mellow like. Folks made jelly out of the fruit. Pawpaw jelly. Possums are great pawpaw eaters. So are 'coons and squirrels.

"And that's what you call a butternut. Don't never pick up a butternut if you don't want to get your hands all brown-stained. It won't scrub off. Only time'll take off the stain. Folks used to use it as a dye to color their homespun."

The tree with the star-shaped leaves of light, gay yellow-green?

"Why, that's a sweet gum," said the hillsman. "The old folks took the ooze and treated sores and skin troubles. Made a sort of chewing gum, too.

"Over yonder's a black gum. The one with the leaves all deep winy red. Them that used snuff always made their toothbrushes out of black gum."

Eventually, the hillsman came to a little creek. The one called Nova Scotia and the falling tongues of maple fire.

"There's sugar maple and red maple and striped maple," he said. "Most all this is red maple. It's good whittlin' wood."

Scattered through the hills were thousands of little trees popping with vermilion and maroon.

These were the dogwood.

The blossoms that shone like stars in the spring were gone.

"The old folks used to steep dogwood bark in whiskey," said the hillsman. "They used the brew for 'the shakes' and the 'ague' It was a good cure."

The hillsman looked off toward the west.

Off beyond the rainbow-colored hills where the pumpkin sun drops ripe.

"Just look at that if you want to see the hand of the Almighty in all its glory," he said. "Just look at the color of them hills.

"There ain't no picture-paintin' artist ever got them colors put down right. There ain't none never will."

Lullaby of Buckeye

Burningtown

MY GRANDFATHER'S UNCLE WAS THE CRADLEMAKER OF the mountains.

His was the hand that fashioned a lullaby out of buckeye and oak and hickory.

Folks said he was the masterest hand in all the land when it come to making cradles.

That was back in the days when everybody that raised children had a cradle to rock them in and soothe them when they were teethin' or when they got fussy.

A home without a cradle was like a man without a wife.

Rich or poor, if you had a baby you had a cradle.

A cradle wasn't a convenience, it was a necessity.

But like so many of the old and useful things, the cradle is only a museum piece now.

It has vanished, and that's a shame and a pity.

Nobody seems to know what killed off the cradle.

Most of the old and useful things disappeared because something came along to replace them.

The homemade candle and the oil lamp, the buggy and the sled, the spinning wheel and the hand-loom were outmoded by things which did their jobs better and easier.

But the cradle just disappeared.

Nobody came up with anything to replace the cradle, oldest and most familiar piece of infant furniture ever known.

"For the life of me," mused my 97-year-old grandfather, "I just can't understand why folks stopped usin' cradles. I never heard tell that cradle-rockin' ever harmed children. Some folks now-a-days will argue that rockin' ain't good for kids. They just let their kids squall their heads off without payin' 'em any mind

"Back when I was a baby, and right up through the time me

and your grandma raised our four children, everybody had a cradle that raised kids.

"My Uncle Eli made cradles for everybody hereabouts. He was the masterest cradle-maker in these parts. Took a heap a pride in 'em. Like he done with the shingles he made. Couldn't nobody turn out better shingles than him.

"When your mama come along he made us a cradle that was the finest and purtiest thing you ever saw. It was made to last and it did. Your grandma rocked four kids in it and then passed it on to somebody. Don't recollect just who, but whoever it was never brought it back and I don't know what happened to it.

"I know when you come along, your mama got to trying to find that cradle and almost raised the roof when we couldn't find it. Of course, Uncle Eli was gone by then, and I had to hunt around for somebody to make a cradle.

"Cradles were few when you were born. And there wasn't but one or two folks around that knew the first thing about cradle-makin'. I got your Uncle Will Cowan at Webster to make you one. He done a fair-to-middlin' job, not being a cradle-maker by trade. But I always did feel bad about you not havin' one of Eli's cradles.

"Eli made 'em out of ash and poplar and oak, but he liked to work best with buckeye. Reckon that was because it was so light and could be hollowed out so easily. And it was pretty wood, too.

"He'd take a short length of buckeye log and work on it like he was makin' somethin' that was gonna hold a king. He pegged it with oak pins to two hickory rockers. The rockers was curved just so, looked like somethin' a feller would turn on a machine now-a-days.

"You could sit there and rock one of his cradles and it never would creep. That's why he used hickory. Rockers out of hickory won't creep.

"There was a thing about a cradle that nobody ever has equaled. A'body could sit by it in a chair and rock the cradle with their foot while they sewed or darned or knitted. A'body could even do their churnin' while rockin' the baby.

"And when the woman of the house had to move about she could keep the cradle nearby so that ever now and then when she passed it she could touch it with her foot and keep it at a slow but steady rockin'."

The Old Man paused and for a moment he seemed far away in time, as if he were sorting out his memories.

"I remember once," he said, "there was a big stir in the settlement. One of the Ropers, a cousin of mine, had a cradle that was kept in the front room. Kept it there long after the children had grown out of it and was sleepin' in beds. It was about the first thing you saw when you went into the house.

"Well, one mornin' this cousin come over to the house about the time we was fixin' breakfast. It wasn't even good daylight. He looked a little peaked and there was somethin' about his eyes that made a man wonder. Looked like he hadn't slept a wink.

"He sat around the fire for a while without sayin' much, and then he finally got around to talkin' about it. Said he reckoned the devil was after him. Your grandma told him that could well be. He didn't seem to pleasure her words.

"At last he started talkin' like a blue streak. Told us he hadn't slept in three nights. It's that cradle, he said. Rocks all night long and no human hand or foot a'touchin' it. Said he'd no sooner get to bed and it'd begin a'rockin'. Told us when he got out of bed and went to it, the cradle was just as still as a settin' hen. Said it only rocked at night.

"Well, this thing went on and on and my cousin couldn't make up his mind what to do. Said he was afraid if he chopped it up and burned it there was no tellin' what might happen to him.

"It got so everybody in the neighborhood knew about the rockin' cradle that rocked of its own accord. But nobody ever saw it a'rockin' though some folks who got curious went over and got in another room and stayed a spell and come away swearin' they heard it, too.

"After about three months my cousin put that cradle in his wagon and went off to Franklin. He come back without it but he never would tell what he did with it. Just said he got rid of it. I always figured he give it to somebody, though I never heard of nobody in these parts ever havin' any trouble with a cradle like my cousin did."

The Old Man chuckled.

"Your grandma always said it was just imagination fed by the peartnin' juice my cousin sipped.

"But there was one thing for certain. It wasn't one of Eli's cradles. If it had of been, you can bet Eli would have chopped it up himself. He was mighty foolish about his cradles."

The Old Man didn't say it in just this way, but you got the feeling that his Uncle Eli put a lullaby in every cradle he made.

After all, said the Old Man, he was the masterest cradle-maker in these parts.

"Too bad," he said, "that folks don't use cradles any more."

A Mountain Man and His Hound Dog

Somewhere in the Blue Ridge

THERE'S A STRANGE AFFINITY BETWEEN A MOUNTAIN MAN and his hound-dog.

It's a thing quite beyond the ken of folks who never have seen a hunter's moon melt behind the hemlocks, or heard the high clear voice of a hound set the hill-echoes to ringing like church bells of a Sunday morning, or felt a dog's cold nose when danger stalks the wild rhododendron thickets.

Somehow a mountain man and a hound-dog just seem to belong together like seed and burr, like sap and bark, and it's worth a man's life to separate them wilfully from each other.

But if a mountain man figures his hound needs killing, then he'll do the killing himself and bury the hound and a piece of his own heart.

And if his hound gets to mean-mouthing and needs a whipping, he'll do the whipping himself, too.

The hound is his and there's an unwritten law of the hills that he's the one to mete out any punishment that needs meting out.

Let somebody else kill his dog or abuse it and he'll grab his rifle or knife, or use his fists or hob-nailed stomping boots.

"There's been more killin's over dogs in the hills than anythin' else," said the old mountaineer, " 'cept maybe over land. A man's got a feelin' for his hounds and he'll trail 'em to hell and back and fight ever' inch of the way for 'em."

The old mountaineer is wise in the ways of woods and animals, and he's been a hound-dog man for fifty years and more. He knows how a man comes to feel about a hound-dog.

He knows that between a mountain man and his hound-dog there is a feeling, an understanding, which the man guards jealously and to which he gives his heart, and sometimes his soul.

In his own simple way he makes you understand that only those who know the solitude and the abiding loneliness of tall mountains and laurel-crowned ridges ever really know this feeling, a feeling which sometimes even transcends a man's love for his son.

There are many stories here in the mountains about men and dogs, of their love and devotion to each other, and how one has died through blind courage and the other has messed up his life because of the dumb one.

Some of the stories are not pretty. Some of them are tragic. And some are filled with the ache that gnaws at a man's insides. But all of them tell of a way of life in the hills.

And all of them are stories that are told and re-told and handed down from one hound-dog man to another, raked up around campfires when twilight melts into the first drift of dark and the shadows float heavy across the mountains.

It is a time when hunters and their dogs wait with the patience that comes with living in a wilderness of fast-running water and thick trees for the hunter's moon to bathe the high reaches with silver and set the wild things of the night to prowling.

Sometimes the old ones, the ones who now must stay by the fire and listen to the bell baying and dream of yesterdays, will remember the famous old hunter of the hills who put his dog above his son.

It's a story poignant as the fragrance of wild honeysuckle.

"I ain't mentionin' no names," said the old mountaineer. "And you ain't to use my name, either. No use of fannin' a dyin' fire that might scorch a'body, even though I don't see how it could. Reckon you'll know who I'm a'talkin' about. Chances are you're some a'kin. 'Course it ain't nothin' nobody's a reason to be ashamed of. Fact is, they ought to be proud. It was all a matter of misunderstandin', or a matter of not tellin' the reason why."

For a moment the old mountaineer stared beyond the fire into the night and the night lay as still as unborn time.

"As a matter of fact," he said, "I got mixed up in this thing, all innocent like, and come within a hair of gettin' shot, maybe killed.

"For the sake of the story I'll call the old man Billy-B. He was as fine an old man as you'll ever run across. Independent as they come. A hunter that couldn't be beat. Lived by a set of rules that was strict as all get-out. But he was a hound-dog man, and his dogs got fit and proper treatment. Loved his hounds, he did. Hunted all the time, daytime and nighttime.

"He was goin' on eighty when this happened. Doctor had told him he had a heart ailment. Told his folks, too. The old man didn't worry none but his folks got all upset and started tellin' the old man to be careful. Got so they tried to keep him out of the woods.

"Well, now, he had as fine a pack of hounds as a man would want. He had one that was especially prime, a hound named Trim. She was the best coon dog that ever hit these mountains. And her and the old man was like fiddle music. They stepped to the same tune. He shore loved her.

"His folks got to worryin' that he'd drop dead some day or night when he was out a'huntin' and they figured the only way to keep him out of the wood was to sell off his hounds. They knew the old man wouldn't hear to it and they figured they'd have to get rid of the dogs when he was off to the store.

"I never knew nothin' about all this. But one day I was down at the county seat, standin' there on the street, when one of the old man's boys come up to me and asked me how I'd like to buy a couple of the old man's dogs. Said they was sellin' 'em off and he figured since me and him was pretty good friends I ought to have the first crack at 'em.

"Well, I didn't want to be too eager, but I'd had my eye on a couple of the old man's coon dogs for a long time. We haggled for a spell and finally the boy told me I could have 'em both for fifty dollars. I knew that any one of 'em was worth $350, at least.

"My first choice was Trim. She was a coon dog from a way back. I give him $25 for her and said I'd have to roust up some more money to get the other one.

"When I went to get Trim the old man's wife said I'd better get her and get away quick before Billy-B come home. She told me the old man wouldn't let me have her. So I got Trim and got away from there.

"I reckon it was a week or so later I was back down at the county seat and met the old man on the street. He come up to me and I said howdy, Mister Billy-B. He looked at me and the tears begun spillin' down his cheeks.

"When he spoke, he said, 'You done me wrong.' Well, I knew right then I was in a fix. I was lookin' at death as shore as God made little green apples, I swallowed once or twice—don't remember exactly—and asked him what was the matter. He told me I'd got his best hound and he wasn't goin' to allow it. I started talkin' real kind like. And then I asked him a question. I says, Mister Billy-B, can you blame a man for buying the best coon dog in the state if he's got the chance. Well, he sort of studied a minute and then said he reckoned not. But, he asked me something that made me want to get away from there. He looks at me and them tears in his eyes, and he says could maybe he go huntin' with me and Trim some time. I could see he was achin' all inside.

"I said, Mister Billy-B, you can hunt with me any time you feel like it, or you can take Trim out by yourself. And I promise you one thing, she'll never be mistreated and she'll have an easy death when her time comes.

"Well, the old man nodded and stuck out his hand and we shook hands and he went on down the street.

"Later on I heard how he went home and faced his boy that sold me the dog. He stood right there and said, 'Son, you've lived with your Pa long enough.' The boy knew what he meant and got out.

"The old man never seemed the same any more. Never once asked me to go huntin'. His wife told folks in the neighborhood that the old man was grievin' himself to death for Trim.

"Well, about six or eight months later, one of the old man's boys died and the one he had told to get out come home for the funeral. The old man moved out to the barn and slept there while the boy was home. When the funeral and the burial was over the old man went to the house and told the boy that sold me Trim, 'Son, it's time you was movin' on.' And the boy moved on. Never come back until the old man died a couple years later."

Some folks, said the old mountaineer, was sure old Billy-B died of a broken heart. Said he just pined away for Trim.

After all, there's an affinity between a mountain man and his hound-dog.

The Gillespie Rifle-Gun

Shooting Branch

THE GILLESPIES HELPED WRITE AMERICAN HISTORY.
They were pioneer gunsmiths and they had a gunshop right here under Forge Mountain in the hills of Henderson County.

Their long rifles tamed the wilderness and talked independence down at King's Mountain.

Many a mountain man who gambled his life on his gun trigger swore by them.

For downright true-firing, the Gillespie rifle-gun spoke right up to anybody or anything on the frontier and a man could be as certain of hitting where he aimed as death and taxes.

The first Gillespies, father and six sons, came out of England about 1700. They settled in Lancaster County, Pennsylvania, where German, Swiss and French Huguenot gunsmiths had begun to do business.

They brought with them the tools of their trade and a heritage of Old World gunsmithing.

It wasn't too long before the fame of their rifle-guns spread far and wide and Lancaster became synonymous with rifle.

Daniel Boone carried a Gillespie rifle-gun in the crook of his arm when he headed out of Pennsylvania for North Carolina and the Promised Land where a man could have wingroom and spit without hitting a neighbor.

Some of the Gillespies followed Boone down into the wilds of the Blue Ridge, a range of timbered peaks that were old when the Rockies were new. They came down the Boone Trail, down through what is now Gillespie Gap and Spruce Pine.

One of them, Mathew by name, crossed the French Broad and followed the Estatoe Trail, an Indian trading path, along Mills River. A half mile down the river he discovered Philip Sitton operating an iron works on the south side of Forge Mountain, a loaf-shaped peak rich in iron ore.

Mathew Gillespie figured he had reached the end of his long journey. This seemed a likely spot for setting up his gunshop. Sitton told him there was need for a master gunsmith.

So Gillespie set down his forge and anvil here on Shooting Branch and began turning out long rifles that made his name legend on the frontier.

It wasn't long until he married one of the iron-maker's daughters, Elizabeth, who proceeded to bear him three sons in a row. And each of them—Wilson, Harvey and Philip—became a crackerjack gunsmith under the patient but demanding tutelage of their father.

They shaped the gunskelps hammered out by their Grandfather Sitton into guns and rifles whose reputation for accuracy spread far and wide.

The Gillespie rifle-gun, long of barrel, slender and graceful of stock with a good deal of drop, or crook, became a frontier legend and even created legends, not to mention a few myths.

No two were identical and yet any man could spot a Gillespie rifle-gun in a wink. Many of them were often ornamented with inlays of brass, German silver or even coin silver. Silver sights adorned some and at least one was turned out with a sight fashioned from Carolina gold.

To the man who owned one, it was a prime superfine rifle-gun, fitting for doing a trustworthy piece of shooting, be it Red Skin, Red Coat, or a grizzly bear.

Of course, a lot of extravagant claims were made for the Gillespie rifle-gun, none of which the Gillespies ever originated and which they were the first to deny.

All they ever claimed was their rifles wouldn't blow up and they would shoot where a man aimed.

And no man ever questioned their true-firing. Well, at least, not more than one and he didn't rightly question the rifle-gun itself. He laid it all to a witch.

At any rate, that's the story that's been handed down about old Neddy McFalls who lived on Cataloochee Creek.

Old Neddy was quite a hunter in his day and he swore there wasn't a rifle-gun in all the land to equal a Gillespie for true-firing. His faith in his Gillespie was a thing that was worth a man's life to question.

But one day when he was out hunting, he got a close-up, broadside shot at a big buck and missed.

Some say the old man figured the world was coming to an end and he didn't have much time to get ready. They say he stood there and looked at his rifle-gun and the cold sweat popped out.

And then he got to studying and decided somebody had bewitched his rifle-gun.

Well, he took off down the mountain and made his way past his house and on down into the faraway cove where he sought out a grannywoman who had a reputation for lifting "spells."

He struck a bargain with her and handed over his rifle-gun and sat by most of a day while the old woman crooned and moaned and mumbled strange words.

Eventually, she handed him his rifle-gun and told him she had lifted the curse.

Old Neddy headed back for his cabin on Cataloochee Creek. When he got home he took his knife and cut an "X" in a tree, stepped off thirty paces, primed his rifle-gun and then took aim.

His finger brushed the trigger and the gun exploded.

He walked over to the tree, not without a little doubt.

He looked at his mark and right there in the center of the "X" was a hole.

After that, old Neddy didn't miss his target too often and when he did, he'd search out the old granny woman.

It never did cross his mind that his eye-sight was getting a mite fuzzy with the years.

The Gillespies could have told the old man his trouble. For they always said their rifle-guns put a ball where a man aimed.

The Gillespies kept right on making rifle-guns here on Shooting Branch until the Civil War.

Philip was the last of the gunsmiths.

And he went off to war and didn't come back. He was carrying a true-firing rifle of his own make when he left.

The iron works fell into disuse. The forge was abandoned.

And a Gillespie rifle-gun became a rare collector's piece.

There is nothing now to remind a visitor that once the famed Gillespie gunsmiths had a gunshop here on Shooting Branch.

The water trompe is gone.

There is no trace of the anvil and hammer.

But now and then you will run across a Gillespie rifle-gun.

There are at least three still around. One is in the rifle collection at the Pioneer Museum in the Great Smokies above Cherokee. Another is owned by Mrs. Sadie Patton of Hendersonville.

On their long barrels are the initials "PG," two of the last rifle-guns made by Philip Gillespie, who was the last of a long line of pioneer gunsmiths whose long rifles helped write American history.

Grandma's Cooking

Little Savannah

IT'S A BUCKWHEAT-CAKES-AND-SORGHUM-SYRUP KIND OF morning. The winds blowing off the Cowees are sharp and the trees are snapping with frost.

Inside the weathered old house, flames crackle along the logs of the hearthfire and stir up old memories.

And the memories are of Grandma and Grandma's cooking.

They are the memories of long-remembered aromas drifting from the kitchen and long-remembered tastes that a small boy somehow loses with growing up, forever haunting and elusive.

They are memories of buckwheat cakes with sorghum molasses and fresh homemade sausage of a winter morning, of Grandpa sitting at the big table in the kitchen and bowing his head and saying the blessing.

They are memories of plain and simple food, and of Grandma greasing a black iron skillet, stirring a pan over the wood stove or cooking ash cakes on the hearth.

Memory can play strange tricks, but when it comes to remembering Grandma's cooking, it's like being with her right there in the kitchen. And the smells are as sharp as the tick of the clock on the mantel.

When the first cold winds of winter began blowing off the high peaks, Grandma got out her special crock for buckwheat batter.

Grandpa grew his own buckwheat and he always had a time every year with the miller who always fussed when Grandpa fetched a turn for grinding. The miller said grinding a turn of buckwheat flour was a waste of his time for the price he got. Said it took most of a day to get his grinder cleaned so he could go back to turning corn meal.

Grandpa made his own molasses, too. Made it in a horse-around mill back of the house from sorghum he grew beyond the creek.

There was always a cruet of sorghum molasses on Grandma's kitchen table. She kept it covered with a white cloth and the only time it left the table was when she had to refill it from one of the jugs Grandpa kept out in the earthen-floor smokehouse.

Grandma mixed up her buckwheat batter the night before so there would be buckwheat cakes the next morning. Grandma passed on before the advent of storebought buckwheat mix, which probably is just as well. For she wasn't one to have any truck with storebought stuff.

Her kitchen was old. But it was as clean as a whistle and neat as a pin. She wasn't one for leaving things lying about. The black iron of her stove glistened from rubbing and polishing.

Unless there was special company, Grandma and Grandpa always ate at the big table in the kitchen. They ate there even when their children and grandchildren came of a weekday.

The dining room was for Sunday, if there was company, or at Thanksgiving and Christmas, times when Grandma sort of out-did herself with a bit of fancy cooking such as pies and cakes and the like. But for the rest of the year, Grandma stuck to plain and simple cooking and plain and simple food.

Somehow, looking back to Grandma's heyday, she seemed to turn out her more tasty dishes in the fall and winter.

Perhaps this was because fall and winter brought fresh pork and fresh beef and such things as backbones and ribs, liver mush and souse meat, squirrel and dumplings, cracklin' bread and hominy, and crisp fried streaked-lean fatback tangy with salt.

Grandma made her own hominy. Folks called it lye hominy. She boiled shelled hard corn in a solution of lye water from hickory ashes poured into the ash hopper back of the house.

In the winter, when the cold winds whined about the house and the snow swirled in from the Balsams, she would fix something like potato soup. And to a small boy coming in at dusk after playing in the snow back on the pine-dotted hill above the north pasture, potato soup never tasted so good. What with a big pone of golden-crusted, steaming cornbread for crumbling in a bowl of potato soup heavily speckled with black pepper.

Grandma was the best potato soup maker there ever was. What she did to it is a mystery, for all that has come after just doesn't seem to have the taste like hers did. Sometimes she would make hash, and it too had a taste that is a memory.

Grandpa was mighty fond of bear meat. Long after he got too old to go bear-hunting, he still managed to get a mess of bear meat from a neighbor or one of his boys.

Grandma didn't care much for bear meat. She said she could eat it if somebody else fixed it. But she didn't have a taste for it when she had to do the cooking. There was something about the smell of bear meat cooking that just took away her appetite.

She wasn't alone in this. Many a mountain woman can't stand to be around bear meat cooking. But Grandma loved Grandpa. She figured if bear meat pleasured him, then she ought to be the one to fix it. She did. Once a year. Grandpa seemed satisfied.

"I reckon," he used to say, "one good bait of bear meat a winter is about all a man can ask for." And he would sort of grin at Grandma. She didn't grin. She just let him talk.

Grandma wasn't one for wasting time with cook books or recipes. She learned her cooking from her mother. And what her mother didn't teach her, she picked up by trying it out on Grandpa. Nobody ever heard Grandpa fuss about Grandma's cooking. And he ate her cooking for most of 60 years running, day in and day out except for the spell he was off in the war getting shot and starving and gnawing on sole-leather soaked in water.

Grandma cooked by rule of finger—a pinch of this and a pinch of that. Her taste buds were sharp and she humored them, and nobody ever fussed with her likes.

Most of her cooking was done on the black iron wood stove, but she cooked on the hearth too. Cooked on it right up until the time she died. Grandpa was mighty fond of ash cakes and hoe cakes. And there's only one place to cook them. That's the hearth.

Of a winter evening when Grandpa came in from finishing his chores, Grandma would bring a pan of cornmeal batter in before the fire and spread it on the hearth. She would let it lay near the fire until the outside crusted up a little. Then she would cover it with hot ashes and let it bake thirty or forty minutes. Or until it got well browned. When it was done she would brush off the ashes with a cloth.

Grandma baked her hoe cakes on the greased blade of a hoe. They were enough to make a man's mouth water. With a glass of fresh sweet milk, her hoe cakes were like nothing on earth. But you could say that about her sweet potato pie, too, or a thousand and one other things that came from her skillet and her hands.

The memory of her cooking is a haunting thing. The yearning for it becomes a flood when the winds blow sharp off the Cowees and the trees snap with frost and there's a smell of snow in the air.

It's a yearning that starts with November mornings.

Like now, when it's a buckwheat-cakes-and-sorghum-syrup kind of morning.

She Shore Loved Her Man

Montezuma

MOUNTAIN WOMEN ARE PLUMB FOOLISH ABOUT THEIR menfolks.

While they may biddy-peck and fault their yokemate behind the door, they'll go through thick and thin for him without asking why.

This is how a widow-woman over in the Alarka mountains put it:

"It ain't for a woman to question the doin's of her man. She takes him on for better or for worse, and it's up to her to make the best of it. Had two husbands myself. Lived with one thirty-odd years and the other some ten or twelve. 'Course, we had our ups and downs, but if either one had told me to stick my head in the fire, I'd a done it."

All of which is by way of introducing Malinda Blalock, a young mountain woman who didn't put her head in the fire but came mighty close to putting it in a cannon barrel.

Chances are she would have got her head shot off if her husband hadn't got himself a good dose of self-applied poison oak.

The saga of Malinda and her love for her man had its beginning back in the spring of 1856 here in the Avery County hills where Grandfather Mountain casts a shadow like a grim prophecy.

That was when she married up with William Blalock, a young giant of a fist-and-skull fighter.

Blalock was the fightin'est man in this neck of the woods. He was known as a fellow who could whip his weight in wildcats. His fists, which some folks claimed were big as hams and hard as flint, had earned him a healthy respect.

They also had earned him the nickname of "Keith" because folks rated him along with another fighter of long and great renown over at Burnsville, an aging hillsman named Alfred Keith.

By the time he and Malinda set up housekeeping, everybody referred to him as Keith Blalock and when he became a graybeard they called him "Old Keith."

Being a fighting man, Keith wasn't one to run from a fight, no matter what the odds.

So, when the Civil War came along, he figured he would have to get in it. Not that he had a hankering for killing, which he didn't. It was just that he had no other choice.

He and Malinda talked it over.

Keith said if he had to fight, then he would fight with the Union. But he told Malinda he was going to stay out of it just as long as he could.

A few days later the conscript law of the Confederacy went into operation, and, though he was a Union man, Keith was clearly subject to conscription.

For the first time, Malinda suddenly realized that she and her man were going to be parted.

For six years they had shared the same cabin. They had never been apart even for a single night.

Somehow, Malinda couldn't see herself being parted from her man.

She told him so.

"I'm a-goin' with you," she said. "That's what I'll do."

Keith protested a bit, but not much.

So, Malinda rustled up a pair of Keith's jeans and cut them down to size. Did the same with one of his shirts and one of his jackets. Then she took the scissors to her hair.

Looking every bit like a young fellow short of the razor-stage, Malinda set out with Keith to enlist in the Confederate army.

They figured the first chance they got they would desert and get into the Union lines.

They made their way out of the mountains and across the Piedmont to Kinston where they joined the 26th N. C. regiment, then commanded by Col. Zebulon B. Vance of Asheville.

Malinda passed muster and was issued a uniform and a musket. She tented with her husband.

She posed as Keith's younger brother and went by the name of Sam Blalock.

She stood guard, drilled and handled her musket like a man.

Nobody suspected that Sam Blalock was a woman.

When they could get off alone, they discussed plans for deserting to the Federal forces.

But Kinston was a long way from the Federal lines and it

seemed there was little prospect of getting closer.

Finally, Keith told Malinda he didn't aim to keep associating with the Johnny Rebs. Said he figured there was more than one way to skin a cat and he aimed to do it.

"If we can't get to the Federals," he told her, "I shore aim to get out of here and go home. I ain't stayin' here."

And then he told Malinda his plan.

She listened and said it just might work, at that.

So Keith waited until he had some time off from guard duty and slipped into a nearby swamp. There he searched out a patch of poison oak. He stripped down to bare skin and rubbed himself with the poisoned leaves.

It wasn't long until Keith's body was all broke out and aflame.

He reported to his superior and was sent off to the hospital in Kinston. The doctors there looked him over and disagreed as to his ailment.

Not being able to agree, they sent Keith back to his regiment where the medical officer shook his head and recommended his discharge.

The discharge wasn't long in coming and Keith left the camp.

He told Malinda he would be waiting up the road for her.

When Keith had cleared camp, Malinda presented herself to Colonel Vance.

"As long as you've sent my man home," she said, "I want to go, too."

Vance gawked. "What's that?" He was thunderstruck.

"Me and Keith Blalock's man and wife," she said.

Vance said he would have to have proof she was not a man.

Malinda said she could give it to him, though she wasn't too anxious.

"But if that's what it takes to get with my man," she said, "then I'll show you, for I don't aim to be apart from him."

And with that she proceeded, in the words of Vance, to display confirmation "strong as proof of holy writ."

Vance hurriedly wrote out her discharge papers.

A little later, Malinda joined her husband down the road and they headed for the high hills and home.

Loggin' Days and Loggin' Ways

Sunburst

THE GREAT LOGGING TOWN, WITH ITS BANDMILL AND neat little rows of houses, is only a ghost of a memory.

The stolid, plodding oxen, snaking the fallen trees from the forest, have disappeared along with the wood-burning logging train.

The broad-axe, symbol of the woodman's quest, leans against the big stone fireplace in the hundred-year-old cabin with its massive hand-hewn logs where I'm writing this piece.

My desk is a 20-foot table sawn from a four-foot-through poplar tree that was a sapling when the folks of Massachusetts were buzzing over the Salem witchcraft trials.

Outside the morning breeze is whispering in the tall, majestic hemlocks and there is the sound of water pouring over the little water-wheel.

Up from the narrow valley, in a world of high bright air and tingling scents and singing white water, the trees rise rank upon rank.

The trees are green against a blue sky.

The world below them has changed.

Only the trees still stand.

And the man.

They are the only reminders of the town that once stood here and of the good, new way of life that came to the people of these mountains half a century ago.

When Reuben B. Robertson came into this country 50 years ago it was still a land where the pioneers made their own legends, just as they had to make everything else.

It didn't take Reuben Robertson long to become a legend, a living legend.

The young man from Ohio, forsaking a career in law to make

paper, saw Sunburst become the nation's model logging town and worked to make the Carolina division of Champion Paper and Fibre Company at Canton a booming industry that for half a century has brought happiness and prosperity to a heap of mountain folks.

Since this is the year that the Carolina division celebrates its golden anniversary, it seemed appropriate to come here where Champion really had its start in our mountains.

As a boy of ten, I knew Sunburst briefly, remembering the big log pond, the giant flume shooting logs out of the mountains, the oxen pulling and tugging their loads, the blast of the mill whistle at noon, the echo of the train whistle rolling down from the hills.

But to really know what Sunburst was like fifty years ago, you must talk to Hope Thomson Robertson, whose father founded Champion, and, who, as a young bride, came into these hills with Reuben Robertson.

Her father, Peter G. Thomson, had stood here in the narrow valley one morning and had watched the sun burst over the mountains.

This was an empire of trees and he was looking for a place to further his paper-making industry. He had decided this was the spot. This would be the place where his logging town would rise.

He watched the sun burst over the mountains and he said, "We'll call it Sunburst."

He sent his son-in-law down here to make the operation go.

Peter Thomson was a wise man. How wise, only the years were to prove.

When Hope Robertson left her home in Cincinnati for the hills of North Carolina she had no idea what she would find. It was to be an adventure that was to turn into a love affair—a love affair with the people and the mountains.

Here in the hundred-year-old cabin, before a fire in the chill of early morning, we sat with her and talked of that first trip and of the days of old Sunburst.

You can never live over the time you first came to a place, just as you never can recapture the lost years of youth, but you can never forget it, either.

The memories burn as bright as yesterday, and Hope Robertson is a lady who remembers well because her years all have been years of happiness.

"My daughter was six months old when we left Cincinnati," she recalled, the sparkle of memory in her eyes, "and Reuben drove us from Canton in a wagon.

"We had to ford the creeks ten times in getting here. And folks would always say they'd make the trip God willing and the creek not too high. There wasn't much of a road in those days.

"Part of the road was made out of logs. That was where it was low and swampy. Logs were cut and laid crosswise and you traveled over them, bumping along. Where it was dirt, it was bumpy in dry weather and muddy in wet weather. You'd mire up above the hubs and the oxen would have to pull you out.

"When I came in here with Reuben it was just the start of the town. Houses had been built for the workers. There was a church and a school and I started the first Sunday school.

"Mother would send me down the lessons they were studying in their Sunday school classes at our church back in Cincinnati and I would use them.

"There were some 350 men working out of Sunburst then. Most of them were married and had their families living here. It was a good sized community. We lived in a cottage near the river.

"I remember there was just one store. It was a little store and not much variety, but we got along.

"I really didn't have time to get homesick. There was so much to do. Since we had so little, we had to do with what we had or make it ourselves.

"I made all my own clothes and clothes for my babies. Coming here made me learn to do everything. You had to do for yourself or do without. It was a good lesson for me."

The fire burned low but the memories burned bright.

And Hope Robertson talked of the bustling town with its loggers and of the logging trains running out of the mountains, fetching wood that made its way down to Canton and the new pulp mill.

But she remembered mostly the things that are close to a woman's heart, a mother's heart.

"I remember that first Christmas here at Sunburst," she said. "That was 50 years ago this December. My daughter Hope was nine months old and it was her first Christmas.

"I told Reuben that we had to have a real Christmas for her.

"The two of us—Reuben and I—went into the forest back of our house and he chopped down a Christmas tree. Mother had sent me a lot of decorations and I decorated the tree. It was a pretty tree.

"Folks in the community had never seen a decorated Christmas tree and we invited them around and had a Christmas celebration. They were wonderful people. From the first I loved them. I've always loved people and these people were wonderful."

For a moment she stared into the fire.

"You know," she said, "I never have regretted coming down here. My people back home said I wouldn't stay two years. I've been here fifty. And I'm happy and I've never had any regrets.

"Reuben and I loved the people from the start. And they loved us. That makes a difference. I remember when we had been here only a short time, one of the men working for Reuben came to me and said, 'We'd go on our hands and knees to the end of the earth for Mr. Robertson'. "

Mrs. Robertson didn't say so, but that was the beginning of the legend.

For in the years that he has been in Western North Carolina, many a man has felt the same way and folks have come to look upon Reuben Robertson as a mountain man, strong and tall and lasting as the mountains.

Other men have come and gone, but he is still here.

No one ever called him a timber baron, a man who denuded the mountains, took his gold, and left.

Reuben Robertson was never reckless with the forests of our mountains.

He never did hack the forests indiscriminately.

"Reuben," said his wife, "always has looked ahead."

He instituted selective cutting in a land where others had skinned the mountains and left them to erode and scar the landscape.

That is why Champion, under his leadership, has won the respect and confidence of the mountain people who think upon him as a mountain man and not a Yankee.

That is why, if you come here to Sunburst, there is nothing to remind you that a logging town ever existed.

The trees still stand.

Where they were felled fifty years ago, new ones have sprung up to keep this section an empire of trees, green and lush.

Only the ghosts of yesterday are still about.

And they live only when Hope Robertson sits beside the fire and talks about Sunburst when it was a great logging town.

First Indian Republic

Cherokee

THERE IS PROUD BLOOD IN THE OLD WOMAN'S HERITAGE. Sometimes when the shadows creep into her cabin in Oconaluftee Indian Village and the log fire is burning low, Aggie Lossiah talks of the grandfather she never knew.

This was such a day and quite fitting, too, for soon it will be the time of the election of a tribal chief to rule over the Eastern Band of Cherokee Indians.

"My grandfather," said Aggie, "was one of the greatest Cherokee chiefs that ever lived. You can see his picture down in the museum."

This was not said in boasting, only in pride, for the Cherokee are not a boastful people. It is the one thing they never picked up from the white man.

Search through the little known history books, read the old and faded documents, dig into the musty archives, and you will agree that the old woman's grandfather walked tall upon the earth.

For he set a precedent in democratic political history that never will be broken.

By free ballot, he was elected to ten successive terms of four years each as principal chief of the Cherokee Nation.

He died in office as chief executive of a government fashioned after that of the United States of America.

Intellectually, he was the greatest chief in the history of the Cherokee people.

In his youth he knew Jefferson, spent most of his prime negotiating with Jackson, came face to face with Lincoln.

In Washington, he was known as the Indian Prince.

Yet, for all his impressive contacts, he was a man of simple and friendly habit, his house ever open to visitors of all walks of life.

He knew humility as Lincoln knew humility. He loved his fellowman as did Lincoln. He hated war and strived for peace, as did Wilson and Roosevelt.

He stood so high in the eyes of his people that they called him Guwisguwi, a rare migratory bird that had appeared long ago in the old Cherokee country, which might have been the egret or the swan.

His real name was John Ross, the mixed-blood scion of a famous Scottish trading family. He was one-eighth Cherokee and seven-eights Scot. He was as much a Scotsman as his great opponent, Andrew Jackson, and fought just as tenaciously.

But he forever was Cherokee-minded.

He was a veteran of the Creek campaign in which the Cherokee established the reputation of their archenemy Jackson instead of shooting him down as some veterans later wished they had done.

He fought alongside Jackson and Houston and Crockett in the War of 1812, and at the Battle of Horseshoe Bend swam the river, in a daring act of bravery, to capture the Creeks' canoes which were then used to effect an attack upon the enemy's fort.

Ross more than anyone else was responsible for remodeling the Cherokee tribal government into a miniature republic with a written constitution.

This republican form of government came into being in 1820.

Under the arrangement the nation was divided into eight districts. Each was entitled to send four representatives to Cherokee national legislature, which met at New Echota, the capital, near the present Calhoun, Georgia.

The legislature consisted of an upper and a lower house. The Cherokee referred to them, respectively, as the national committee and the national council.

The principal official in the government was the president of the national council. Because he had shown great leadership, this office fell to John Ross.

Meanwhile, Sequoyah invented his alphabet, and overnight the Cherokee became a literate race. This led in 1828 to the adoption of a constitution, development of a system of industries and home education, and establishment of a national press.

The constitution was predicated on the Cherokee assumed sovereignty and independence as one of the distinct nations of the earth.

This bold step drew the immediate wrath of the authorities and people of Georgia, and set off the first argument for state's rights, with Georgia asking the United States government what it proposed to do about the "erection of a separate government within the limits of a sovereign state."

And as the battle raged, Ross dreamed that one day a new star would be added to the flag of the United States and that star stand for a state the like of which had not yet been received into the Union—an Indian state, the State of Cherokee.

But this was not to be, and John Ross found himself spending most of his time in Washington fighting the removal of the Cherokee to new homes in the West.

His knowledge of the writings of Jefferson enabled the Cherokee to present memorials of dignity and moving appeal to Congress.

He almost won the fight. He lost it by one vote.

Throughout the long hard battle, Ross's people trusted him, sometimes almost blindly.

Even when the Cherokee were removed to what is now Oklahoma in 1838, he continued to fight.

His wife, Quatie, was among those forced to leave their homeland. And she, like some 4,000 other Cherokee, died on the overland march which has come to be called the Trail of Tears. She is buried in Little Rock, Arkansas. Her picture hangs in the Gilcrest Museum in Tulsa, Oklahoma.

A few years ago when four tribal leaders retraced the Trail of Tears to Oklahoma, Aggie's son was on the journey, vice chief of the tribe at the time.

There in the museum, McKinley Ross saw the picture, the first he had ever seen of his great-grandmother. And in Oklahoma City he saw the great hand-painted mural depicting the Trail of Tears, in which John Ross is shown trudging along in the great exodus.

John Ross never gave up the fight for his people.

He died in Washington, August 1, 1866, at the age of 76.

Before he died he sat in the White House and talked with Lincoln about his people. He was concerned over what might happen to Cherokee because of their Confederate alliance.

"I can promise you," Lincoln told the old man, "that it will not rise up in judgment against the Cherokee."

They buried John Ross in Philadelphia, far from his hills of home.

But he lives in the memory of an old woman who is proud of the blood in her heritage.

And sometimes when the shadows creep into her cabin in Oconaluftee Indian Village she talks about the grandfather she never knew.

A Frontier Gipsy

Valle Crucis

FOLKS IN THE HILLS STILL SING OF BLACK JACK DAVID, but few ever heard of Johnny Holsclaw.

And that's a shame, for Johnny also knew how to charm the heart of a lady.

He was a sort of frontier gypsy who cast a spell over a mountain belle with his outlandish tales of strange paths he had traveled and faraway places he had visited.

Like Black Jack David of ballad fame, Johnny filled her head with tree-top tall promises he couldn't keep and ended up listening to a song of thanks when she learned he had deceived her.

Johnny Holsclaw wandered into the Watauga highlands about 1816.

Among other things, he was a hunter.

This was a virgin land where hemlock and spruce and balsam stood like whispering sentinels on the hills and clear streams, rippling with trout, tumbled through the valleys.

It was a place where a man could hunt deer and bear and have himself a passel of wingroom. The kind of place a man never had to give a bother about neighbors.

Johnny Holsclaw picked out a spot over on the waters of Elk at the Big Bottoms and built himself a bark shanty.

Just eight miles from his diggings, the settlement of Valle Crucis was beginning to shape up and among the settlers was Bedent Baird.

But for the most part, Johnny kept to himself and for years refused to have any traffic with the folks hereabouts.

He never came visiting and when he happened to meet up with somebody in the woods while out hunting, he made it a point to explain he was just a wandering hunter.

But along about 1826, Johnny got to feeling mighty lonesome

and reckoned it was time to start looking for a helpmeet.

So one day he set out across the mountain and come into the valley here where he started visiting about among the families in the settlement.

When he stopped by the Baird home dinner was just being put on the table and he was invited to break bread, which he did.

Across from him sat the colonel's youngest daughter, Delilah, already a woman at fifteen and a belle of the frontier.

Her beauty was a thing to behold.

Johnny Holsclaw figured right then and there that she was the girl for him.

When dinner was over, the menfolks moved to the fire and lit up their pipes and talked.

Johnny did most of the talking. He told them he was from Kentucky. Now there, he said, was a place abody ought to see before he died. Why, there wasn't enough gold in all creation to get him to settle some place else.

No, sir, he said, there was no finer place in all the land. Why, Kaintuck was a heaven of a place and he was heading back in a few days.

Like many another girl, Delilah Baird had her dreams.

She listened to Johnny Holsclaw and reckoned she never would be happy until she got to Kentucky.

Young fellers in the settlement had been after her for some time to marry up but she had turned them all down.

Listening to Johnny Holsclaw, she told herself she wouldn't say no if he asked her.

Now, Johnny, for all his lonely recent years, knew the way with a maid and he knew better than to press his attentions too quickly.

He stayed on at the Bairds and talked more and more about the fabulous land of Kentucky.

And pretty soon Delilah was asking him questions and feeding his ego.

Johnny knew he had her charmed. He told her of strange paths he had traveled and faraway places he had visited. He said it was too bad she hadn't seen some of the things he had seen.

So it was he wooed her with his tales.

Finally, he managed to get Delilah off alone.

And that's when he started making all sorts of outlandish promises. He told her he wanted to take her to Kentucky. He said if she would say yes to marrying up with him he'd go right in and ask her pa.

But Delilah said no and then yes.

She would marry him and go to Kentucky but she knew if he asked her pa that her pa would say no.

"Then," said Johnny, "run away with me."

Delilah said she would.

They made their plans and when night came on they slipped out of the house when the others had gone to bed and headed into the hills.

Johnny Holsclaw liked to have walked Delilah to death.

He took her up one mountain and down another, across streams and through rocky ravines.

Delilah kept asking when they would get to Kentucky and Johnny kept saying it wouldn't be too long.

Maybe it was a week, maybe it was longer. Nobody knows and Delilah never did say. But eventually Johnny brought her to his bark shanty on the waters of the Elk.

"This is Kentucky," he said.

Delilah kissed him and hugged him and said she reckoned she never would go back to North Carolina and the Valley of the Cross, for this sure was a beautiful place.

Not for one moment did she dream that the home she left was only eight miles away as the crow flew.

She was to be kept in ignorance of this startling fact for many years.

Meanwhile, she set out to make Johnny Holsclaw never regret bringing her to this far-off wonderful place.

And Johnny took his ax and built them a cabin and made her chairs and tables and a bed.

She gave him children and cooked for him and told him of her love for him.

Johnny would smile and then take off on a bear or deer hunt and be gone for days.

But Delilah didn't seem to mind. She watched over her brood and nursed her happiness.

Sometimes, when there were just she and the children sitting around the fire at night all alone, she would sing some of the old tunes and old ballads.

There was one in particular. The one called Black Jack David. Perhaps it was because it reminded her in a way of Johnny and her.

Folks in the mountains had been singing it a long time. It had been fetched over from the old country and changed to fit the times.

Maybe it made her love Johnny all the more when she sang:

> "*Black Jack David came ridin' through the woods,*
> *Singin' so loud and merry*
> *That the green hills all 'round him rang*
> *And he charmed the heart of a lady*
> *And he charmed the heart of a lady.*
>
> "*How old are you, my pretty little miss,*
> *How old are you my lady?*
> *She answered him with a 'Gee, he, he.*
> *I'll be sixteen next summer,*
> *I'll be sixteen next summer.'*
>
> "*Come go with me, my pretty little miss,*
> *Come go with me, my lady:*
> *I'll take you across the deep blue sea*
> *Where you never shall want for money,*
> *Where you never shall want for money.*"

Well, hadn't she and Johnny jumped the traces and come all the way to Kentucky? Johnny had sure charmed her, and she wasn't one bit sorry.

The years passed, and then one day Delilah was out with her children in the woods. They had strayed far from home when she suddenly stopped and listened.

She shushed the children and bent her ear toward a far-off hill.

Why, it's a cow-bell, she said.

She listened some more and said it sounded just like a cow-bell her father used to have.

Curious, she and the children searched out the cow.

She went up to the cow and looked at the bell.

Why, it can't be, she said. But it was. It was her father's cow-bell.

And then the cow turned and started off across the hill.

Delilah followed along and came to the top where she could look down into the valley.

And there she saw her old home.

Well, of all things. How could that be?

So she went on and came to her father's house.

Everybody was glad to see her. Said they didn't know what had happened to her or where she had gone, except they'd figured she had run away with Johnny Holsclaw.

Delilah stayed only a little while but promised to come back for a visit.

When she got home, Johnny was there.

She didn't fuss with him.
She just hauled off and told him she had been home.
Just across the mountain, there, she said.
Johnny sort of grinned.
Delilah smiled.

"I want to thank you," she said, "for taking me off and making me think I was in Kentucky. It don't matter that this ain't Kentucky. I couldn't have been no happier."

And then she reached up and put her arms about his neck and kissed him.

And they lived happily ever after.

Somehow, it seems a shame nobody has ever written a ballad about Johnny and Delilah.

But even if Johnny didn't get a ballad like Black Jack David, he got a line of elegy from Delilah.

She thanked him for deceiving her.

Alum-Root

Of an Angel and a Giant of a Man

Hendersonville

THE FADING RED OF A SUMMER TWILIGHT TOUCHED THE marble angel and spun just a whisper of a halo about its head.

Back in the hills, the time-lost hills of a stonecutter's son, the first frost had come and with it a breath of autumn-come-Saturday and the prelude to the blaze that is October.

Between the marble angel and the turn of the season there is a thing that brings to mind the young giant of the mountains whose words of prose and poetry will live as long as man can read.

Each in its way was a part of him and each was a part of his tune.

For him they represented the fable and mystery of time, and he wove them into his writings and made of them something to be recalled and remembered.

He made of autumn and October in the hills a tapestry as vivid and colorful as nature's own brilliant-hued canvas.

And he took a marble angel and gave it a halo and sent men on a 20-year search for it.

They found it long after he was dead.

They found it here in Oakdale cemetery.

In all the world there probably is none as famous as this one.

For it is the angel that Tom Wolfe was referring to in his memorable *Look Homeward, Angel*.

There is a picture of it in the current issue of *Life* Magazine which is telling the story of Wolfe in a two-part series.

The identification of the marble monument here as "the angel" of Wolfe's *Look Homeward, Angel* was made just seven years ago.

At the same time, it was substantiated that not one but several angels stood on the porch of Wolfe's father's marble shop in Asheville over a 25-year period.

But the angel here is the only one that answered the description given by Tom Wolfe in his writings, first in *An Angel On the Porch* which was his first short story. It appeared in *Scribner's* and later was incorporated as a chapter in *Look Homeward, Angel*.

As described in his story:

"... it had come from Carrara, in Italy, and it held a stone lily delicately in one hand. The other hand was lifted in benediction. It was poised delicately upon one phthisic foot."

In another place he referred to the lily as a "stip" which technically the flower is, while the other angels that stood on the porch of his father's shop carried either wreaths or unidentified flowers.

Until 1949 there had been a dispute about the identity of the angel.

There were some who insisted that Tom's "angel" rested in Asheville's Riverside Cemetery. Others said it was in a cemetery in Waynesville or Haywood County, while others still insisted the real "angel" was in a cemetery at Whittier.

Mrs. Wolfe herself said it was not in Asheville. She said she believed it was here in Hendersonville.

So it was the search narrowed and came to an end in Oakdale cemetery where the marble angel marks the grave of Mrs. Margaret Bates Johnson.

Several years ago Mrs. Sadie Smathers Patton, the Hendersonville historian, was visiting Oakdale and discovered that the angel needed repairing.

Mrs. Patton discovered that a piece from the raised hand had broken off. This fragment lay nearby. She had it replaced. She also discovered that the entire angel was loose on the base. She had it reset.

Some who had searched for years thought the angel might even have been shipped out of the country.

For in one of Tom's stories he mentioned that it had been bought by Queen Elizabeth. But his mother cleared that up quickly. She said Tom had just changed things around in the story.

Actually, the angel here was purchased from Tom's father in 1906 by the Johnson family. That would have made Tom six years old at the time.

Tom wrote that the angels his father bought at great cost and had sent from Italy were the joy of his heart.

As a boy they impressed him, one in particular—the one he made famous.

Just as he wrote that the stonecutter of *Look Homeward, Angel* had been impressed as a boy and wanting more than anything in the world to carve delicately with a chisel.

"He wanted to carve an angel's head," Tom wrote. "But he never found it. He never learned to carve an angel's head. The dove, the lamb, the smooth joined marble hands of death, and letters fair and fine—but not the angel."

Tom Wolfe made of the angel remembered as a boy on the porch of his father's shop a sort of symbol.

It was something that had to do with time and the turning of the seasons.

The angel and October signified both sorrow and delight.

The angel was a "haunting sorrow for the buried men" which he felt in the golden warmth of October when there was "an exultancy for all the men who were returning" to the hills of home.

Soon it will be October. Tom Wolfe's month.

For back in the hills the first frost has come.

And here in Oakdale cemetery the fading red of twilight touches the marble angel and spins just a whisper of a halo about its head. And the marble angel and the turn of the season nod to one another.

In the trees the wind whispers lines out of a book and they are lines that sound like the ones created by the young giant of the mountains—Tom Wolfe.

Blue Eyed Grass

Mountain Balladeer Singing Reporter

South Turkey Creek

THE OLD-TIME MOUNTAIN BALLADEER, WHO NOT ONLY WAS a singing reporter but a sort of singing historian, is about as scarce as the old Model-T.

But his homespun ballads, like the old Model-T, were fashioned to last.

They have. And the pure, genuine, unadulterated stuff—tangy as a persimmon, lively as hard cider—will still be around, for all the bumps and knocks, when all of today's radio hits have turned to dust.

But, be that as it may, the art of old-time ballad-making is almost a thing of the past.

Few remain of the traditional mountain balladeers who dealt with courtship, love and marriage, the old maid and the scolding wife, the rocking cradle—troubadours who sang of real things as they actually happened, who chronicled the humble incidents of everyday life.

Once they were as thick and sturdy as mountain chestnut but, like the mountain chestnut, they have died off or grown too old to have a care about making up ballads.

And the young ones somehow seem to lack that instinctive knack for putting simple experiences of life into an immediate and direct musical speech.

Maybe it's because the mountain people no longer are isolated and no longer have to depend on the ballad-maker for their news and their history.

Roam the mountains from the Blue Ridge to the Smokies, search out the hidden coves and the valleys, run down the scrape of a lively fiddle or the rasping twang of a banjo, hunt as you will for an oldtime balladeer. . . .

Mark it a rare find if one turns up.

About the only ones still around who can qualify are Samantha Bumgarner, the fiddlin' ballad-woman of Love Field south of Sylva and Bascom Lamar Lunsford, the Minstrel of the Appalachians, who lives here on South Turkey Creek.

Samantha is bound to a rocking chair by rheumatism and her fingers are gnarled with arthritis and although it's been many a day since she turned out a ballad, she keeps scrawling ideas on paper and now and then the rhymes run through her head.

Lunsford is too busy making the world conscious of the old ballads and old tunes to compose any new ones. He's busy collecting the old ones and recording them.

There are others, to be sure. Others who now and then whittle out a ballad as a whittler whittles a pretty for his own pleasure.

But for the most part the natural gift for ballad-making and improvisation has all but been lost here in the mountains.

The once great output is dwindling, even if the art is not wholly lost.

The work is still lonely and isolated.

But even if new ballad-makers are not being born, even if new ballads are not being written, the old ones are still around.

The old ones can not even be submerged by the fabricated tunes of Tin Pan Alley and Hollywood. The old ones can take it.

And somehow when the old ballads are sawed out on a fiddle and plunked out on a banjo and sung by some rusty-voiced Homer, there's a feeling here of what music must once have been like before it became a business.

And for those who might get an idea that the old earthy music has disappeared, then all they have to do is gather with Bascom Lamar Lunsford at his annual Mountain Folk Festival in Asheville or visit with Sam Queen over in Maggie Valley.

But there was a time when every mountain town and community had its street singers and street musicians.

Any Saturday you could find them singing the old ballads and playing the old tunes and making up some on the spot, on the spur of the moment.

The mountaineer, who was always supposed to be feudin' or moonshinin', has yielded ballads old and new, songs, fiddle tunes, party and square dance songs, folk hymns and blues.

They tell of building a tunnel through Swannanoa Tunnel, of a swain who lost his love atop Old Smoky by courtin' too slow.

The one about Cripple Creek was about a stream near here. And Dogget's Gap can be seen from above Asheville. There's one about "Italy" which is a mountain community and not the country of the boot. Others have been written about such highland places as "Quebec," "Canada," "Egypt," and "Jerico."

More and more the old ballads are being sung and played.

Out of them grew what outlanders termed "hill-billy music." And now folks have prettied up the name and are calling it "country music," which must make many a mountaineer smile.

But for all this, time was when old-timers believed that such fiddle tunes was tantamount to reserving a seat in Hell. Especially, when folks got to singing and fiddling about the gal called Cindy.

Of course, the young folks didn't pay no mind to the old-timers.

Like Cindy, they just couldn't keep their feet virtuous when the cry of the fiddle and the twang of the banjo was heard.

And they laughed as they sang:

"Cindy got religion, had it once before,

When she heard my old banjo, she 'uz the first one on the floor."

Mountain folks always have liked to sing and play the fiddle and banjo. Even today, when three or four folks get together of a night around the fire and are having a good time, somebody will break forth in song. And strange as it may seem, out come the old ballads, the old songs.

Sooner or later, they're singing "Darling Cora," a heroine who was not to be trifled with on a dark night, for she was a gal "with a .44 buckled around her, and a banjo on her knee." Or they will come up with "Careless Love," maybe "Little Turtle Dove."

These are songs that become more dear with each passing yar.

And group singing is a custom old as the hills and as indestructible.

Songs keep on being born and disappearing with the seasons.

But the ballads live on.

They got their start as the world's first newspaper and informal history book.

They came into being as a sort of tabloid record of battle, adventures and scandals when an illiterate community depended for its news on the troubadours who roamed the countryside.

They were fashioned to last. And they have.

And it's a shame and a pity, and somehow sort of sad, that the traditional mountain balladeer has not kept pace.

He's either dead or dying or got himself a musical education, which is about the same.

For today's balladeers, writing for Tin Pan Alley and Hollywood, have lost the touch that made the old-time mountain balladeer not only a singing reporter but a sort of singing historian as well.

So, shed a tear for the old, the old-time mountain balladeer.

Potlikker and Cornpone

Sunset Farms

A MOUNTAIN MAN ONCE DESCRIBED HIS NOTION OF HEAVEN as a land flowing with cornpone and potlikker.

He made his comment, appropriately enough, while pleasuring his palate with a brimming dish of potlikker and "crumble-in."

Some folks may think he was trying to be facetious. They would be wrong because, forsooth, he was a plumb fool about this pot-and-skillet brew and actually believed the proverbial milk and honey of the promised land couldn't touch it as a steady diet.

But, be that as it may, he was not alone in his judgment or in his taste, and he considered as dishwater anything served up for potlikker which substituted the basic vegetable of his Scotch-Irish heritage.

Many a mountain man before and since has felt the same way about cornpone and potlikker which, albeit a simple dish, binds together the taste of both the folks that have and the folks that have-not.

All of which is by way of taking down the muzzle-loader—the one that talked at King's Mountain, naturally—and wading right into a peart controversy over what is and what isn't real potlikker.

But before a culinary shot is fired it's necessary to take a good look at how the potlikker fuss started and what all the feuding is about.

Innocently enough, the *Wall Street Journal* up in New York set it off by publishing a recipe for potlikker, to wit:

"For potlikker, put a large piece of fatback in the pot with a tasty green vegetable, preferably cabbage. Boil long and vigorously. Then throw away the cabbage and sip the hot potlikker from a soup bowl. Excellent with cornpone."

This brought a somewhat indignant howl from Paul Flowers of *The Commercial Appeal* down in Memphis, Tenn., who said everybody knew the only real way to make potlikker was with a hambone or a home-cured jowl, compounded in a black iron kettle by adding red peppers, maybe an onion, with turnip greens preferred, although admitting cabbage is mighty good.

Then George McCoy, one of our associates who has a knack for waxing enlighteningly on the editorial page of the *Asheville Citizen*, came up with his own recipe, arguing that neither of the others really filled the gastronomical bill.

Like Flowers, he agreed on a hambone or "a generous piece of streaky bacon," and also announced a decided preference for greens—"turnip or mustard or mixed or collards." But he ruled out peppers and onions.

McCoy was more specific than Flowers in the proper use of cornpone, allowing "it's real good for sopping up the potlikker."

Well, first off we must point out that Memphis-On-The-Mississippi and Babylon-On-The-Subway are poles apart in distance and taste, and that there's a disquieting heresy in McCoy's stand on potlikker.

To mountain folks whose tastes are simple but keen the only real, honest-to-goodness potlikker rightly commanding the name is that brewed in a black iron pot from quartered cabbage cooked with a ham shoulder and pods of red peppers.

They should know. After all, from time out of memory they have fed potlikker to their children about as soon as they arrived on this earth and got big enough to sit up and demand nourishment.

Besides, back when this region was being opened up folks were too busy fighting Indians or wolves or grooving together a cabin or clearing a piece of land for fancying up cabbage in the pot.

Ed and Rubye Bumgarner who operate Sunset Farms, an establishment long famous for its food, are a couple of potlikker connoisseurs who are horrified by some of the recipes.

Both are mountain born, and in cookery Rubye can hold her head high, can foot it on an even basis with the world's best and can outstrip the rest, while Ed is no slouch himself with the skillet.

"It beats me," said Ed, "how some folks can get so all-fired twisted when it comes to something as simple as potlikker. Seems like these fellers who are giving out with their recipes don't get to eat much cornpone and potlikker, else how could they be so balled up.

"Take this thing of making potlikker out of greens. Now that's a real humdinger. Just imagine trying to eat turnip greens with enough water in 'em to be that juicy.

"And it's downright sinful to suggest throwing away the cabbage.

A mountain woman would no more think of doing that than she would of throwing out the ham shoulder.

"Why, potlikker as served by mountain folks is a one-meal dish, and cornpone is as much a part of it as cabbage. They go together like ham and eggs or chicken and gravy.

"Even if a feller was starving to death he wouldn't think of sitting down to a dish of potlikker without a pone or two of cornbread to crumble in or sop with.

"The only pure way to eat potlikker is to crumble in cornpone and spoon it out or break off a piece of cornpone and sop up the juice like dunking doughnuts.

"I might say right here that you don't cut cornpones. They are broken at the table when they're served.

"Another thing, this New York recipe tells you to sip the potlikker from a soup bowl. Now, ain't that a frazzlin' way to take potlikker!

"Of course, some of the old folks would drink it out of teacups. That was fit and proper as well as handy but not customary.

"And it's a rare thing that potlikker is ever served in a mountain home to company. You might say it's kept, like the best whiskey, for the home folks."

At this point, Rubye came up with her recipe for potlikker. A recipe handed down from her mother and her mother's mother and on back until the line gets hazy.

"To do it right," she explained, "you put the ham shoulder in and let it cook in a pot of water a long time. Just let it simmer for two or three hours. Then you take your cabbage. You take the core out and cut the cabbagehead in four pieces and put them into the pot.

"You use a tablespoon of salt and fourth of a tablespoon of black pepper and two small pods of red pepper.

"Once the cabbage is put in the pot you cover it and let it simmer about two hours, adding water to maintain the original volume. After the last water is added you let it cook about 20 minutes."

Ed grinned and licked his lips.

"Now, that's real potlikker," he said. "The pure stuff. As mountain as cornpone and molasses."

And for a moment you half way expected him to echo the same sentiments of that other mountain man who once described his notion of heaven as a land flowing with cornpone and potlikker.

And That's to Say Buncombe

Dellwood

THEY CALLED HIM "OLD OIL JUG."

The sobriquet was a hearty tribute to his talent for talking the people's language.

He gave the world a synonym for hum-bug, apple-sauce, tall talk, pie-in-the-sky, and political clap-trap.

He made the name buncombe a byword among English-speaking people.

He wrote it into every dictionary in the land.

Folks have been using the word some 130 years to describe "talking merely for talk's sake" but few know the name of the man who gave it a special meaning or that his home was here on Jonathan's Creek in Haywood County.

About the only monument he ever got is a historical marker erected by the N. C. State Department of Archives and History. It's just down the road from here on U.S. 19.

The name on the marker is that of Felix Walker, Revolutionary officer, member of Congress.

And therein lies a story.

Felix Walker was one of the first settlers in this section.

That was back around 1800 when Buncombe County stretched all the way west to Tennessee and Georgia.

Old Jonathan McPeters had been the first white man to take up land here and carve out a homestead right next door to the Cherokee Indians.

The creek that ran through his lush valley holdings got to be known as Jonathan's Creek.

About 1805, Walker came this way and talked McPeters into selling him some land. Walker was in his early fifties then.

Even so, he was a rather flamboyant man. He was suave of manner. He had a reputation for bombastic political speaking. He was a lawyer by choice, a merchant and farmer by necessity. He was such a fine electioneer that folks referred to him as "Old Oil Jug," a sobriquet he wore with pride.

He was chairman of the first board of commissioners of Haywood County. He was serving in that capacity when plans for the first county courthouse were approved.

As a pioneer business man, Walker cut quite a figure. He had a store in Waynesville, one on Scott's Creek in Jackson County, and another at Quallatown in the heart of the Cherokee domain.

His trading posts earned for him a good living and gave him an opportunity to pursue his love for politics.

When Haywood County was formed he ran for clerk of court but got beat by Colonel Robert Love who founded the town of Waynesville.

But the defeat didn't stop him. He just raised his sights and started talking.

In 1817 he was elected to Congress from the Asheville District and re-elected in 1819 and 1821, retiring from politics in 1823.

While in Congress, Walker made his pitch for the history books and the dictionaries.

And it was a good pitch.

The long debate on the famous Missouri Compromise was coming to a close in the Sixteenth Congress.

The legislators were weary of talk. They wanted to vote. They wanted to go home. They were just plumb tired of talk.

But Felix Walker had other ideas.

His thoughts were not so much on the Missouri question as they were on the folks back home, his constituents who had sent him to Washington.

While the House was impatiently calling for the question, the old mountaineer got to his feet and said he wanted to be heard.

Several fellow members gathered hurriedly about him, pleading and begging with him to keep his mouth shut.

But Walker wouldn't budge.

"The people of my district expect me to make a speech," he argued. "I'm bound to do some talkin' for Buncombe."

Well, he did.

It was a masterpiece of fence-sitting.

When he finished a colleague asked him:

"What in the tarnation was the purpose of all that talk?"

Walker looked at him, then replied:

"I was just talking for Buncombe."

And that's how the word buncombe became the definition for

"talking merely for talk's sake."

That's how a politicalism was born.

Overnight, buncombe became a part of our language.

In time to come it was shortened to "bunkum" and "bunk."

By 1828, "Talking to Bunkum" was an old and common saying in Washington when a member of Congress got to making one of those hum-drum and unlistened to "long talks" that lately had become so fashionable.

Newspapers in 1841 said "there is a deal of 'speaking for Buncome,' or as some would call it, 'for grandeur,' in our legislative assemblies nowadays."

In the people's language, buncombe came to mean "stuff," "nonsense," "humbug," more often with reference to legislative action designed merely to satisfy or impose upon public opinion,

As a critic back in 1847 said of a speech:

"To sum it up, it is a little of government—a great deal of bunkum, sprinkled with a high seasoning of political juggling."

Be that as it may, Felix Walker planted the word firmly in our vocabulary and folks are still using it.

And that's not bunkum.

Carolina Lily

Charming Old Lady Makes Fine Moonshine
A Cabin in the Blue Ridge

THE SLANTING RAYS OF AN AFTERNOON SUN CAME THROUGH the tiny window and fell across the shawled shoulders of the old woman sitting in the splint-bottomed rocking chair.

Her gnarled old hands lay folded in her lap like a cat napping. A tiny cap of age-yellowed lace sat atop her head of snow-white hair. A gold locket hung from a black ribbon about her wrinkled neck. The toes of her black comforts peeped out from beneath the hem of her black calico dress.

She reminded me of a painting I had seen once in the Luxembourg gallery in Paris. A charming and serene arrangement in black and gray called "The Artist's Mother." It was by an American painter named Whistler.

But the resemblance belied the old woman's way of life and the ancient craft she practiced in the loneliness of her remote mountain-top homestead.

"I don't talk none about my affairs," she said. " 'Specially to folks I don't know nothin' about."

There was a note of finality in her voice. The story I had come seeking from her own lips seemed lost. I turned to the man who had fetched me over the torturous, winding trail to her cabin.

"Aw, go on, talk to him," he said. "He ain't goin' to give you away. He'll fix it so nobody'll know 'cept them that do already. He ain't goin' to turn you in. Besides, I'm here to vouch for him, ain't I?"

The old woman studied a moment. She stared at me out of eyes blue as Wedgewood cameoware. Finally, she nodded her head, like she was nodding to herself.

"Somethin' tells me I oughn't to speak up," she said. "But if you say it's all right, I reckon maybe it is. Ain't many times I've found your judgment wantin'. But this is somethin' it don't pay a-body to speak of. It could get me into trouble with the law. Now, what is it you want to know?"

She unfolded her hands in her lap and reached for the snuff-stick on the table beside her chair. It lay beside a tin of snuff that shared space with a coal-oil lamp and a worn leather-bound Bible out of which hung a faded, wrinkled piece of red ribbon.

"Huh? How I got started?" She chewed a moment on the snuff-stick. "Why, my pa put me to it. Reckon I wasn't more'n sixteen. He come down with the miseries and had to take his bed. There was just me and him a-livin' here then.

"With him sickly, it was either me to do the makin' or else starve. Pa's stuff was mighty good. Why, it was spoke for quick as he got one run off and before he could get another started. Kept us in meat and coffee and sugar and flour. And a store-bought dress now and then for me.

"Pa never had no qualms 'bout whiskey-makin'. He never figured it was a sin like some folks do. He always said if the gover'ment could make it, he reckoned it was his right to make it, too. Girl, he would say, what's fittin' for one is fittin' for all. He had his still off there in the thicket and the govern'ment had theirs off yonder over the ridge.

"Once, before he took his bed with the miseries and couldn't get about, not even to chop wood, he took me across the ridge and showed me the gover'ment's whiskey-makin' still. It was a heap bigger than pa's but he said the whiskey wasn't nowheres as good as his. Pa said they single-footed theirs. He always double-footed his, same as me.

"What's that? You ain't acquainted with double-footin'?" She cackled. "Laws-a-me, you don't know nothin'. And you mountain-raised. Why, whiskey ain't fit even for the hogs 'less it's been double-footed. That's runnin' it through the still twice. Takes longer but it's the only way to make whiskey worth the callin'."

She paused and looked toward the door as shoe-leather scraped against a loose board on the porch. A tall, lanky man, bareheaded and grinning, stepped into the room. She nodded her head toward the bed pushed against the wall. He shuffled over to it and sat down, still grinning.

"He can't talk much," she said. "Somethin's the matter with his tongue. Hard of hearin' too. Lives here with me and helps me with the work. Does most of the whiskey-makin' since it's got so I can't get about so well. Jugs it up and keeps it hid so I don't know where it is. That way, if the law comes I don't have to tell no lie.

"Well, now, where was I? Oh, yes, I was a-tellin' about double-footin'. As I was a-sayin', whiskey's got to be double-footed to be the real stuff. But there ain't many, I reckon, that makes it that way any more. Pa always said a feller that wouldn't take the time to double-foot ought to have to drink every drop of his own makin's and he'd get religion mighty quick."

She paused again. The tick of the old-fashioned clock with its glass door and swinging pendulum on the mantel above the fireplace was loud in the room. Suddenly, there was the buzz of a recoiling spring and the clock struck off the hour of five.

"Some folks would say the truth ain't in me for what I'm 'bout to speak," said the old woman. "But it's true as Bible-fact and I want you to know it's such. These lips of mine ain't never tasted whiskey. Not once in all the years of makin'. And if I live 'till next October I'll be 87.

"Guess you're goin' to ask how I know good whiskey if I ain't tasted it. Well, I've got ways. Same as Pa had. I can tell by the looks and the smell. Tell by the way it beads when it's shook up in the jug. Then, folks tell me. Ain't never had nobody to complain. And I'll tell you, a heap of folks has come up the mountain in my time.

"Of course, ain't so many as there once was. Store-bought whiskey's too easy to get. And gettin' in here's kind of troublesome since there ain't nothin' but a trail. Folks got so they can't walk. Even the law-fellers leave me alone."

She laughed a thin, high laugh.

"Don't know as though I blame 'em. It ain't walkin' country. Besides, they wouldn't find nothin' if they did come. Why, they could walk right over my still and never even know it. Don't reckon there's another place like it in creation. Seems like it was made not to be found out. I ain't sayin' which way it is, but if I led you right up to it nearly, which I ain't got no thought of, it would baffle you.

"Like I was sayin', them law-fellers wouldn't get nothin' but a mighty tiresome piece of travelin' if they come this way. I ain't been off the mountain since I was nineteen. One trip was enough for me. Took the mule Pa had and held on to his tail goin' and comin'."

The old woman was silent for a moment. She looked off through the door and across the yard to the field of ripening corn.

"Reckon my days are about over," she said. "Some how, I've got a notion that's my last crop of corn out there."

The sun was going down red. Shadows gathered in the room.

The old woman nodded to her handyman on the bed. He slipped out of the room. He was gone only a moment. When he returned, he carried a towsack that bulged at the bottom.

The man who had brought me to the cabin laid a five-dollar bill on the mantel and picked up the sack and slung it across his shoulder.

The old woman kept to her chair.

"Come again," she said. "Come soon."

At the door, I looked back.

She looked for all the world like the woman in that painting I had seen once in the Luxembourg gallery in Paris.

Wild Sweet William

October's a Mountain Prophecy

Pumpkintown

ACROSS THE AGELESS HILLS OCTOBER CASTS A LONG GOLDEN shadow pregnant with mountain prophecy.

In the corn-fodder fields along the winding little creek the pumpkins sit like gold marbles on a Chinese checkerboard.

Sagging orchards steam with amber spice.

An old man in a weather-stained old hat, a hickory apple-mall in his hands, bends over a cider mill.

Blue smoke drifts out across the cove where sorghum juice, fresh from a horse-around cane mill, simmers over a hickory-fired furnace.

Full-grown lambs bleat from the hilly bourn.

A redbird whistles softly from a garden-croft.

A two-horse wagon, piled high with hay, creaks along a country road bordered with a palisade of browns, reds and yellows. . . .

From the Blue Ridge to the Smokies, across the Balsams and the Cowees, the year is on the wane and it is autumn.

It is autumn and autumn's golden month of October.

It is a time of color, scent and sound.

Every common bush is afire with God.

The splendour falls on mountain walls and mountain tops.

The smoke of many a calumet ascends to heaven again.

Off beyond the horizon all the winds of winter gather.

Time flies, suns rise, and shadows fall.

The leaves are falling from the great oak at the meadow's edge. They are falling from all the trees.

It is October and autumn in the hills.

And there is something that sets the gypsy blood astir.

Maybe it's the dry rustle of leaves on the ground . . . quail feeding at sunrise, roosting at daydown . . . the chit-chat of an idle squirrel . . . thunder rolling and arguing and shaking the clouds over Grandfather Mountain.

Perhaps it's a bird at break of day, singing a song so mystical and calm and so full of certainties . . . an owl calling, cool dews falling . . . bells ringing from a white church steeple.

October is a time to walk on a rainbow trail.

It's a wind in the heart and fire in the heels.

It's fodder-pulling time, sorghum-cane cutting, molasses-making, acorns falling, persimmons ripening.

It's a mountain woman in Watauga grating cabbage on a homemade shredder to begin a batch of kraut.

It's a time when the old ones study the sky for weather-signs, a time when the frosts begin walking down from the hills.

It's homely men at the crossroads store, tall tales and tall talk.

It's fiddle music and square dancing.

It's a coonskin tune by a homespun bard.

It's a covey of grouse on autumn leaves.

It's the ground covered with tattered gold.

It's a curve in the road and a hillside clear-cut against the sky, a tall tree tossed by the autumn wind, and a white cloud riding high.

It's a mountain woman in Haywood or Henderson making applebutter.

It's an old man settling down in a rockingchair before a log fire.

It's a hillsman shouldering his gun and leaving his scythe in the rain and the sun.

It's the scarlet of maple and oak that can shake a'body like a cry of bugles going by.

It's a rich pumpkin pie that calls back the past.

It's sometimes wind and sometimes rain.

It's dusting off the quiltin'-bars and picking out a pattern for a quilt.

October is a burst of glorious color and then a stark bareness.

It is a time when the serenade of spring is lost in the nocturne of autumn.

It is a time of hope and joy and sorrow.

It slips away and the world is full of solemnity and a pathetic sense of old age.

But before it goes, hound music already is ringing through the hills.

For October means the hunter can take down his rifle and stalk the black bear.

And the old ones wonder out loud what winter will be like. They read the signs, governing their predictions by bark on the trees, the fur on animals, the behavior of birds, the thickness of corn shucks.

In the forests there are footsteps. The squirrels are scurrying about where the acorns are falling. They are filling their storehouses in the hollow trees with food for winter.

And here on Pumpkintown, fast under Cowee in the Jackson hills, the barns are bulging and the pantry shelves are loaded.

The harvest is good and folks are thankful.

The old ones nod their heads.

Over the land there is a patchwork of reds and yellows.

The old man at his cider mill lays aside his hickory apple-mall. He wipes a gnarled hand across his brow. He looks out over the land.

"I've lived a long time," he said. "Watched the seasons come and go nigh on to eighty years. Folks call this autumn. I call it God."

Across the ageless hills October cast a long golden shadow pregnant with mountain prophecy.

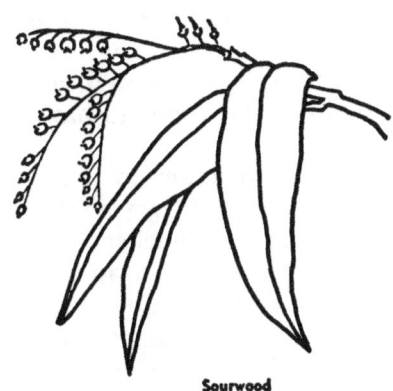

Sourwood

"Pucker Mouth"

Persimmon Creek

THIS IS THE STREAM THE INDIANS CALLED TSA-LA-LUI, which is to say "pucker mouth."

It flows through the rolling hills of Cherokee County where the gnarled, now leafless persimmon trees stand heavy with the autumn ripeness of their wrinkled yellowish-red fruit.

When Hernando DeSoto tarried for a spell near here on his gold-seeking expedition through the Carolina hills, the Indians introduced him to dried persimmons and tickled his palate with a bread made of persimmons.

The gold-mad conquistador arrived before the strange fruit, which he called prunes, had formed on the trees and he moved on before the Indians had an opportunity to lure him into sampling a green persimmon.

All of which probably was just as well, for this DeSoto was a man with a quick temper who seems to have been born without a sense of humor.

Naturally suspicious, his reaction to biting into a green persimmon and feeling his mouth drawn awry with much torment likely would have sent him into puckerish screams he had been poisoned and would have meant the head of the chief.

Others since, including a certain Captain John Smith who was a connoisseur of women and food, particularly the Indian variety, have had unluckily the unforgettable experience of biting into an unripe persimmon.

Such strangers to the fruit, which scientists say was growing hereabouts more than 50 million years ago, have given the persimmon a bad name. All because they couldn't tell a green one from a ripe one. On the tree, that is.

But they found out quickly enough when they bit into a green one.

For an unripe persimmon puckers the mouth even more than alum and the puckery taste hangs on for a full day. The taste begins to worry the mind that maybe it is permanent.

As a result these folks, in all probability, never again will have the courage to sink a tooth into a persimmon and for the rest of their lives low-rate a fruit that is really a mouth-watering delicacy when ripe or whipped up into a pudding.

But to folks who know their persimmons, who know when they should be picked, this wild-growing fruit that nature serves up each autumn as a tasty dessert to the squirrel and the 'possum is something that makes strong men drool.

Why, there are folks who can hardly wait from one season until the next for persimmons to pop out on the trees. They are a rabid clan and woe be the man who fails to talk in superlatives about the persimmon within their hearing.

Time was when the mountain man looked to persimmon-ripenin' time as a time to run off a barrel of persimmon beer or persimmon brandy.

Many a mountain man preferred such beer or brandy to corn liquor, both as to flavor and headiness.

But it took a good man to handle it.

Zeb Vance, the mountain-born man who made a name for himself as governor and U. S. Senator, once recommended persimmon brandy as a steady beverage for long-winded speakers.

He said there was nothing like persimmon brandy to make a man keep his mouth shut. He said a feller with a couple good slugs of persimmon brandy under his belt just seemed to lose all interest in speech-making.

A few folks still make persimmon beer or persimmon brandy but they are fast disappearing, even though the long-accepted recipes for these astringent drinks have been preserved by a heap of folks.

Back during the American Civil War, Confederate soldiers boiled persimmon seeds as a substitute for coffee and their families back home who were sweating out the Yankee blockade made persimmon syrup and persimmon vinegar.

But persimmon vinegar disappeared as soon as the menfolks came home from the war. At least it did here in the mountains, when the menfolks discovered what was going into it.

For persimmon vinegar was a concoction made of three bushels of ripe persimmons, three gallons of corn likker, and 27 gallons of water.

It was a cheap way of making vinegar, but some of the veterans argued it was a waste of good corn likker.

They had their own ideas about how corn likker was meant to be used.

Be that as it may, persimmon vinegar managed to hold out for a while but eventually just passed into the limbo of things remembered.

Folks who never have seasoned greens with persimmon vinegar or tasted persimmon beer or persimmon brandy are nevertheless downright fools about persimmon pudding.

In fact, there's a heap of folks all over the country that look on persimmon pudding as just about the tastiest dish anybody ever set on the table.

For lovers of persimmon pudding, it's something to smack the lips over and dream about whether served hot or cold, with whipped cream or hard sauce.

And strangely enough, all the best cook books now include a recipe for persimmon pudding. But they don't stop there. They include recipes for persimmon salad, persimmon cake, persimmon custard, persimmon whip, persimmon jelly dessert, and jellied persimmons.

But none of them has a recipe for persimmon bread.

And even the Cherokee Indians who were making such bread when DeSoto came this way some 400 years ago have forgotten how to make it.

Which is really a shame.

For DeSoto and some of the earlier explorers who came after him described persimmon bread as quite tasty, something that tasted sort of like gingerbread.

And none of the Cherokee ever bother with dried persimmons any more.

But the persimmons still grow.

They grow here along the stream the Indians called tsa-la-lui, which is to say "pucker mouth."

And the gnarled, now leafless persimmon trees, heavy with the autumn ripeness of their wrinkled yellowish-red fruit, conjure up a time when persimmons were an important article of diet among the Indians.

It's a shame the white man has not made better use of the persimmon, too.

A Tear For a By-Gone Era

Turnpike

EVERYBODY WHO FUSSES ABOUT THE HIGH PRICE OF LIVING should shed a tear for the good old days.

Time was when a'body could buy a passel of groceries for a dollar and eat right well for a spell.

That was back when the likenesses of Lincoln and Grant flaunted their clipped beards on a dollar bill that was almost twice the size of the ones folks handle now-a-days.

Every now and then something comes along to bring a slight tear to the eye of an old-timer who knew this country "when."

Sometimes a souvenir of the past is uncovered that causes folks who never knew the old days to sort of wish they had lived back then.

The register and account book of the old Turnpike Hotel is just such a souvenir.

Its yellowed pages, filled with names and purchases, tells a part of the fabulous story of the mountains when Col. J. C. Smathers was the Boniface of the Great Western Turnpike—a horse-and-buggy thoroughfare from Asheville to Waynesville and beyond.

Colonel Smathers was a man of remarkable character and a jack-of-all-trades.

He was a rock and brick mason, a carpenter and shoemaker, a tinner, painter, blacksmith and plumber, a harness and saddle-maker, a candle maker, farmer, hunter, storekeeper and bee raiser, a glazier, butcher, fruit grower, hotel-keeper and merchant, a physician, lawyer, politician and rail-splitter, a cook, school master and gardener, as well as a Bible scholar.

He was born near Canton in 1828 and when he was 84 he could still run a good foot race and throw most men in a wrestle "catch-as-catch-can."

As operator of the Turnpike Hotel, which now is a tumble of

ruins, he became known throughout the land as a man who set a good table and kept his guests comfortable and happy.

But this is not the story of Colonel Smathers, albeit there's a good one about his life and times.

This is the story of a big dollar bill and the price of things back in 1885 and 1886.

The record he and his wife kept on the operation of the Turnpike Hotel is the story of an era when ham was selling at thirteen cents a pound and coffee could be had for twelve cents a pound.

Colonel Smathers paid $6.50 for 52 reams of hotel paper and envelopes. Got his flour at six dollars a barrel, eggs at ten cents a dozen, chickens at ten cents a piece, and butter at ten cents a pound.

Honey sold at nine cents a pound, and freight on eleven pounds come to seventy cents. Table salt was ten cents and starch eight cents a pound.

A carving knife and fork sold for $1.50, a tin cup for a nickel, a whisk broom for a dime, and four lamp chimneys could be bought for thirty cents.

Beef sold at five cents a pound and a barrel of hominy fetched five dollars.

A night message by telegraph to Charleston, S. C. was fifty-five cents and a straight message to Asheville was thirty-one cents.

Colonel Smathers paid $7.80 for two pair of blankets, 25 cents for a trunk lock, and 15 cents for a box of silver polish.

When he had to replace knives and forks, dishes, mattresses and bedsteads, he ordered in quantity from Asheville and New York.

A dozen dinner plates come to $1.10. Butter knives were 25 cents each, plated dinner knives 16 cents each, and covered butter dishes fetched 50 cents each.

Colonel Smathers paid $10 for four mattresses and eight dollars for six feather-beds. He laid out four dollars for a maple bedstead and $1.50 for two small tables. He purchased two large fire pans for 20 cents and a coffee pot for a quarter.

Even in those days folks who operated hotels believed in doing a bit of promotion and advertising.

Colonel Smathers printed up circulars to advertiese special rates and paid a boy fifty cents to distribute them in Asheville.

When he reduced his rates for room and meals he carried daily advertisements in the *Asheville Citizen* for a week and his bill came to $1.50.

Back in those days the Turnpike Hotel was charging $1.50 a day for room and three meals. A dinner cost a traveler fifty cents.

In addition to the overnight guests traveling by stage on the Great Western Turnpike, folks came from all over the country to spend a week or more.

For these longer-staying guests, Colonel Smathers kept a stable and rented out horses and buggies and wagons.

A horse and cart was rented out for $1.50 a day. A horse and buggy could be had for a dollar a day and a horse for fifty cents.

Lodging without meals must have been cheap. One entry showed where a man got six nights lodging for 75 cents.

Among the names of visitors in the register were Mayor George H. Smathers of Waynesville, Judge Shufford of Tarboro, W. H. Weaver of Asheville, W. L. Bingham of Bingham's School, and W. F. Tompkins of Webster.

Colonel Smathers, unlike the run of hotel men, was not superstitious. He flaunted the figure thirteen and had a room in his hotel with that number.

There's really a heap of history in this old register.

It's the story of a bygone era, and it makes a'body shed a tear for the good old days.

Maypop (Passion Flower Vine)

Give Me a Good Corn-Cob Pipe

Burningtown

THE OLD MAN GREW UP IN THE JEANS-BRITCHES AND WOOL-hat era when the corncob pipe was all the go.

"In my time," he said, "I've made lots of 'em. Just lots of 'em. Smoked a heap of 'em, too. A corncob makes a mighty fine pipe. Gives a-body a right pleasurable smoke. You don't hardly ever see one nowadays though. But back 80 or 90 years ago...."

The Old Man paused to put a match to his pipe.

When he begins like that, there's a story in his sights and there's not much a man can do but listen. Especially if the wind is capering and there's a smell of frost in the air and a good log-fire blazing.

Such are the moments when the Old Man, nursing his pipe, re-stages a collection of homespun scenes from a time gone by. And for all his 97 years the old man's recollections are as studied and carefully correct as, he likes to say, a cane-totin' judge's charge to a jury.

"No, you just don't see folks smokin' corncobs any more," he said. "But back 80 or 90 years ago most ever'body smoked a corncob. They was all the go. Womenfolks smoked 'em, too. That is, them that was along in years. After they got past fifty or sixty. It was sort of looked on as sinful for a woman below that to smoke a pipe. Now chewin' and dippin' was common for womenfolks, both young and old, but that's somethin' I'll leave for tellin' another time.

"Like I said a minute back, I've made lots of corncob pipes. Reckon I was about ten years old when I turned out my first one. By that time I'd commenced thinkin' about pipes. Seein' the others smokin', you know.

"Well, I had me a pocketknife and one day I told some of the grownups I could make a corncob that would smoke just as good as theirs. I did. I made me some. Folks went to usin' em. Anybody that wanted one, I'd sit down with my knife and make 'em one.

"Course, I knew my pa would lay into me with a hickory if I smoked. I never started smokin' until I was about fifteen. But I made pipes right along. Reckon I made forty or fifty a year.

"Done my pipe-makin' in the fall of the year. That's when folks made 'em. That was the only time of the year you had cobs. Folks burned corncobs back then for fires. There's nothin' like corncobs for a good fire.

"Well, when you done your corn-shellin' you'd save out some cobs for pipes. You used the biggest ones you could get. Picked out ones that was big enough to hold four or five goodsized thimble fulls of tobacco.

"Then you'd get by the fire at night or just any place and take your pocketknife and start right in. First off you'd trim off the outside where the grains run. Take off the rough part and get down to firm cob.

"Once you got the cob all smoothed you started hollowin' it out. You had a piece about two inches long. You bore in from the top with the blade of your knife and cut it around until you cut it all out and had you a good deep bowl.

"When you had it all hollowed out you took a burnin' iron to fix a place for the stem. The burnin' iron was a long thing. About as big as your little finger. You could burn anythin' with it.

"You got the burnin' iron red hot and worked it into the cob down near the bottom. Didn't take no time at all to burn a hole through the cob.

"Then you fitted your pipe-stem to the hole. Used cane for the stem. The cane come from the creek bank. There was a sight of cane back then. It didn't grow so big. Just right for pipe stems.

"There wasn't much pith in the cane. But there was enough you had to take a wire and run through the can and push it out. The pith come out altogether, all in one piece, and looked sort of like pipe-cleaners you buy in the store nowadays.

"Sometimes you'd treat your pipe bowls with honey or apple juice. We called it flavorin' our pipes. Everybody didn't do it. But I always liked a flavored pipe. Made a good tastin' smoke. I'd pour just a little bit of honey down into the pipe and work it into the cob with my finger. And sometimes I'd pour a little bit in when I loaded my pipe. Just let it soak down in the pipe. Sure give it a good flavor.

"A-body could make a pipe just about any size he wanted. If you wanted a big one, you made a big one. Same with middle-sized. Small ones was just a waste of time in the makin'. Too short a smoke.

"You always made your pipes out of white cobs. You worked the outside with your knife until it was plumb slick and looked like it had been polished. After usin' it a time it started coloring' up just like any pipe'll do.

"A corncob pipe would last a long time. Much as 12 months, I guess. They wouldn't burn through. Just smoked up and got a cake like a pipe's supposed to do.

"Folks back then would gather around the fire and smoke their pipes. Only smoked three times a day. That was always after meals. While the womenfolks was clearin' away the dishes the menfolks would get up from the table and sit by the fire and smoke.

"There wasn't no smokin' outside while you was workin' in the fields or doin' whatever work you was about. That was when you done your chewin'.

"Nobody much bothered with store-bought tobacco in them days. Fact was, it was hard to come by at stores hereabouts. Ever'body grew his own tobacco. Ever'body had a little patch. If a-body run out he went to one of his neighbors and borrowed or bought some to tide him over until his crop come in.

"You kept your tobacco stored where it wouldn't get damp. It was tied in hands, leaves and all. When you got ready to smoke you'd take a leaf and crumble it up with your hands and pour it into your pipe."

The Old Man paused. His pipe had gone out. He struck a match and touched the flame to it. He puffed it into life again.

"A-body has to use a lot of matches smokin' a pipe," he said. "Back when I was comin' on matches was scarce. Cost a heap of money, too. What we had was pipe-lighters. Made out of paper rolled up in thin pieces about seven or eight inches long and crooked over at one end. You took your light from the fire and put it to your pipe.

"I've been smokin' a pipe way over 80 years now. Never tried but one box of cigarets. I've smoked a few cigars. But a pipe is the thing I like best for a good smoke.

"How much tobacco do I smoke? Well, a can lasts me about two weeks. Maybe a little less. Been smokin' about that amount all my life. No, I don't chew no more. Done no chewin' for thirty or forty years.

"Course I give up corncob pipes a long time ago. Use store-bought pipes altogether now. But I tell you, a good corncob's hard to beat.

"You know some folks say smokin's bad for a-body. I can't see it ever hurt me. Fact is, I think pipe smokin's good for a-body. Lots of folks smoke a pipe and I've yet to hear the first one say it hurt 'em.

"There's nothin' like sittin' by the fire and smokin'. Gives a-body a right peaceful feelin'. Tasty, too. That is, if you've got a good tobacco. I like mild tobacco. Don't want it so strong. Never was one for strong tobacco. Yes, sir, a pipe's the best smoke there is. And a corncob pipe makes a right good smoke. I've got me one I smoke ever now and then."

The Old Man's pipe had gone out again. He knocked it gently on the hearth and then put it in his pocket.

Then he sat looking into the fire.

And you had an idea that his thoughts were faraway in time.

Back in the jeans-britches and wool-hat era when the corncob pipe was all the go.

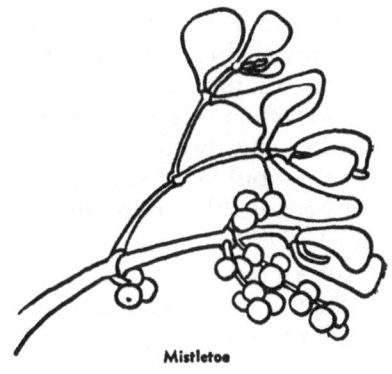
Mistletoe

Old Chimney Monument to Past

In the Alarka Mountains

THE SPILT-MILK-MIST OF FIRST MORNING LAY UPON THE high, hidden cove where a tottering old stone chimney stood all alone.

Back in the hills a whippoorwill sounded a requiem to the night and the dawn ran down the valleys of the wind, tracking the sky with coral.

But way off here at the back side of nowhere there was only a brooding, weary silence and the gray mist seemed reluctant to leave the cove.

The hillsman paused at the edge of the abandoned clearing and stared at the lonely old chimney feebly standing attention.

Somehow it roused silent whisperings of his imagination.

Maybe it was because of the hillsman's affinity for the homespun past, long-ago years when this was dark wilderness and a man only had to build a cabin and dwell in it to be king of a mountain top, a grove of hemlock, a bubbling spring.

Or perhaps it was because the hillsman looks upon lonely old chimneys with a knowledge that once they were sort of temples of a pioneer people whose sacred hearths were their altars.

There was really nothing unusual about this particular old chimney that had caught the hillsman's eye and set him to wondering.

The hills were studded with others like it.

In roaming the mountains from Watauga to Cherokee, the hillsman had stumbled upon many an old chimney standing alone in some hidden cove or out-of-the-way place where folks seldom go.

He had come to think on them as silent witnesses of a bygone era.

And always, as now, they seemed to ask the same question: Why did they go away?

This was a question the hillsman pondered, too.

And in pondering it, other questions came to mind and made of his brain a picture-maker.

Standing in the dayspring, the hillsman pulled his eyes from the old chimney. He let them walk about the cove. Past the stubborn remains of an orchard. Down the briar-grown path to the spring. Across the little stream. And then back to the old chimney.

Once upon a time, something had drawn a man to this far-off cove and he had taken his axe and grooved together a cabin. With his hands he had fashioned a chimney.

Now the cabin was gone. Only the chimney remained.

The chimney had been built to stand, to last, to endure.

No one remembers the man who built the chimney and lived here.

Nobody knows why he went away.

It could have been a death, worn out land, the lure of smoke in the valley.

Or it could have been he was one of those people destined almost never to be the oldest living citizen of a given community.

But whoever he might have been, he was a good man with his hands.

For the old chimney belies its looks.

At first glance it seems tottering and feeble, ready to crumble into ruins and return to the lonely earth.

But close examination reveals that it's really a sturdy piece of construction.

And somehow you get the feeling that the man who built it must have been kin to the builders of the pyramids.

It was built to last until time is a pinch of mold.

Perhaps it will.

For the old chimney has been here a long time.

This one and the others that stand abandoned in the hills could tell quite a story if only they could talk.

Each is a witness of a bygone era and all of them have looked down on the joys and sorrows of family life and the pageant of untold years of history.

The times and the men they once knew were great.

Maybe they knew Daniel Boone or Davy Crockett or Andy Jackson.

Around their hearths much has happened.

Not so much that would rate mention in the history books but a heap that goes to make up the heritage of a people.

Like the songs they sang, the music they played.

Thinking on this, the hillsman tried to imagine what the man was like who once lived here and what he thought when he knew he was going away or going to die.

The hillsman saw him as a tall, lean man with an axe in one hand and a rifle in the other, a God-fearing man.

When he came into the cove he was young. He could squint across a creek and knock out a deer's eye with his muzzle-loader. He carried his powder in a cow's horn and at 50 he could chew his bullet lead into bullets.

He cleared his land and raised the things he needed.

He was content to live back in the hills and work with his hands.

He raised a family. His boys grew up and went out of the cove. His daughters grew up and married and went off to live in the valley.

But he and his wife stayed on until they died or got so old and feeble that one of the sons, or maybe it was a daughter, finally made them come live with them.

That's when the cabin began to crumble and decay.

One by one the barn and corncrib and the springhouse rotted and crumbled.

In time, all that remained was the old chimney.

The fields returned to weeds and briars and new growth.

Folks seldom came this way.

There was no reason for coming.

It was way off at the backside of nowhere.

The cove was forgotten.

Only the chimney stood to remind the wanderer that a man once lived here.

The hillsman who came into the cove at dawn stumbled on it only by chance.

And he paused to stare at the old chimney and wonder.

The old chimney roused whisperings of the imagination.

The sun had chased the gray mist from the cove when the hillsman turned back up the trail.

He paused once and looked back down into the cove.

The old stone chimney stood like a stark monument to the past.

Gritted Bread

Burningtown

THE OLD MAN IS RIGHT PARTIAL TO GRITTED BREAD. "Finest bread you ever tasted," he said, "but folks now-a-days just don't make it. Reckon it ain't highfalutin' enough for 'em."

At 97, which he figures gives him certain unarguable rights, the Old Man has his "druthers" about many things, mostly about the choice of what he had rather sit down to in the way of victuals.

This is not to say, or even hint, that he is fussy or finicky about his eating. For, small though he is, his appetite is a wonder to behold and he likes to point out that he's a hearty eater.

But when it comes to bread, he'd druther bite into a pone of hot gritted bread baked in a greased skillet than to have buttermilk biscuits three times a day, seven days a week, and he's a plumb fool about buttermilk biscuits.

The subject of gritted bread popped up, as such rare and outdated topics have a habit of doing, when the Old Man returned for a visit to the old home place which has a way of reminding him of old customs and old things now relegated to the limbo of memory.

The afternoon sun was spinning golden mists over the land and the corn was tasseling in the fields that checkered the valley like green in a patch-work quilt.

A timid breeze, tip-toeing down from the high hills, set the greening corn blades a-flutter as the old man measured the growth of the corn with his eyes.

"Won't be many weeks now," he said, "before that corn'll be ripe enough for makin' gritted bread. 'Course, nobody takes the time any more to work up gritted meal.

"Huh? Gritted meal? Mean to tell me you don't know what it is? Why, boy, it's the finest thing a man ever made. Better'n waterground. Law me, yes! Makes up the sweetest bread you ever tasted. If I could have gritted bread all the time, I wouldn't give you a nickel for all the other corn meal that's ever been ground.

"Why, there's as much difference between bread made out of gritted meal and bread made out of water-ground meal as there is between sugar and salt or peaches and green persimmons.

"When I was a boy, and right up till I moved to town some years ago, we always had gritted bread on the table. That is, we had it as long as fresh corn held out.

" 'Course, there's only a certain time in the year a'body can have gritted bread. That's the time between when corn gets ripe enough to eat and when it gets too hard to eat."

The Old Man chuckled, and his grandson knew a memory had popped up to tickle him.

"Why, it was a sight to see folks when corn started sproutin' back then," he said. "They'd stand around watchin' the corn grow, their mouths a'waterin', plumb fidgety to get it eatin' size. Me and my brother had a time seein' which would be the first to spot when the corn reached grittin' size. I remember once he sat up half the night in the corn field a'testin' corn ears, thinkin' by mornin' they'd be right for pickin'. He come in to breakfast empty-handed and Pa told him he was plumb crazy. My brother looked real sheepish. And to make it worse I went out to the field right after breakfast and found a patch of corn that was grittin' size. He was fit to be tied.

"Now, once your corn gets grittin' size, you get out your grittin' board and make your meal for cookin'. You've got to cook it while it's fresh and milky.

"Some folks bought their gritters but most of 'em made 'em. I made mine. And I made lots for other folks, too. They was better than the store-bought kind.

"For my gritters I'd get me a board about two foot long and about six inches wide. Then I'd buy me some tin, somethin' like roofin' tin. Good bright tin. I'd cut me a piece to fit my board and stud it good with nail holes, making it all rough on one side.

"The rough side was the grittin' side. When you got your holes in it you'd take the tin and tack it on the board, just the sides and one end and you'd tack it down so it'd be sort of cupped up.

"Then you'd take the fresh ears of corn and rub 'em up and down over the rough side. The meal would run down through the little holes and onto the board and out the end that wasn't tacked down. You had a pan or somethin' to catch it in as it run out.

"Made the sweetest corn meal a'body could imagine. Didn't take long, either. Why, in four or five minutes you could grit enough meal for a big family. I've gritted many a pan full.

"As soon as the corn was gritted you carried the meal right to the kitchen where you wet it and put in the milk and salt and poured the batter into a greased skillet."

The Old Man smacked his lips.

"When that bread come out of the pan all crisp and brown and steamin'," he said, "it made a'body's mouth water. And when you broke off a hunk and buttered it and put it in your mouth—well, a'body couldn't ask for anythin' better."

The Old Man paused. In the silence, he looked wistfully toward the tasseling corn. When finally he spoke there was a sort of come-back-oh-lost-ways in his voice.

"Maybe," he said, "just maybe we could have us some gritted bread. The corn'll soon be grittin' size and I still know how to make a gritter. Looks like if we gritted the meal your mama wouldn't mind bakin' the bread."

Yes, at 97, the Old Man is right partial to gritted bread.

Maypop (Passion Flower Vine)

Ballad Singers Becomin' Scarce

Balsam Gap

THE TRUE SINGERS OF MOUNTAIN BALLADS ARE GETTING TO be almost as rare as the jew's-harp and the dulcimer.

They are dying out or being educated, which is the same.

The few purists that are left form a unique clan, bound together by tradition and a proud heritage that can be traced back to Elizabethan England.

They include such apostles as Bascom Lamar Lunsford of South Turkey Creek, Artus Moser of Wilson's Cove, Virgil Sturgill of Oteen, and Samantha Bumgarner of Love Field.

They sing the old ballads and the old folk songs the way their grandmothers and great-grandmothers sang them, throaty and natural as can be.

They sing them as tunes remembered, tunes handed down by word of mouth, thus losing none of the freshness of the untrained voice with its folksy flavor.

But their kind is passing, and when their singing style—the true traditional style—finally disappears, something will pass that is truly of the mountains and nothing will bring it back.

Tunes that never knew any instrument but a fiddle, a dulcimer, and a banjo are winning popularity with big orchestras as program spicers, but they are a far cry from the traditional rendition.

The bands are stepping up the tempo and changing the key. The tunes are being prettied up and fobbed off as the real thing, played and sung by trained musicians, choirs and soloists who give them an operatic twist.

Folks who never have heard the true singing of the old tunes are being told that this is real mountain music.

Oh, brother, how wrong can you be!

As a matter of fact, about the only relation between the songs as now played and sung and the old-timy ones are the words, and even they are not always recognizable.

Recently when I bemoaned on Edward R. Murrow's nationwide news program that mountain music—real mountain music—was disappearing, I received a letter from a listerner telling me the folks up at Berea College in Kentucky were keeping it alive. My correspondent said he was sending along a recording by the college choir to prove it.

Well, I've just received the recording, and I'm disappointed.

I had expected to hear the throaty naturalness that marks real ballad singing, that freshness of the untrained voice which sets the true ballad singer apart from all others. And I listened expectantly, but in vain, for the plaintive twang of the dulcimer.

True, they were the old ballads. The words were those that had been sung throughout the Southern Appalachians for centuries, but they were rendered by voices that had been trained and coached.

Missing was the spirit, and the feeling.

But don't get me wrong. The voices were beautiful, cultured and trained. And Berea is to be commended for taking a step to perpetuate the words of these priceless old ballads.

Yet, there was something missing. Only those who have heard Lunsford or Sturgill, Moser or Aunt Samantha, will know or recognize the difference.

It's sort of like taking a majestic balsam tree out of its natural setting and putting it right smack in the center of a desert.

Virgil Sturgill, a mountain man dedicated to the preservation of the old tunes and the old songs, probably expressed it best.

"The only way to sing a ballad," he said, "is to sing it the way you heard your grandmother sing it. When I start to sing a ballad I just close my eyes and think back 40 years and remember the voices and how they sounded, and I try to sing the song with the same pitch of that memory.

"You've got to have a feeling, a sense and an enjoyment of the song. You've got to sing it in a natural pitch. You've got to sing it like your grandma or your mama sang it, duplicating all the sounds. And when you do, then you are singing in the traditional style.

"You've got to remember, too, that these old ballads were not set to music. The tune was handed down by word of mouth from one generation to another.

"But folks now—the professionals, that is—have taken the old ballads and proceeded to set them to music on paper. When they do that they lose the freshness of the untrained voice and the traditional style.

"You've got to remember that the old time ballad singers and balladeer, for the most, were simple folks, unlearned, unlettered and often illiterate.

"They sung the songs as they had been sung before them.

"I sing them in the traditional style, the way I learned them from the old timers. And now my son is learning them. He sings them the way I sing them, echoing the words the way I render them. That's the only way to learn to sing ballads."

Sturgill then called attention to the modern trend of labeling popular songs as ballads.

"This is most regrettable," he said. "Tune in your radio almost any time and you'll hear folks talking about ballads when what they're talking about are popular songs.

"Take for instance the song now up at the top on the hit parade, *Sixteen-Ton*. It was written by a boy from Kentucky. It's a folksy song but it's not a folk song.

"When authors write songs and the songs are played and sung by trained musicians then they are not authentic folk ballads. Only if the origin of the song is unknown and learned by word of mouth does it become an authentic ballad. For that makes it something that belongs to the folks.

"Even the old ballads are being changed. Not so much the words. But the tempo and the key. They are giving them an operatic twist. Thus they lose their folksiness.

"They are too refined and too near scientific styling to be authentic renditions

"I believe that the real essence of true folk singing has to do with the attitude and the mind of the performer, a sort of acting out of the words, a recreation in sound of the tale the ballad tells."

Sturgill agrees with many an old timer that most of the ballads almost sing themselves, without benefit of printed tunes.

But most folks now are depending on printed tunes to shape their style.

And that's why the true singers of mountain ballads are getting to be almost as rare as the jew's-harp and the dulcimer.

When Anvil-Shootin' Rocked the Hills

Burningtown

MY GRANDFATHER REMEMBERS WHEN GUN POWDER WAS as much a part of Christmas as eggnog stew and peppermint stick candy.

"Back when I was a-growin' up," he said, "we saved our fireworks for Christmas instead of the Fourth of July, and a feller without a pound of black powder to spark his celebratin' was a mighty lonesome feller.

"Folks now-a-days don't celebrate like we did. Reckon if they was to go around firin' off guns and shootin' anvils and settin' off charges of black powder they'd get theirselves into a peck of trouble."

For a moment the Old Man looked off across the Burningtown hills. There was that look in his eyes when he starts rummaging through his recollections that go back almost a century.

"We sure did use up a lot of black powder back in them days. But we had us a lot of fun. Reckon we scared a lot of womenfolks. Of course most everybody back then was used to a lot of shootin', but the noise we made around Christmastime was sort of like a war a-goin' on.

"We called it serenadin'. We fellers would all get our guns and our bag of black powder and meet up some place on our horses and then start goin' through the community, shootin' as we went.

"We loaded our guns with tow wads. That was so nobody'd get hurt. That's the way we made our blank shots. Back in them days there wasn't no blank shells that you could buy at the store.

"There'd be a whole bunch of us, 15 or 20, and we'd ride up to a feller's house and start shootin'. Pretty soon the door would open and they'd invite us in and give us gingerbread and apples.

"Some of the more frolicksome would take their guns in the house and stick 'em up the chimney and fire 'em. You never heard such a noise. Sounded like the chimney and the house was a-blowin' up.

"Then we'd ride on and visit somebody else. We'd keep at it until way up in the night. Did I tell you that we only done this the night before Christmas? Well, that's when it was. Did our serenadin' the night before. Never on Christmas. Maybe you'd hear a few shots early on Christmas morning.

"You see, back then, the fellers serenaded the night before and come Christmas day everybody would get together and go on a big rabbit hunt. That was a custom back then.

"After I got married and moved over to Hog Rock in Jackson County we'd celebrate with all kinds of shootin'. We'd take an augur and bore holes in the trees and tamp in black powder and set it off. Bore five or six holes in one tree. It'd tear them trees to pieces and make a noise like a cannon.

"I reckon if I took you over to Hog Rock I could still show you some of them trees we busted up.

"There was somethin' else we used to do when I was a boy. That was shootin' anvils. Huh? Never heard of anvil shootin'? Why that was one of the finest things ever. For real noisemakin' you can't beat an anvil.

"We'd pack black powder real tight into the round and square holes of one anvil. Then we'd take another one and put it on top of the charge. When we lit the powder both of them anvils would ring out with a clang that could be heard in the next county. 'Course, you'd sometimes ruin the anvils, de-horn 'em, you might say.

"Some of the stores got to keepin' firecrackers. But they wasn't much big and didn't have much powder in 'em. Wasn't much noise to 'em. They was what you called Chinese firecrackers and they cost five cents. That is, five cents a pack. But most of us spent our money on black powder.

"When we'd meet up around the store that's when we'd have some fun with them firecrackers. Somebody would light one and throw it under somebody's chair. We'd pick a feller that was a-leanin' back and when it went off it would cause him to jump and the next thing he'd be there on his back in the floor and everybody a-laughin' at him. If he was a good sort he'd take it all in fun and then set everybody up to a drink of cider or a drink of whiskey.

"Back in them days all the stores in the country had a whiskey barrel at Christmas time. Me, I'd take the cider."

The Old Man said he had no idea how the custom of firing guns and anvils and firecrackers at Christmastime started in the South.

In the North, such celebrating is done on the Fourth of July, not at Christmas.

Actually, there seems to be little reason for this fundamental difference between the two sections of the country in celebrating Christmas.

Some have claimed that the reason folks in the South shoot firecrackers and guns at Christmas time instead of on the Fourth of July is because of something that happened during the Civil War.

The seige of Vicksburg was lifted on the Fourth of July and folks said that is why Southerners refuse to celebrate.

"I don't rightly know why we did all the shootin' and noise-makin' at Christmas time," the Old Man said. "It was a custom that was being carried on long before the war. I remember my pa tellin' me about how when he was a boy they shot rifles and anvils.

"Seems like I recollect somebody sayin' that when there was just a few folks livin' here in the mountains that one family would fire off his gun if he wanted help or wanted 'em to pay a visit. You know them was the days when folks lived two and three miles apart. It was a lot easier to fire a gun and let 'em know you was a-comin' than it was to send somebody over."

The Old Man paused, looked off into the hills that now were deep in shadow.

"Of course, we done a lot of other things at Christmas time besides serenadin' that ain't done now. But I'll have to tell you about that another time."

Somewhere in the dusk there was an echo of a gun-shot.

He cocked an ear for a moment and somehow you had the feeling he was still remembering when gun powder was as much a part of Christmas as eggnog stew and peppermint stick candy.

Frog Rains Mighty Common

Burningtown

THE OLD MAN LISTENED TO THE THUNDER ROLLING A reveille to the hills and the hill-born.

"It's booin' for 'taters," said the Old Man. "Booin' up a 'tater-diggin' rain."

To the southwest, the sky was black with prophecy. Rain-bearing clouds raced out across the Nantahalas and a wet wind hustled down the ridges.

"That's what you call a lazy man's rain," said the Old Man. "A feller that don't have no hankerin' for workin' in the fields is always mouthin' 'bout how daytime rain is the best kind of rain But I was always for rain at night. That's what you call a poor man's rain. Let's him work in the day-time."

The Old Man looked out across the fields, there at the head of the valley. Thunder rolled through the hills. The rain raced into the valley like a puff of pipe-smoke.

"Back when I was a boy," said the Old Man, "the Indians had a name for spring and summer rain. Called it she-rain because it made things grow."

By now the rain had swept down the valley and was pounding the earth with a steady downpour which the thirst-starved earth sopped up.

The Old Man looked into the rain and watched while the earth drank.

"There's all kinds of rain," he said. "Soft rain and hard rain. Warm rain and cold rain. Dog day's rain. That's a slushin' kind of rain. There's frazzlin' rain which ain't no rain at all. Just a few drops. And there's a drizzlin' rain that ain't much better."

He paused. Suddenly there was a twinkle in his eyes.

"Reckon you're acquainted with frog-rain and fish-rain. What's that? Never heard tell of it. Maybe not by them names, you ain't.

But you've seen it. That you have. Why it's the kind of rain that rains frogs and little bitty fish and worms.

"Why many's the time I've seen it rain frogs and redworms and fish. Not all at the same time. This is that kind of rain. Just wait till it stops and then get out and about. Why, the ground'll just be covered with little bitty frogs not much bigger than your thumb-nail. And redworms. Why, they'll be all over the place.

"Now if it didn't rain 'em, I ask you where they come from? You just look. They ain't there before such a rain. Everybody will tell you it ain't uncommon for it to rain frogs and redworms.

"Now a fish-rain is somethin' else. You ain't as likely to find as many fish-rains as frog and worm rains. But they come ever now and then. Search out rain puddles after a rain. If it's been a fish-rain you'll find a heap of fish no bigger than a fair-to-middlin'-sized maple tag.

"They ain't tad-poles. They're fish. You usually find 'em along the roadside after a quick thunder storm. They're about an inch long. Now and then you'll run across one up to two inches."

The Old Man paused. He grinned.

"Reckon you've got your doubts," he said. "Don't know as I blame you. But folks would learn a lot of things and see a lot of strange sights if only they'd pay attention to what goes on about 'em."

The Old Man prides himself on paying attention to everything, whether it's little, fair-to-middlin', or downright big.

"Nature's a right handy teacher," said the Old Man. "She talks all the time. Day and night. All you got to do is keep your eyes sharp and your ears tuned up to catch what she's sayin'.

"Why, there's signs ever which-a-way if a-body'll take the time to read 'em. Folks got along right well when there wasn't no almanacs or fancy do-dads to prophesy what the weather was a-goin' to do.

"Next time you pass a corn-field, take notice of the corn. If the blades are twisted from the heat you can look out for rain.

"There's a heap of ways of tellin' when rain's a-comin'. A raincrow croakin' durin' the day will bring rain by tomorrow. Any time you hear jaybirds a-frettin' unduly and a-fussin' like all-get-out you can look for bad weather.

"You've seen these whirligusts. Some folks call 'em devil-dancers and little whirlwinds. Any time you see one of 'em a-layin' down the road you can count on rain for certain.

"Now when there's honey-dew on the trees and leaves it's a dry weather spell set in.

"Reckon you've noticed that sometimes a creek seems louder than usual. Like it wants to bust out and go a-shoutin'. When it gets that-a-way, look out for rain."

The rain had slacked off. The earth had drank deeply. The sky was beginning to clear. The thunder was only an echo in the hills.

"Time was," said the Old Man, "when rain was mighty welcome. That was when I was a-farmin'. It's still mighty welcome to farm folks. But I'd druther have a poor man's rain now-a-days. Day-time rain keeps me all shut up so I can't get about."

There was a faint suggestion of sun and the Old Man's eyes matched it.

"Maybe," he said, "we ought to see if it was a frog-rain."

Deer's Tongue

Never Cuss a Man's Houn' Dog

Somewhere in the Blue Ridge

BIG SAM'S TONE WAS KIND AND OLD BILLY-B'S EYES WERE prideful and the combination told their story. The two old cronies were over their pout and everything was all right again.

A hound-dog, a super-prime coon dog, had set them against each other and brought them to a hair-trigger stand-off across a campfire, one with a rifle, the other with a bare knife.

"Things like that happen in the hills when a man berates another man's hound-dog," said the old mountaineer, the one they call Gramps. "Only the good Lord knows why one or both of 'em weren't killed. Just one of them miracles, I reckon, a thing for which there ain't no answer."

This was part of the story of Trim, the huntin'est coon dog in all the mountains—maybe in all the land—and of old Billy-B, the famous old hunter who put his dog above his son.

"I told you about how old Billy-B's boy sold off Trim, thinkin' he was doin' the right thing for his Pa, and how the old man run the boy off from home," said Gramps. "That's a mighty hard thing for a man to do, to turn out one of his own and shut his mind against him. But then maybe you've never owned a hound-dog. Especially one like Trim.

"Old Billy-B raised her from a pup. He was a master-hand with dogs and he trained her well. Hunted her for six years. Long enough to let her steal his heart and his soul. And then I come by her, like I told you.

"To understand how old Billy-B felt about her and how I got to feel about her, you've got to know somethin' about Trim. She was a small red hound, one-eighth feist. Prettiest hound-dog you ever saw. And the smartest.

"Now some folks'll boast and brag about their dogs till they're plumb out of breath. Why, they'll 'tribute powers and wisdom to their dog that no dog has. Of course, it's a man's privilege to brag when he's got a good hound-dog. That is, just so long's he don't cast no slurs on somebody else's while he's a'doin' his braggin'.

"Be that as it may, a'body didn't need to let his tongue run loose about Trim. She done her own braggin'. Done it like a good hound should. The proof's in the end of the trail come daybust.

"You never saw her, so I'll have to tell you. Trim was the best dog I ever owned, and I've had some mighty fine dogs in my time. She had 256 coons to her credit when she died. She never failed to tree a coon that she barked on the trail."

The old man paused, and in the firelight his eyes were wistful with memory.

"Yes, sir-ree, she was some dog. You knew of a certainty when she barked she was after a coon. She wouldn't bark at nothin' else. She was what you'd call a straight coon-dog.

"I remember once a bunch of us was out a'huntin'. The dogs was out a'trailin' and we was a'followin' along. When a dog's a'trailin' they'll bark one way and when they tree they'll change their bark and bay. If you know your dog you can tell when it's a 'trailin' and when it's a'treein'.

"Well, I knew my Trim. And I heard her a'bayin' about a mile off. She had the prettiest-soundin' voice you ever heard. Somehow when you heard her it made you think of heaven. It was that kind of pretty.

"When we got to her she was a'settin' back on her haunches with her head turned up a'bayin' at a tall hemlock, She was all by herself. The other dogs had gone on. One of the fellers said, 'That dog's a'lyin'.'"

The old man smiled.

"For a minute I saw all red and was about to mix up with this feller. Then I thought better of it. But I knew Trim wasn't lyin'. And I said so. Just wait till daybust, I says, and you'll see who's lyin'.

"Well, we built us up a fire there at the foot of that hemlock. There wasn' no moon and no stars that night and the night was very dark. Trim struck right there by the tree a'bayin' nightlong.

"Then it was daylight and then the sun come up and the sun come through them hemlock branches. I could see a knot of fur in the top. Took my rifle and fired away. Somethin' come tumblin' down, breakin' limbs as it fell. It was the biggest coon I ever saw. I never said a word. But I looked straight at this feller who'd accused my Trim of lyin' and he looked real sheepish. Then he said, 'That dog don't lie'.

"Well, that closed the issue. And because it was closed, it was forgotten. I never had no hard feelin's but I was mighty proud. Trim had stayed there all night a'bayin' while them other dogs had gone off huntin' elsewhere. She didn't move. Showed she was smarter'n all the rest of 'em put together.

"Gettin' back to old Billy-B. He got a real scare once over Trim. I always said if the old man had heart trouble, like they said he did, then he should of dropped dead that night I'm about to tell you about.

"The old man and one of his boys was out with some fellers coon huntin'. Well, the dogs got to barkin' around a tree and one of the fellers thought they'd treed a coon.

"Old Billy-B spoke right up and said somethin' peculiar was a'goin' on. Said he couldn't rightly explain it but he didn't figure there was a coon in the tree. Said Trim wasn't a'bayin. Then he looked around for her and didn't see her.

"One of the fellers shined a light up in the tree and there was somethin' starin' back at 'em through a fork in the tree, eyes all a'shinin'.

"By this time, old Billy-B figured he knew what was happenin'. There was two or three of his other dogs in the hunt besides Trim. One of the fellers said he was goin' to take a shot at whatever it was and he was sure it was a coon.

"Well, the old man said go ahead but he told 'em to make sure they didn't shoot his dog. One of the fellers blazed away and somethin' tumbled out of the tree. The old man went over, his boy a'followin', and it was one of old Billy-B's hounds, not Trim. This feller what shot the dog said he was awful sorry. Old Billy-B never said a word. He just stood there a'cryin' and his boy a'cryin' with him.

"The two of 'em gathered the dog up in their arms and the boy and the old man started home with it. When they got home they told the family and the family cried and the old man and the boy cried some more.

"I reckon if it had of been Trim there'd been a dead man on the mountain that night. The old man shore loved that Trim.

"Which gets me to when him and Big Sam had their run-in. Him and Big Sam had growed up together. They'd hunted all over together. Yarned together and slept together. They was as close as brothers, maybe closer. And both of 'em was mighty prideful about their dogs.

"Reckon they never had words but twice in all their lives. The first time neither one of 'em got mean-mad. But the second time was somethin' else again,

"This last time I was along when they got into it. And it all started over somethin' that had got 'em to mouthin' against each other the first time.

"Big Sam that first time accused Billy-B's Trim of runnin' one of his dogs out of a race and makin' her no count any more. Billy-B was pretty calm about it but he told Big Sam it just wasn't so and he never wanted him to mention it again.

"Well, for goin' on three years Big Sam hunted with Billy-B and never mentioned Trim runnin' off his dog. But along comes this night I'm tellin' you about and we was all around the campfire a'yarnin' and a'rakin' up old hunts when Big Sam hauls off and asks Billy-B does he remember the time Trim run off his hound.

"Billy-B jumped up like a mad wasp, his rifle in his hand. He aimed it across at Big Sam. 'I told you never to mention that again,' said Billy-B. 'I told you I'd kill you if you did. And now you've done it.'

"Big Sam had been a'whittlin' as he talked and he was curlin' off shavin's with a knife that had a blade about five or six inches. One of them mean-lookin' knives. Well, he got to his feet, that knife in his hand and it a'pointin' at Billy-B.

"It was a shore ticklish situation. The rest of us knew it was no time to say a thing. We just kept our mouths shut tight and got out of there. Left the two a'standin' there facin' each other, neither one sayin' a word with their mouth but sayin' a plenty with their eyes.

"Ever' last one of us knowed there was goin' to be a killin' on the mountain that night, maybe two. Figured Billy-B would get in one shot and Big Sam, who was a giant of a man, would get to Billy-B with that knife no matter if he had a bullet in his heart.

"Well, we went on down to the foot of the mountain to where the wagon road was that run off around the hill to Billy-B's and Big Sam's and built us a fire and waited to hear a shot.

"When daybust come on we still hadn't heard nothin' and we didn't know what to make of it. Then about that time we heard somebody a'comin' down the trail and there was Billy-B and Big Sam a'walkin' along like nothin' had ever happened.

"Billy-B done the talkin' to us. Said he reckoned they was just a couple durned old crazy fools. Said they stood off up there by the fire all night never sayin' a word and a'waitin' for the other to make the first move.

"We still didn't know what to make of it and we kept quiet.

Billy-B said, 'I got weary of holdin' my rifle on Big Sam and told him I wasn't mad no more. Big Sam said he wasn't neither. So we shook hands and come out. It's a closed issue, boys. You needn't worry no more about us. Both of us are gettin' too old for that kind of stuff.'

"Well, you know, them two seemed closer after that. Then Big Sam died, died in his sleep. And it wasn't long till I got Trim and then old Billy-B died.

"But you never can tell what a man'll do when somebody berates his hound-dog."

Blue Eyed Grass

June's a Whippoorwill A-Callin'

Truelove Mountain

IN THE CAROLINA HIGHLANDS, JUNE IS A WHIPPOORWILL a-callin' and the sap a-runnin' wild.

It's singing on the mountain and dinner on the ground.

It's courtin'-time and marryin'-time.

It's blue skies and golden mists.

It's she-rain come down from the clouds to cleanse the earth.

It's the ancient hills proclaiming the mystery and miracle of enduring life.

It's a mountain flower kingdom that was old when the Gardens of Babylon were new.

It's azalea and rhododendron and laurel turning the landscape into a mad confusion of mauve, purple, pink and white.

June in the mountains is the answer to an old man's prayers and a young man's dreams.

It's June-bugs on a string and fire-flies in the night.

It's a hoe-down and a stomp-down.

It's fiddles a-cryin' and feet a-shufflin'.

It's Sam Queen, King of the Square Dancers, cutting a pigeon wing and riding a short loper.

It's Marcus Martin, last of the old-time fiddlers, resining up his bow.

It's Samantha Bumgarner, the banjo-pickin' ballad-woman of Love Field, crooning a tune.

June in the mountains is a mountain maid with flowers in her hair and stars in her eyes.

It's a climbing moon upon an empty sky and a bee singing to her groom.

It's Wallace Bradley, the "Bee-Keeper of the Smokies," quoting an old saw:

> "A swarm of bees in May
> Is worth a load of hay.
> A swarm in June
> Is worth a silver spoon.
> A swarm in July
> Is not worth a fly."

June in the highlands is milk-spilt mist at crack-of-day and a flaming scarf at daydown.

It's lambs gamboling on a hillside and goats climbing toward the sky.

It's bear hounds lazing and sunning themselves on a cabin doorstep.

It's a bear cub staring at a tourist.

It's the glory and freshness of a dream.

It's poke-sallet and greens.

It's a mountain farmer greeting the dawn from the fields and twilight from the furrows.

It's barefoot boys heading for the swimming hole in the bend of the creek.

It's berry-pickin' time and jelly-makin' time.

It's bloom-time of the passion-vine, galax, trumpet creeper, mountain camellia, and the wild orchids.

It's morning-glories, honeysuckle, and wild strawberries.

It's the cry of bull-bats in the pink of evening.

It's the noise of a hidden brook singing a quiet tune.

June in the mountains is a time when rainbows come and go.

It's the marriage of spring and summer.

It's a time when a mountain man in some far off land yearns for the hills of home.

It's a time when the old, the very old, get a hankering to wander where the woodbine twineth and the whangdoodle mourns.

June is a shaft of sunlight slanting through a balsam grove like a lane to heaven.

It's the hum of a spinning wheel and the whackety-whack of a loom.

It's box-suppers and fried chicken.

It's family reunions and going back to the old-home place.

It's all these things and more.

Especially in the mountains.

For here, June is really a many-splendored thing.

Rustic Imagery Disappearing

Alarka

THE RUSTIC IMAGERY ONCE SO PECULIAR TO MOUNTAIN folksay is disappearing.

The old timers who were the beatin'est folks you ever run across for expressing themselves simply, albeit colorfully, are few and far between, and the young folks just don't seem to have the knack.

And that's a shame, for conversation these days could do with a shot of homely poetry, pungent wit, and simple wisdom.

One of the old timers who was seldom at a loss for a word was Israel (Wid) Medford over in Haywood County.

When he lacked other means of expression, a coinage of his own would come from his lips.

Once when interrupted while telling a story, he turned to the feller and said: "Just tend to broilin' your bacon, Jonas, and let me travel to suit my own legs." After that, the feller stuck to minding his own business.

Once, he described a bear as "lean as a two-acre farmer's horse, after corn has been a dollar and a half a bushel for three months, and roughness can't be got for love or money."

He was so familiar with the hills he allowed "What I don't know about these mountains ain't of any profit to man or devil."

"Why," he said, "I've brogued it through every briar patch and laurel thicket, and ain't I been with Guyot, Sandoz, Grand Pierre, and Clingman over every peak."

He called his rifle a "nail-driver," and when he was out camping and said "Hand me some Old Ned from that suggin o' mine," he was referring to fat pork in a pouch.

There was many another like him who had a way with words.

Back during the election campaign of 1904, a mountain man confided that "the people around here is so poor that if free silver was shipped in by the carload, we couldn't pay the freight."

This was a section where some of the land was so poor "it wouldn't raise a cuss-fight" and where "the chickens ran wild and scratched for a livin'."

When John Davis lived in the Smokies there was a certain razorback hog that gave him so much trouble he swore "it would cross hell on a rotten rail to get to my tater patch."

One of his neighbors had a gun whose hammer wouldn't stay cocked. "The dad-burned thing," he said, "won't stand roostered."

In every mountain community there were folks who made pleasure of gathering and spreading news. Once when talk got around to one of these fiddle-cryers, an old mountaineer said:

"You can hear the news jinglin' afore he comes within gunshot."

These news-spreaders and news-gatherers had a way of trying to cover up their mission by saying they were "jes' cooterin' around," "saunterin' about," "spuddin' around" or "shacklin' about."

Cooter is a box-turtle, spuddin' means toddling or jolting along, shacklin' is a loose-jointed way of walking.

A feller had a cabin up the road that was described as being so small "you can't cuss a cat in it without gettin' hair in your teeth."

If a man was described as "feisty" or "brigaty," it meant that he was stuck on himself and wanted to show off.

Some of the ridges hereabouts are "might nigh straight up and down, and, as the feller said, perpendic'lar."

There'd been a runction over on Hazel Creek. Some of the folks standing around were discussing it. "If a feller'd treated me the way Alf did," one said, "I'd get me a forty-some-odd and shoot enough meat off his bones to feed a hound-dog a week."

In the talk that was, it was not uncommon to hear a mountain man say "them clouds denote rain" or "he is blind but he can discern when the sun is shinin'." And a woman that was forever nagging was one who "kept faultin' us all day."

If a feller was in a hurry he "took his foot in his hand and lit out," and when the elements were cloudin' up you could count on "a rainin', windin' spell."

My grandfather still says "back this letter for me," a phrase unchanged from the days before envelopes, when the address had to be written on the letter itself.

He knew a feller that was "born tired and raised lazy."

When a'body comes a'visiting he is liable to say "lift your hat and rest your wrap."

The old timers who had a way with words are few and far between. And the rustic imagery once so peculiar to mountain folksay is disappearing.

Old Way of Life Dying

Big Cove

LET'S CALL HIM LITTLE JOHN LITTLEJOHN.
It's a good Indian name, and proud.

He's eight, going on nine. Not much bigger than a bear cub. Just about hoe-handle high, maybe. Bright as a new Indian-head penny.

His eyes are chinquapins. His hair is as black as the raven. His high cheek bones are the heritage of a thousand years and more. His skin reflects the tint of the Dawn Man.

When he walks he turns his toes in, naturally. His feet are only a whisper on the fallen leaves.

He traces his ancestors back to a chief who made talk with a certain Hernando DeSoto, the first white man to come this way some 400 years ago.

One of his ancestors was the chef who prepared a banquet for the visiting Spanish Dons and introduced barbecue.

His grandfather, four times removed, had a hand in saving the day and the life of Andrew Jackson at the Battle of Horseshoe Bend, albeit regretfully years later when Old Hickory tried to exile the entire Cherokee Nation.

His kinsmen were among the small band that hid out in the Great Smokies and said they would die starving or fighting rather than leave their homeland. They did neither. But they stayed.

Because of them, Little John Littlejohn is growing up in the old Cherokee homeland.

And, yet, he is destined to become a stranger to his heritage.

For a way of life as old as the hills is disappearing into the limbo of cob-webbed memories.

The old order is changing.

Chances are Little John Littlejohn, symbol of every little Cherokee boy of eight going on nine, will grow up without ever knowing or learning the things that are a part of his heritage.

The wisdom of his people will fall before the white man's twist of education.

There will be no old man to translate the signs of nature.

There will be no affinity of the sun and the moon and the stars.

He will no longer look to the earth as the source of his food and his self reliance.

He will not feel the thing that his elder brother, his father, his uncle has felt when they were forced to leave their homeland, even for a short time.

The earth, the mountains, that pulled his kinsmen back—from universities, from wars, from "success" in the white man's world—to feel one with it, to die upon it. . . .

These he will not feel.

For the old order is changing. An older way of life is dying. It is disappearing. And no one is doing anything about it.

Little John Littlejohn, in a sense, is all alone.

There isn't a medicine man around to pass on the wisdom and secrets of ancient tribal ritual.

Old Creeping Bear, the one who taught the young, is dead.

Runaway Swimmer is a name that means nothing to him, albeit he was the greatest of Cherokee shamen, priests and storytellers.

Little John Littlejohn probably will be no better than his white college roommate in tracking a bear.

He will grow up in the white man's ways. He will take to the white man's customs. In time, Little John Littlejohn will be a white man, in every way.

For a way of life as old as the hills is disappearing. . . .

The old Cherokee dances are dying. Nobody dances like they used to. The patterns are hazy. The spirit is gone.

Indian ball, once the most rugged sport in all the world, is a farce. The blood and bets and thunder are only memories of the old, the very old.

The ancient techniques in basketry, beadwork and woodcarving are forgotten.

Only a few still raise real Indian corn, the kind with many-colored grains, and Indian beans, the kind that produces rainbows.

There are only a rare few still around who could teach Little John Littlejohn how to make a dugout canoe from a poplar tree.

By the time he goes to college, chances are he will have a hard time finding someone to show him the art of making blowguns and blowgun darts out of thistle.

He probably will grow up never learning to speak his own language. And the odds are a million to one he will never be able to write his language, never be able to take advantage of the opportunity given him by an illiterate named Sequoyah, who invented the Cherokee alphabet.

Little John Littlejohn is learning English and English grammar in the white man's school. But no one is trying, or offering, to teach him Cherokee. And by the time he goes to college, unless something is done and done quickly, Sequoyah's invention will be only a record in the history books.

Although he is only eight going on nine, Little John Littlejohn is lost to his heritage.

In all the land of the Cherokee—a tiny mountain domain of 56,000 acres—only a few medicine men, a few wise old men, still are alive.

And before many moons they will be gone.

With them will vanish a way of life, a wisdom no white man has ever had.

Little John Littlejohn and all the little Indian boys of eight going on nine will grow up with only twice-told tales to tell.

For the old ones are too old.

And they no longer practice their magic.

At least, not openly.

For the young are disbelievers.

And the old have their pride.

This is something that shouldn't happen.

For the ancient way of life of the Cherokee is something that should be preserved.

Little John Littlejohn is only eight, going on nine, but his heritage is disappearing.

Tomorrow it will be gone.

No Cause to Be Lonesome

Somewhere in the Hills

THE RAIN HAD PASSED, THE LEAVES WERE DRIPPING, AND the sun made diamonds everywhere.

Hearth-smoke drifted up from the little cabin nestling gray and lonely in a clearing at the head of the cove.

A fence of rived palings laced with gourd vines circled the cabin. Scarlet sage stood like red-coated sentinels on either side of the sagging gate. The "flying ciphers" and the "pretty boys" nodded in the fence corners.

She sat on the vine-wreathed porch in a splint-bottomed chair. The years had made a Madonna-like mask of her face. There was a look of the age-wise in her kindly blue eyes. Her hands, old and worn and leathery, lay empty in the aproned lap. A black, knitted wool shawl hugged her bent shoulders.

"Folks hardly ever come this way," she said, "except if they want somethin'. And that ain't often."

Her voice was soft. Almost like a caress. And, yet, there was a hint of sadness in it. Something wistful. A yearning for something known in a long-ago year and then lost.

"It's been that way for nigh on to thirty years now," she said. "Ever since I got to be a widow-woman. At first it was mighty lonesome livin' here all by myself. But in time I got used to it. I wouldn't have it no other way.

"Of course when my old man died the children wanted me to come into town and live with them. I told 'em this was my place and this was where I'd stay till they put me in the ground."

She paused and looked off beyond the field of corn and the little patch of sorghum, there to a little shelf on the hillside where a picket fence marked the family burying ground.

"I couldn't move away and leave my man over there all alone," she said. "We come in here together. That was back in '85. I'd just turned eighteen. We'd been married two years. He cleared this land and built this house. My first-born was barely a year old."

She remembered how it was back then. How her man had set out the apple trees and the peach trees. How he had made her a spinning wheel and a loom and some quilting bars.

She remembered how she went into the fields and helped him raise their crops. How she took a turn at plowing and hoeing, pulling fodder and cutting cane.

"That was before the children got big enough to work," she said. "But even then I done my share of work outside. I've always believed in workin'. That way abody has somethin'."

She paused and looked at her worn hands. They had done a man's work.

"I ain't as peart as I once was," she said. "My hands ain't as strong. Have to get somebody to come in and do the plowin' for me in the spring. I don't raise much. Just enough to do me. My wants are few.

"I try to raise enough stuff to share with the children. A feller across the ridge makes molasses on the shares for me."

From her garden comes tomatoes and beans for canning. She has blackberries and wild strawberries and grapes and apples and peaches for the gathering.

"There's more than enough for my wants," she said. "I make a little money sellin' what I don't use or give to the children. It buys my coffee and sugar and meat."

Being alone, she has no one to carry her berries and vegetables to market. She must make the long trip into town herself. It's a five-mile walk.

"When you've got nobody to do for you," she said, "you do it yourself or it don't get done. I don't mind it. Walkin's good for abody. I do my travelin' before the sun gets up. Ain't as worrisome then."

What about her children? Couldn't they arrange to make the trips to market for her?

"They live too far away," she said. "Besides, they've got their own to think about. They've got jobs that keep 'em busy. That's what happens when you move into town. Goin' all the time. Keeps 'em so busy they don't get out to see me more than once or twice a year.

"Maybe you've heard of my youngest boy. He's a lawyer. They keep him so busy about the only time I get to see him is when I go into town. He's on the go all the time."

There was no bitterness in her voice. There was nothing to

hint of any sadness she might feel over the indifference of her children toward her.

Never once did she complain that she had been forgotten.

And, yet, she is alone and lonely. An old woman living alone in a forgotten cove deep in the hills.

"Lonesome?" she said. "Only now and then. Like when it rains or snows and the weather keeps me shut up in the house. Maybe I get a twinge of lonesomeness then.

"But when I do I take my Bible and read and the lonesome feelin' goes away. Or I sit by the fire and think about all the good times me and my man had together here when there was just the two of us.

"Long's abody can keep busy doin' things they won't tend to bein' lonesome. Idle hands brings on lonesomeness. I don't let mine idle if I can help it.

"What's that? Scared of stayin' here by myself? Law me, no. Ain't nothin' to bother me. All the varmints has been gone ever so long ago.

"When me and my man first come here there was bears and panthers. They used to get our hogs and our young calves. But there ain't none around here no more. Besides, I ain't got no hogs. Don't even have a cow no more.

"My children can't understand why I won't go live with them. But I tell 'em it wouldn't be like home anywheres but right here. I'm satisfied to stay right here. Been here most of my life and I aim to finish it out right here."

The old woman looked off again toward the burying ground. She smiled.

"There ain't no cause," she said, "to be lonesome."

Johnny Holsclaw Gets a Ballad

Valle Crucis

AT LONG LAST THERE'S A BALLAD ABOUT JOHNNY HOLSCLAW, a frontier gypsy who knew how to charm the heart of a lady, and Delilah Baird, a mountain belle who knew when to hold her tongue.

Theirs was quite a romance, and nobody ever will know why the balladeers failed to recognize that Johnny and Delilah were prime subjects for a ballad.

But now, after more than a hundred years, Johnny and Delilah have got a ballad.

And it's the kind that has had fiddles crying, banjos ringing, and folks singing since the first wandering ministrel meandered into the hills strumming the news in a sing-song cadence.

The ballad of the frontier gypsy and the mountain belle was inspired by a piece I did some time ago recalling their love affair.

A hill-born woman read it and agreed that it was a shame nobody had ever got around to immortalizing Johnny and Delilah in song.

Mrs. Aubrey Jennings, who used to live out at Cherokee and now makes her home in Washington, decided she would do something about it.

So she sat right down and began writing.

When she finished she had a ballad of 21 verses.

She called it "The Ballad of the Woman Who Knew When to Hold Her Tongue."

It tells the story of Johnny Holsclaw and how he won the heart and hand of Delilah Baird by promising to take her to Kentucky and ended up by taking her just across the ridge from her father's home.

Johnny, who could and did spin outlandish tales of far-away places he had visited, completely fooled Delilah into believing she was in Kentucky by wandering for days in the hills and never really going any place.

Through the years, Delilah stayed in their cabin and raised a family and never had reason to believe that she wasn't away off in Kentucky.

It was only when she strayed one day out across the fields and up the near mountain and heard the sound of a cow's bell that she learned Johnny had told her a big fib.

The cow bell led her to her father's home.

But when she returned to her own cabin and to Johnny, she didn't light into him and give him what-for.

She just smiled at him and said:

"I want to thank you for taking me off and making me think I was in Kentucky. It don't matter that this ain't Kentucky. I couldn't have been happier."

That's the story. And here's the ballad Mrs. Jennings wrote about Johnny and Delilah.

He came when winter winds blew loud,
   He came when stars were bright,
He sat before her pappy's fire
   And charmed away the night.

He knew the grace of barren bough
   The lace of brittle fern;
Their steps were light on winter moss
   Where partridge berries burn.

And ever through his talk there ran
   A shining magic theme:
The wonders of Kentucky
   Where a man could work and dream.

There soil so rich grew tulip trees
   Full twenty feet around,
No wonder 'possums were so fat,
   Persimmons weighed a pound!

And so come green-up time they wed,
   They waved her kin goodbye
And journeyed where Kentucky trail
   Wound upward toward the sky.

Love put a rainbow 'round his head,
  He kissed her when he durst;
The ragged, scarlet maple buds
  For very love did burst.

On thru shade and on thru shower
  They wandered many a day
Until he led her to a spot
  All green and white with May.

He kissed her once, he kissed her twice—
  Her breath came back to say
Kentucky was a lovely land,
  A heavenly place to stay.

He built a house of logs and dreams,
  She chinked with love and mud;
The smell of summer filled the home
  From flowering bush and bud.

So there they lived and there they loved,
  Three children made them merry,
As young love changed to married love
  Like blossom into berry.

The children climbed with her to seek
  Blue berries for a pie.
She rested, breathless on the moss
  To watch the clouds float by.

She hushed the children in their play.
  She cupped her hand to hear
A tinkling, long-forgotten sound
  That fell upon her ear.

They followed fast upon the sound
  Where cattle stopped to browse,
Those bells she knew, from long ago,
  Bedecked her pappy's cows!

She led the children by a branch
  Down through the ringing wood,
Where far below beneath its oak
  Her pappy's cabin stood.

Her kin folks took her by the hand,
  Their eyes were soft with tears.
They said her lads were bonny and peart,
  She lightly wore her years.

They sat them down while sun was high
  To ham and turnip greens,
To biscuit, cornbread, corn-on-cob,
  To milk and good green beans.

They talked on the porch in the settin' chairs
  Till she 'lowed she must be on her way
If they got back across the mountain
  Before the close of day.

Before they reached their cabin door
  They heard him shout her name,
And never the lamp had seemed so bright
  As into his arms they came.

"Oh, where'd you go so far from call?"
"We went to see our kin—
"They hugged and fed us, kissed our ma,
  And said to come ag'in!"

His doubtful look she met with smiles
  And never a word did say
Of why he had taken such days and miles
  To come so short a way.

Come ladies young and ladies old,
  Now profit by this song
Of one who kept her happiness
  By wit to hold her tongue.

Yes, this ballad of Johnny and Delilah was a long time in coming.

But now that it's here, maybe folks will take to it and fill the mountains with the story of the frontier gypsy who knew how to charm the heart of a lady and the mountain belle who knew when to hold her tongue.

Mineral of the Rainbow

Corundum Hill

SOME FOLKS CHASE RAINBOWS ALL THEIR LIVES AND NEVER discover the fabled pot of gold.

Other save their breath and stumble onto a fortune.

Then there are those born with infinite patience who wait for the rainbow to come to them.

Such a man was Hirman Crisp, a mountain farmer who had gumption enough to recognize the truth that gold is many things.

In the summer of 1868, while plowing and hoeing his fields here on Cullasaja Creek in the Macon County hills, he turned up a lot of queer looking stones.

They were enough to make a man spit out a few persimmon-like words when his plow-point or hoe-blade struck one.

But, be that as it may, Crisp took time enough to examine them and recognize in their rainbow coloring that they were uncommon, perhaps valuable.

So he gathered up a few specimens and carried them with him the next time he went into Franklin where he showed them to some of the folks.

They didn't create much interest. Folks said they were right pretty and let it go at that.

Eventually, however, a specimen reached Asheville where it aroused the interest of General Thomas L. Clingman, a former U. S. Senator.

Clingman knew the rock for what it was and immediately took the stagecoach for Macon to investigate Crisp's find.

At Franklin, Clingman hired a horse and rode the seven miles out to the Crisp farm where the farmer guided him about his property.

Clingman found that the mineral occurred in the livine rocks. He dug pits at the base of this hill and also on Ellijay, where he washed out considerable gravel, seeking to locate gems without success.

Naturally, Crisp was anxious to learn the name of the rocks he had discovered in his fields. Clingman told him the true name of the mineral was corundum.

Corundum, Clingman explained, was remarkable for its hardness and that in its finer varieties formed a valuable gem-stone.

Crisp further learned that the transparent varieties were known as ruby and sapphire, while the impure massive forms were known as emery. Also that corundum gems included Oriental topaz, Oriental emerald, and Oriental amethyst, the term Oriental being used to distinguish corundum gems from other, softer stones having the same name.

In the meantime, Dr. C. D. Smith, a well known authority on minerals, and A. D. Ledford purchased the property from Crisp.

Mining operations were started in 1870 by Colonel C. W. Jenks of Anderson, S. C. and Corundum Hill was born.

There was no market for corundum and operations came to a halt after two years.

Then in 1876, Dr. H. S. Lucas of Chester, S. C., who a few years earlier had discovered an emery mine in his native state, heard of the corundum property here and figured he was in for some stiff competition in the abrasive business.

So Lucas came to Franklin and set out to purchase the property, the negotiations being handled by Kope Elias, a local attorney.

When he had obtained the property, Lucas resumed mining operations as the Hampden Emery and Corundum Company.

He mined Corundum Hill for 24 years, selling it in 1900 to the International Abrasive Company, which worked it about a year and then discontinued operations.

In 1917, when the United States became involved in World War I, it developed that the only supply of corundum available was here at Corundum Hill or in Turkey, and Turkey was an enemy country.

The deposits here, therefore, became of great value to the United States.

It wasn't long until the mines were operating full blast to supply the country's war needs.

For two years, Corundum Hill was the nation's only source of supply for corundum, a stone used to manufacture bearings in electrical apparatus, watch jewels, and abrasives.

Large quantities of corundum were shipped out of Macon during those two years, being hauled by ox-wagon to Dillsboro, some 25 miles distance, and put on train cars there.

During its years of operation, Corundum Hill produced more than 10,000 tons of corundum which sold at an average of $200 a ton.

A crystal of the stone found when Jenks was operating the mines weighed 356 pounds—the largest specimen ever known.

Through the years, crystals of gem quality have turned up, ranging in value from a few dollars to as much as $5,000.

Most of the corundum taken from Corundum Hill was in course pebble and sand form.

It was conveyed from the mine to the mill in troughs filled with running water, sort of like wood flumes used in timber operations here in the mountains years ago.

Nobody ever did know for sure how much Crisp got for his property where he made his rainbow find.

But he never was one after that to argue that a'body couldn't find a pot of gold at the end of the rainbow.

What he discovered wasn't yellow but it was gold none the less.

In fact, those rocks he turned up must have reminded him of the rainbow.

For corundum is a mineral of the rainbow.

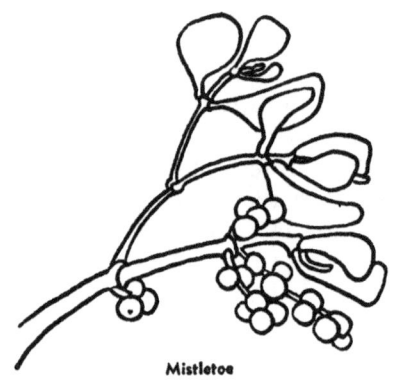
Mistletoe

My Mountain Woman

Sylva

SHE HAS MANY FACES.
I can not tell you her name, for she has so many names.
She is young and she is old, and yet she is ageless.
They'll never mold her likeness in bronze.
No Rembrandt or Rockwell will ever come along who can put her on canvas.
Chances are she never will be memorialized by poem or song.
The world will little know or little care that she has walked upon the earth.
But she is my nomination for the Woman of the Year in the hills.
She is a weaver in Mitchell, a midwife in Haywood, a krautmaker in Watauga, a land agent in Buncombe, a nurse in Swain, a teacher in Jackson, a historian in Henderson, a widow in Macon.
She is a farmer's wife in Madison, an innkeeper in Polk, a doctor in Graham, a mother in Clay, a Sunday school teacher in Avery, a newspaper publisher in Burke, a welfare worker in McDowell, a club woman in Transylvania, an office worker in Yancey.
In her way, she is a part of every mountain community.
And every mountain community is a better place to live because of her.
She is hope and faith and charity.
She is an evening prayer and a morning hymn.
And in a way, she is a part of you and a part of me, and she has your heart and she has my heart.
She asks nothing and gives much.
She knows the meaning of suffering and travail, and there are times when she is a sister to loneliness, yet she never complains.
Folks think of her as an ordinary woman, because the things she does are neither spectacular nor world-shaking, albeit she is quite extraordinary.

Perhaps it is because the things she does are the things expected of her.

She is the lonely widow with heavy heart who soothes the heart-pains of others.

She's the anonymous friend who shares her own small earnings with the needy.

She is a woman who remembers her own meager education and has dedicated her life to providing scholarships to boys and girls who are poor.

She is a self-appointed Samaritan who travels lonely roads and walks lonely trails to answer the beck and call of those in distress.

She is a woman whose hair matches her heart.

She is the one who never married because she gave her life to God and became a missionary.

She's a young farmer's wife who shuts her eyes to pretty clothes so they can pay off the mortgage on the farm.

She's a mountain woman who holds her tongue unless she can speak good of a neighbor.

Her god is tolerance and her patron saint is courage.

She's tasted hardship and bitterness but she refuses to be bitter.

She's overcome handicaps because she is mountain-born and because she is strong like the mountains.

She's a woman who recognizes that little things are important.

She has the gift of stilling a baby's cries and inspiring good in others.

Her hands are red and leathery, like a man's, for they have done a man's work.

Neither rain nor snow nor the blackest night keeps her from going where there is distress or sadness or suffering.

Her home is a haven for the lost, the wandering, and the lonely.

She shares the warmth of her fire with any and all.

She shares her food with the hungry.

She thinks of others first, herself later.

Her heritage is as old as the hills and her independence is a thing of which she is proud.

My Woman of the Year lives on yonder mountain or in the cove at the head of the creek or where the new bungalow sits or just down the block.

Sometimes, more often than not, she walks alone.

In a crowd, she has a way of losing herself.

She is too busy to gossip, too busy to feel sorry for herself.

The things she does are as natural as breathing. She does them without thought of fame or recognition, for she is a mountain woman, born and bred to the principle of live and let live.

So pause and give thought. Chances are she is your next door neighbor.

Or she may be sitting in the same room with you.

She has many faces and she has many names.

In her way, she is somebody's Woman of the Year.

At first glance, you probably won't recognize her.

And only with her passing will somebody pause to say:

"She was a good woman. She will be missed."

In that moment, the things she did that went unsung and unpraised will come to mind, a recognition and a realization that the deserving do not have to be spectacular or notably prominent.

You will remember that in her way she walked tall upon the earth.

You will remember a million little things that in recollection become big and wonderful and unselfish things.

Pause again. Lift your eyes.

She has many faces.

I can not tell you her name, for she has so many names.

She is young and she is old, and yet she is ageless.

No Rembrandt or Rockwell will ever come along who can put her on canvas.

But she is my nomination for the Woman of the Year in the hills.

Perhaps she is yours, too.

For you probably know her name.

He Rightly Knowed B'ars

Lickstone Bald

THE OLD BEAR-HUNTER SAT CROSS-LEGGED BEFORE THE campfire shewering a slice of salt pork in the bubbling flames.

His hatchet-shaped face, razored clean except for a reddish, walrus-like mustache, gleamed like a copper skillet. The firelight ran its fingers through his thick, sleet-gray locks.

The bear hunter was Wid Medford, master hunter of the Balsams. It was a fall night in 1880, off here in the hills above Waynesville. The day's hunt was over and Wid was rustling up some grub for a couple outlanders bent on putting him in a book.

Being a right sociable sort, Wid had invited the two fellers to brogue the mountains with him so they could see him in action. The names they give out to the old man were Zeigler and Grosscup.

As Wid turned the salt pork in the flames he talked up a storm. The writing fellers were all ears and what Wid told them they put in a book called *Heart of the Alleghanies*.

"What I don't know about these mountains," he told them, "ain't of any profit to man or devil. Why, I've fit bears from the Dark Ridge country to the headwaters of the French Broad.

"I've brogued it through every briar patch and laurel thicket, and ain't I been with Guyot, Sandoz, Grand Pierre and Clingman over every peak from here to the South Carolina and Georgia lines?"

One of the fellers spoke up, wanted to know what Wid meant by brogued.

"Crawled, that's what it means," said Wid. "Just as you'd have to do if you pursued every point of the mountains. If you went through Hell's Half Acre, if you slid down the Shinies, or climb the Chimneys."

"Yes," said Wid, turning his attention to a boiling pot of coffee, "that day was a tough one. It was a hot summer day. We, that is Bill Massey who's almost blind now, Bill Allen who give up huntin' long years ago, my brother El, me and several others—we started a bear on the Jackson County line nigh Scott's Creek in the mornin'.

"Well, we drive till after noon, and in the chase I got below here. I heard the dogs right on top of Old Bald, and a-bearin' down the ridge top I was on.

"Powerful soon, I seen the bear a-comin' on a dog trot under the trees. He was a master brute, four hundred and fifty pounds net. Thinks me to myself. Gun first, knife next. For, you see, I was clean played out with the heat and the long run, and I was in favor of bringin' the thing to a close.

"So I brought my old flint-lock to my shoulder. This is the very gun I had then." He tapped the battered stock of a six-foot, black-barreled, flint-lock rifle. "I wouldn't have your cap arrangements. This kind never misses fire. And rain never touches it, for this here kiver to put over the pan keeps it dry as a terrapin hull."

One of the fellers said, "Go on with your story."

Wid cut his eyes at him.

"Just ten' to broilin' your bacon, Jonas," said the old man, "and let me travel to suit my own legs. I fetched my gun to my shoulder and fired.

"Well, the brute never stopped, but I knowed I'd hit him, for I had a dead sight on his head. And like blockhead whiskey, a ball that black bore always goes to the spot.

"He's a thick skull varmint, I thought. I dropped my gun and pulled my knife. On he come. He didn't pay no more attention to me than I'd been a rock.

"I drew back a step, and as he brushed by me I lent over him, grabbin' the hair of his neck with one hand, and staubed him deep in the side with the knife in the other. That's all I knowed for hours."

"Did you faint?"

"Faint?" said Wid, sticking out his chin. "You ass, you don't reckon I faint, do you? Women faint. I fell dead. You see, all the blood in me jumped over my heart into my head, and of course it finished me for a time."

"What about the bear?"

Wid grinned.

"It lay dead by the branch below," he said. "Staubed clean through the heart."

Somewhere off in the hills an owl hooted. There was a small of frost in the air.

Wid kept talking.

Folks in Haywood who knew the old man used to say they didn't know which Wid liked the best—hunting or talking.

He had a right smart reputation for both.

Zeigler and Grosscup couldn't have run into a more colorful character to put in their book. He was an honest-to-goodness mountain man.

Being the tenderfeet they were, the two outlanders assumed that Wid's life had been just one long, rugged experience.

One of them asked him:

"If you had it to live over again, knowing as much as you do now, how would you live?"

Wid popped his gums. He answered quick as a bear-trap triggered shut.

"I'd get me a neat woman," he said, "and go to the wildest country in creation, and hunt from the day I was big enough o tote a rifle-gun until old age and roomaticks fastened on me."

Wild Sweet William

Tell Weather By Rhododendron's Curl
Banner Elk

AS MOUNTAIN WEATHER SHARPS WELL KNOW, IT'S A SIGN of winter for a fact when the rhododendron leaves begin to droop and then roll inward until they remind a'body of old-time homemade pipe-lighters such as grandpa kept by the hearth.

In the cloud-nestled highlands hereabouts, where rhododendron lavishes the mountain slopes and the rocky coves, the weather sharps are keeping one eye on the long glistening leaves and the other on the elements.

Between the two, what with some help from the almanac and a feeling in their bones, they make weather prognosticating as easy as falling off a log and a heap sight less uncertain.

Like the old timer who reckoned there was no need for a clock if a'body had a good crowin' rooster, these mountain weather prophets figure a'body's a plumb fool to squander money for a store-bought thermometer when the mountains are thickety with rhododendron.

They'll tell you, with a wisdom born of the hills and of hill-living, that a'body can depend on rhododendron as a gauge for cold weather with the faith of Scripture.

All a'body's got to do is make a habit of studying the leathery green leaves and know their tell-tale signs.

Everyone of them is a thermometer, nature's own special agent for measuring the cold when winter comes to the mountains.

To the weather sharps, a rhododendron leaf reacts the same way as mercury in a store-bought thermometer.

Its droop and curl tells the temperature.

Until cold weather comes on, until winter storms the high peaks, the thick leaves of the rhododendron stand out like rabbit-ears.

But when the temperature drops, they begin to droop.

As the mercury falls lower, the edges begin to curl under.

The colder it gets the tighter the curl becomes.

When it reaches zero, the entire leaf is rolled.

From then on as sub-zero sets in, the leaf takes on a sort of hard brittleness and a blue-greenness.

To those who have devoted years of constant study to the leaf thermometers, there is a familiarity of the tightening curl that is as easy to read in terms of degrees as the markings on a store-bought thermometer.

Patience and a keen eye for detail have made them experts in a rare art which sometimes borders a little on superstition and crystal gazing.

But the old timers argue if a'body sets his mind to it and has a knack for setting and watching he can look at a rhododendron leaf in the winter and tell right away exactly how cold it is.

Chances are a real reader of the rhododendron thermometer won't be off more than a degree from the mercury register of a store-bought thermometer.

Of course, a'body doesn't come by such a knack over night.

Most anybody can read the simple signs.

But when it comes to the fine reading, then that calls for more years than a few at studying rhododendron leaves and measuring their curl right down to a hair's-breadth with the eye.

Folks who fall in this category are rare and far between these days. They are all old timers, born and raised in the mountains, folks with a pleasure for the old things which they figure still have their use.

Of course, their eyes are not as keen and sharp as they once were, but even though their eyes have grown dim their fingers are sensitive and they can come close to gauging the cold by just feeling a rhododendron leaf.

Like so often, the young ones are indifferent to learning the secrets of the rhododendron leaves and are satisfied to get their weather temperatures from a store-bought thermometer.

And that's a shame. For the old timers are disappearing.

And with them is disappearing many of the old but good and useful ways, customs and lore. Things that should be preserved because they are a part of our heritage.

Maybe if you'll come this way you will run into some of the old timers, mountain weather sharps who are really good prophets and who take time to read the signs.

They are the ones who know that winter's a fact when the rhododendron leaves begin to droop and then curl inward until they remind a'body of old-time homemade pipe-lighters such as grandpa kept by the hearth.

Sword of a Preacher

Sylva

THE OLD MAN, THE YEARS OF NEARLY A CENTURY LEANING on his cane, shuffled out of the hot sun and into the cool quiet of the sanctuary.

An usher guided him to a front pew where he sat a moment with white head bowed in contemplation and then raised his eyes to the cross back of the choir.

On another Sabbath 81 years ago the Old Man had professed his faith in God and written his name into the membership of the Tellico Methodist Church in the hills of Macon County.

He was 16 at the time and was courting my grandmother whose father, Barnard Wild, was a Methodist preacher. It was during a protracted meeting and he had ridden four miles by horseback to attend.

Those were the days when a preacher whose sermon lasted only an hour was considered to have done no more than skim the cream from his text.

It was a time when a harangue of 90 minutes was regarded as just a fair-to-middling job.

The preacher capable of two solid hours of thundering hellfire and damnation was considered a rightly powerful sword against sin and the devil.

Barnard Wild was a sword of a preacher and folks flocked from miles around to hear him preach, coming by horseback and muleback, by wagon and afoot.

He was conducting the protracted meeting at Tellico when my grandfather came to his hour of decision.

"It was an awful powerful meetin'," the Old Man recalled. "The church was filled and runnin' over, mornin' and night. Seemed like folks was starved for the Word. It was a sight to watch folks profess their religion. The meetin' lasted a week and a half."

That first day the Rev. Barnard Wild held out his hand and asked for converts, my grandfather walked up to him and spoke out his convictions and publicly accepted Jesus Christ as his Saviour.

"Soon as the service was over," the Old Man said, "I went to my brother and told him to take my horse back home. Told him I was goin' to stay there till it was finished and I didn't want to impose on folks where I was goin' to stay any more than I had to. Didn't want them to have to feed both me and my horse."

After that, my grandfather followed the Rev. Wild wherever he preached. Got so he was neglecting his work on the farm, but his father never complained.

Four years later he married the Rev. Wild's daughter and they set up housekeeping of their own and went to all the meetings together.

"Some of 'em," the Old Man said, "lasted as much as two weeks. All of 'em was for more than a week. Don't have that kind of meetin's any more. Seems like folks don't have as much time now-a-days as they did back then for religion.

"Besides the protracted meetin's we had preachin' every Sunday. Twice a day. Had it in the mornin' and at night. Sometimes there'd be preachin' in the afternoon.

"Most times folks would bring their dinner and there'd be dinner on the ground when the mornin' preachin' was over and then folks would visit till it was time to start again.

"Folks was awful friendly back then and liked to get together. About the only time they got to see each other was when they come to meetin'.

"We had prayer meetin's regularly back then, too. Had 'em on Wednesday nights. Most of the prayer meetin's was held at somebody's house. One week it would be at our house and the next at somebody else's, and so on.

"I remember one time me and your grandma went to a meetin' at a neighbor's and had been asked to spend the night. It was a log house and the chimney was made of sticks and mud. The mantel was just a log.

"Well, it was in the winter time. Cold as it could be. They built up a big fire and kept puttin' on the logs. That chimney caught on fire and there was the awfulest time you ever saw. Broke up the meetin'. Everybody was a'carryin' water from the spring to put out the fire. Finally got it out and everybody went home.

"I'd just bought me a fine new hat. Cost me two dollars. That was all hats cost back then. The best hats, that is. Well, in all the scramblin' around and leavin' after the meetin' broke up and the fire was put out, I got to lookin' for my hat. Couldn't find it no place.

"The only hat left in the house besides the hat that belonged to the man where we was holdin' the meetin' was an old worn out hat. We tried to figure out whose it was and couldn't.

"About a week later I got my fine hat back. The preacher had carried it off. Said he just grabbed one and left. He'd asked all around and it took him a week to get around to me."

The old church on Tellico where my grandfather professed religion was torn down several years ago and a new one built.

"Didn't seem quite the same," the Old Man said. "I loved that old church. Why, it was sort of like it was a part of me."

When he was a young man the Tellico churchhouse, like many another country church, was a real power that furnished the farm folks not only a means of salvation but a place to go and an opportunity for an exchange of news and views.

But times have changed.

And as the Old Man sat listening to the quiet voice of the young minister on this Sabbath morning, bringing a message that held his attention, I wondered, if by chance, a recollection of Tellico had come to him.

I wondered, too, when the hymns were sung, if he recognized any of them and if in his mind he was singing the old ones, the familiar ones of his youth, which he sings to himself sometimes when he sits on the porch at home.

The sermon over, he picked up his hat and his cane and shuffled back down the aisle and into the sun.

He stood a moment in the churchyard, the laughter of children about him, and I wondered how many, if any, of the folks who were there realized that the Old Man with the cane is the oldest member of the Sylva Methodist Church.

Old-Time Shape-Note Singing Still Lives

Dutch Cove

THE HEART-STIRRING VOICES OF THE FASOLA SINGERS CAN still be heard here in the highlands where folks never have lost the feeling for Christian harmony.

They are a unique coterie, practitioners of "do-ra-me" or "fa-so-la" singing, who apply Elizabethan names to the notes of songs made in pre-Revolutionary America and sing them with the help of the 155-year-old "patent notes."

Their patron saint is "Singing Billy" Walker, a pioneer singing teacher and song writer from whom thousands of our ancestors received their first notion of music.

As a young man from upper South Carolina, "Singing Billy" first came this way more than a century ago to introduce and make the gift of song an integral part of religious services.

He was a wandering troubadour of the shaped-notes, sometimes referred to as "buckwheat notes" because in his own song book the heads of the various shapes were somewhat suggestive of buckwheat kernels.

There was a triangle for fa, an oval for so, a square for la, a diamond for mi. These shaped notes assisted folks in learning to sing by the fa-so-la system which Walker made famous throughout the South and which is still practiced today.

The old-time shaped-note singing lives here as a sort of memorial to "Singing Billy," and each year on the second Sunday in September the fasola singers gather at Morning Star Methodist Church in the cove to join in Christian harmony without the support of any instrument.

They call it "Old Folks Day," a time when all the old folks return to this historic settlement to keep alive an old folk custom, and if you want to sense the reality of the "old-time religion," then come along and listen to the hymns they sing.

"Singing Billy" would be mighty proud of the folks of the cove.

To understand this traditional singing, you must know something about the people and their ancestors, the country and the times past, and, of course, you have to know about "Singing Billy" and his Southern Harmony hymn book.

The men and women who came here as pioneer settlers shortly after the American Revolution found much of their spiritual strength in the peculiar gift called fasola singing or Christian harmony.

When they first came their hope was anchored to the axe, the rifle, and the Bible—their trinity for survival.

Once they had built their cabins, cleared their fields, and stocked their larders, they were then able to turn attention to providing for their spiritual needs.

So it was not long until little groups here and there began to gather at such times as their ever-pressing duties allowed for study and reading from the treasured Bible.

Books were few, if at all, and many a child learned to read from this same cherished Bible.

The circuit rider, or occasionally a preacher, managed to visit the little flocks scattered through the valleys and the mountain coves. But these were rare occasions.

Gathering first in the little cabins, attendance of the mountain folks at any kind of religious service soon proved too great for such accommodations.

Camp meetings, held at some central place in a settlement, were introduced and brought a new way of life to the mountains. At such meetings, the Gospel was preached two or three times a day.

And it was through these meetings that a need for congregational singing, as a means of expressing pent-up emotion, began to make itself felt.

There were a few bits of old chants remembered from the long ago and occasional hymns made familiar by the followers of John Wesley.

Gradually, through contact with other and older communities, and on their trips into the Low Country, a limited number of folks here in the mountains gained some familiarity with the work of early music writers and teachers.

However popular tunes heard and made known through such sources might have proven, even if books could have been obtained, few could read the notes and there was little means of learning the symbols representing the tunes.

Unlike the ever popular ballads fetched by the pioneers from the old country, the singing of hymns by folks of the early denominations here was made possible by one of their own generation.

The gift of song as a part of their religious services was given to them by a man whose recognition of the opportunity for a contribution to the development of the section came shortly after he had entered on what was to be his life's work—the teaching of singing.

The man was William Walker who was known far and wide as "Singing Billy."

He was born on Tyger River in Union County, South Carolina, in 1809, and while still a child moved to the Greenville-Spartanburg district.

He seemed to be born with music in his soul. From the very beginning he sought to learn all he could of music. In this he was encouraged by his mother.

Shortly after he was 20, the first known volume of his compositions was published under the title "Southern Harmony."

He was so well established in a few short years in the career he had chosen that he knew he could never turn back. And from then until he died in his early 80's, he roamed the country teaching folks to sing, setting up singing schools in sparsely settled communities, and turning out song books of his own making.

While many of the songs were set to tunes of his own composing, "Singing Billy" also turned to some of the world's greatest composers, thus assuring the mountain folks a familiarity with the works of famous musicians.

In indicating the sounds used in his fa-so-la book, each note was represented by a character of differing shape. This made the reading easier for those who had had so little opportunity to learn to read at all.

The fa-so-la method, in use by other early song writers, was not entirely unknown in the mountains where before "Singing Billy's" coming a few scattered copies of Sacred Harp, Harp of Columbia and other like books had found their way.

The fame of the singing master, the one called "Singing Billy," and his book, the one called *Southern Harmony*, was not long in spreading through the southern states, where annual classes of singing school were taught by him or by someone trained by him.

The new singing school introduced by Walker to the young people of the strict Quaker, Covenanter Presbyterian, early Methodist and Calvinist Baptist families of the mountains opened up a new and fascinating pleasure.

At the same time it furnished a means for praising God, even in the midst of the rude frontier reaches of the mountains.

As means of travel improved, the singing classes became regular seasonal events.

When crops had been laid by, and before time for the fall harvest, every little community in the mountains had a session of "singing school."

Walker described his method of teaching thusly:

"Not more than one in every fourteen can make a musician, but every person has time and tune, more or less, so all may learn to sing.

"We are pleased to know that while our work accommodates the masses or the millions by the character notes, it is none the less suited to the scientific and profound."

So "learning to sing" gained new recruits from session to session. Before a great while the terms of the singing schools had become a preliminary preparation for the annual camp meetings.

Whatever social life existed in the scattered settlements, it centered around the old song book, and many a courtship had its start at the yearly fa-so-la class.

In the years to come there would be fa-so-la singers growing up throughout the mountains and, even with the advent of musical instruments and musical accompaniments, the "do-ra-me" or "fa-so-la" singing would hang on to form an ever-living link to the past.

The Fa-so-la Singers of Dutch Cove

Dutch Cove

WHEN IT'S LAYING-BY TIME IN THE HILLS THE FASOLA folks gather with their old-time shape-note song books to carry on a musical tradition that goes back more than 200 years.

William Billings, the Boston tanner's apprentice who scribbled his first hymn tunes on cowhides with chalk, really started it, albeit "Singing Billy" Walker, the South Carolina troubadour of the shaped-note, carried it to the people.

The original hymn songs "Singing Billy" thought up in his own head and set to music caused folks to sing who had never sung before and made of his *Southern Harmony* song book a best-seller second only to the Bible.

The book became the treasured possession of thousands and was passed down from one generation to another to become the hymnal for camp meetings, revivals and get-to-gethers such as Old Folks Day and Homecoming.

And even though "Singing Billy" has been dead 75 years, his *Southern Harmony* is still around and the fa-so-la tunes are still being sung, particularly here in the cove.

The Smathers and the Rhodarmers have seen to that.

And come Sunday, the fa-so-la singers will gather at Morning Star Methodist Church for their annual old-time shape-note singfest which is called Old Folks Day.

Carried on without a break for 66 years, it is one of the unique folk gatherings in the mountains.

The Christian Harmony singing will be led by Quay Smathers of Canton. And in the choir of some fifty to sixty voices will be Mrs. Lester Smathers who is just about the best fa-so-la singer in all the land.

There's really nothing quite like Old Folks Day as folks observe it here in the cove.

It's something that is fine and wonderful, a thing rooted in the land and the folk culture of the mountains.

Old Folks Day usually comes on the second Sunday in September.

That's when it's laying-by time, when the days whisper of autumn, when folks look to harvest and there's a rising joy in their hearts.

So they come to the old church, back to this shrine of early days.

They come from all over, family after family.

They begin gathering long before midmorning, long before Sunday School is called.

The old ones grow nostalgic, speaking from hallowed memories recalling when they were young, remembering the little country school, the singing classes, the camp meetings, the congregation grandpa welded into a church body.

There's a morning service and music from a choir of trained voices rising above the organ.

Once the services are over, the folks file out of the church to mingle under the shade of the great oaks.

Tables blossom under the trees. It's time for dinner-on-the-ground.

It's the housewife's place in the sun, her moment of glory. And her cup is full as folks shift from table to table, sampling and enjoying the heaping mounds of fried chicken, spiced peaches, grandmother's famous pound cake.

But under and over it all is a compelling sense that the real event, the main purpose of the gathering, lies ahead.

Before the last table can be cleared and the baskets stored, an expectant hush falls on the crowd.

Those who a moment before were filled with laughter now turn their steps toward the church door.

They crowd through and into the church and the pews fill.

On the same platform where earlier the earnest young preacher had exhorted his people, there now appears a group of elderly men and women.

Each carries his old Christian Harmony song book.

They file across until the choir seats are filled.

Quay Smathers stands in front of them, a leader with the confident assurance of his following. He leafs through his book, picks the opening number.

Sounding the tone to set the pitch, he raises his hand. The fa-so-la singers open their mouths and the words roll full-throated:

> "I love the volume of Thy Word,
>   What joy and life those leaves afford,
>   To souls benighted and distrest.
>
> "Thy precepts guide my doubtful way,
>   Thy fear forbids my feet to stray,
>   Thy promise leads my soul to rest."

With the sonorous tones of this Sixth Century Gregorian chant borne aloft, the old-time singing has started.

Now they come, one after the other—

The tunes Martin Luther once sang, words that strengthened the martyr John Huss when flames raged around him, old English melodies, Hayden's "Creation." . . .

Sunlight in wavering bands filter through the huge stained-glass window, bringing to life its legend:

"Sacred to the Memory of the Old Christian Harmony Choir."

Touched with this glow, the fa-so-la singers carry on their moving tunes.

The graveyard glimpsed from the open door is the resting place of many a member who had in other times filled the choir.

Through the afternoon the tunes slip by, one after the other.

Finally, the last tune is ended.

The crowd quietly, almost solemnly, begins its homeward journey.

But there is no spirit of sadness among parting friends.

Instead, there is something that seems to carry a promise that this will all come again, again in another year.

And so, Old Folks Day ends. Another old-time shaped-note singing is over.

As the dove folds its wings and slips into the haven of its nest, so the hearts of the departing, bound in the spell of memories, softly turn back home.

And in their ears is an echo.

It is an echo of the refrain of the fa-so-la singers of the hills:

> "Oh, come, angel band,
>   Come and around me stand.
>   Oh, bear me away, on your snowy wings,
>   To my immortal home."

November's Full of Hound Music

Sylva

NOVEMBER IN THE HILLS IS AN INVITATION FOR THE OLD man with the scythe who lurks along the years to come inside and set a spell before the fire.

For November belongs to the wind and the rain.

It is Indian Summer sighing in the trees and snowy breath on every breeze.

It's a 'possum-hunter's lantern winking in the night, a fox-hunter's fire crackling applause to tall tales and hound music.

It's valleys drifted with leaves, crisp and rattly in the wind.

It's the hills from Watauga to Cherokee berry-bright and firelight-gay.

It's the friendliness of wind-tossed smoke, stealing from hearth and chimney.

It's the season turning from gold to gray.

It's frost on the pumpkin and pumpkin pies in the oven.

November is birds taking wing.

It is something that has told the flashing Tree Swallow that soon it will be time to go, something that has whispered "snow."

It's a cabin standing on Lonesome Mountain in a long silver rain and a cow-bell tinkling as the herd comes home.

It's a shaft of golden sunlight slanting through a balsam grove like a lane to heaven.

It's a farmer with the harvest behind him in a rocking-chair before the fire rocking the wrinkles from his mind.

It's sheep-bells on a hill, the hum of a spinning-wheel, the whack-aty-whack of a loom, the ring of a wood-chopper's axe.

It's a doe and her fawn etched against the sky on Pisgah.

It's baying dogs and a bear crashing through the rhododendron along the slopes of Mount Mitchell.

It's the sound and fury of a wild boar hunt among the heights of Santeetlah and the Snowbirds.

It's a handful of snowflakes flung over the high tor called Clingman's Dome.

It is frost marks in ditch-mud, rime on Grandfather Mountain.

November is grouse exploding underfoot and rocketing into a thicket.

It's a farm boy of Shoal Creek in a canvas coat and a red cap with a 16-gauge in the crook of his arm cat-walking through a field of broom-sedge.

It's a fox barking in the starlight, an owl asking midnight questions.

It's a time when pancakes and molasses and fresh homemade sausage belong on the breakfast table.

It's a time when a man gets a hankering for potato soup at suppertime and a hot pone of cornbread to crumble in.

November is apples in the cellar, dried fruit in the pantry.

It is a bouquet of dried onions above the kitchen stove, strings of red peppers, pods of okra, dried pumpkin strips.

It's a jug of fresh molasses, a jar of sourwood honey, a crock of homemade kraut.

It's a flour sack filled with dried beans-in-the hull which mountain folks call "leather-britches."

It's pickled beans and pickled peaches, pickled beets and pickled onions.

It's apple cider with champagne beads of authority.

November is wild turkeys gobbling in the brush on a high hill and stuffed turkey on the tabled harvest of God's bounty.

It's hog-butchering and cracklings and sage and pepper in fresh sausage.

It's lard-makin' time and soap-makin' time.

It's chittlin's seasoned with vinegar, brown and crisp.

It's liver-and-lights, backbones-and-ribs, souse-meat and liver-mush.

November is mournful winds playing leapfrog over the tree-tops.

It is naked woods and meadows brown and sere.

It is a gray squirrel in the limber top of a hickory tree, graceful as the wind, a Pavlova in the air.

It's a groundhog sniffing the wind and scurrying back to his den to sleep until spring.

It's corncob tales around a stove at the country store.

It's a hymn of thanks and a whispered prayer.

It is a clean-limbed birch laughing in the wind.

It's the last chance a man has to get ready for what December and winter will bring in the way of snow and cold.

November somehow suggests old lace, rare old lace.

Perhaps it is because there is beauty even in the weather-beaten, worn things, the cracked, broken, torn things.

These are symbols of age.

And November is the aging year.

But there is a gracefulness and a proudness in the aging.

For November in the hills makes a fiction of the poetic lines that these are melacholy days, the saddest of the year.

To the hillsman, November is neither dour nor dowdy.

November is the highlands of balsam and hemlock in a green lace party dress over a holly slip with clusters of red berries.

It is a glittering night, a multitude of stars, a crisp blue day, a whispering wind.

November in the hills is all these things and more.

But most of all, it is a time of thanksgiving.

Carolina Lily

Day of the Rived Shingle

White Oak Creek

THE PONDEROUS OAKS STILL TROOP ACROSS THE HILLS BUT the hand-hammered froe and the hardwood maul—tools of the pioneer shingle weaver—have gone the way of the broadaxe and the footadze.

The log cabin is only a history-book symbol of a homespun era and a roof-raisin', once 'most as merry as a wedding, is a faraway memory.

Of the axemen who could notch and mortise and tenon, join and rive, few are still alive.

Some of the old ones, such as my grandfather who grew up here in the Macon County hills when the ringing swack of the axe echoed the sound of a people claiming their Godsend, were master hands at cracking out shingles.

In that faraway youth of his, the Old Man rived many a shingle.

Looking back over his years of four score and ten plus seven, he remembers that folks sort of considered him as just about the best shingle weaver hereabouts.

"In my time," said the Old Man, "most folks roofed their houses with rived shingles. Made 'em out of white oak. Shakes, they called 'em.

"Now, when it comes to lastin', a roof of properly hand-rived boards'll last four or five times as long as them cut with a saw. Last a heap longer'n any these new storebought shingles.

"A'body could cover his house with hand-rived shingles and figure they'd last a life-time. Not like now when a'body has to keep a sharp look to his roof and spend a heap of money coverin' it ever ten years or so.

"Why, a hand-rived shingled roof was good for 50 or 60 years, maybe longer. I've heard tell of some that was covered with rived oak shingles that lasted more'n a hundred years.

"There's an old house back over on Burningtown with shingles I cracked out back when I was a boy. Still good. Ain't but a few of 'em that's had to be took out and replaced."

The Old Man learned the art of cracking shingles out of white oak blocks from an uncle who was a master hand with axe, broadaxe, footadze, froe, hardwood maul, and knife.

"My Uncle Eli," said the Old Man, "was just about the best shingle cracker there ever was. Everybody put a heap of faith in his rived boards. He was a steady worker. Never talked much when he was a'workin'. Just went about his business.

"I remember when I was about ten or twelve he got me off and started showin' me all about rivin' boards and doin' other things. He made the best buckeye cradles you ever saw.

"By the time I was sixteen or seventeen I was gettin' all the shingle work I could do. Folks used to come from all around to get me to make shingles for their houses. Got so my father figured I wasn't much help around the farm. Said all I done was rive boards. But he was right proud of me."

The Old Man's hands are gnarled now. They are only skin and bones. They're sort of curved into a mold. Like they're holding an axe or a froe or a hardwood maul.

"Time was," he said, "when it wasn't nothin' for me to crack out six or seven hundred shingles a day. Best I ever done, I reckon, was 916. You want to know how I remember? Well, I'll tell you. Uncle Eli was always talkin' about how nobody had ever matched the day he cracked out over 800 shingles.

"Well, I kept hearin' him talk about it. And I sorta set my sights on beatin' him. Took me a long time. Riving boards is slow work. You've got to know how it's done. Just ain't ever'body can rive boards that'll last or do right in a roof.

"My father said wasn't no use to try to beat Uncle Eli. He said Uncle Eli just had a knack for rivin' boards that nobody ever had and never would.

"But I figured I was pretty good, too. And I laid my plans. I got me a big pile of oak blocks and had 'em all piled up back of the house. One mornin' I got out there just at daybreak and set in. I went at it hard and steady.

"Wasn't nobody to bother me. And I cracked them shingles. Wouldn't even stop for dinner when they called me. Come sundown I had a mighty fine stack of shakes. I'd kept count and I knew I had beat Uncle Eli. I called my father out and told him what I'd done. He looked at the pile of shakes and said maybe he'd better count 'em. Then he called two of my brothers and they set in. It got dark before they finished. But next mornin' they finished up and when the last one was counted Pa looked at me and said we'd better go over and see Uncle Eli.

"Well, we saddled up the horses and went over to Uncle Eli's. When Pa told him what I'd done, Uncle Eli just sat there and never said a word. Then he said he reckoned he'd have to believe it since he knew Pa as a truthful man.

"I never said nothin' to nobody about what I'd done. Never mentioned it to folks down at the store. But Uncle Eli started talkin' about it. Seemed like he was right proud of me. He told folks about it and said he'd learned me how to rive boards."

The Old Man grinned at the memory.

"After that," he said, "folks would come by just to watch me rive boards."

To turn out proper rived shingles, that is, with froe and maul, the old man said a'body had to have two good hands and time a'plenty and a good supply of white oak blocks.

"There's heap more'n just crackin' out a oak block," he said. "You've got to know how to split it. You've got to split it with the grain of the wood. Then the shingle won't curl. That is, if it's properly placed."

Rived shingles covered the first roofs of the pioneer's cabins here in the mountains.

The boards were thin, narrow, split strips about half an inch thick. They were four to eight inches wide, two to three feet long.

They usually were made of oak or hickory and split with a froe. A froe being a long-bladed tool with a handle at one end. The blade was driven into the wood by the stroke of a hardwood maul on the back edge. Then the boards were split off or pried off.

A tough young white oak was selected for a maul. It was cut off close to the ground. The handle was trimmed with axe and smoothed with pocketknife.

"Ever'body used white oak for shingles," said the Old Man. " 'Most ever'body did. Though some used chestnut and poplar.

"Now when it come to layin' the roof, there was a certain time a'body had to lay his roof if he didn't want the shingles to cup or twist. Had to lay 'em in the light of the moon.

"Yes, sir, there's never been nothin' for lastin' like a hand-rived shingled roof. But don't nobody use 'em any more."

The Old Man looked out across the hills where White Oak Creek meanders down from under Wayah Bald and into the Nantahala River.

The ponderous oaks trooped across the hills.

"There's many a shingle in them trees," said the Old Man. "Pity that they're goin' to waste."

His eyes stared into the mists as time spun the earth toward sunset.

And looking on the oaks, his eyes somehow seemed to sort of take on a gaze into time of his faraway youth when he was a shingle weaver.

Back when the hand-hammered froe and the hardwood maul were the tools of his art.

But now they are only a memory, slipping into a limbo, going the way of the broadaxe and the footadze.

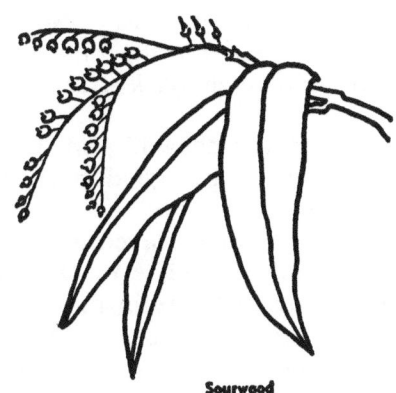

Sourwood

Pine Resin Made Finest Chewin'

Burningtown

BACK WHEN MY GRANDFATHER WAS A BOY IN HOMESPUN jeans, springtime in the mountains meant "gummin'-time."

This was long before Mr. Wrigley discovered the wonders of chicle and gave birth to a nation of gum-chewers.

"When I was a boy," my grandfather recalled, "there wasn't no storebought chewin' gum to be had. We got our chewin' gum out of the woods.

"Come spring, when the sap was risin', we boys would get together of a Sunday and head for the pine ridge. We called it goin' gummin'. And we'd fetch back pine resin. That was our chewin' gum.

"Pine resin made the finest chewin' gum you ever chewed. It was good and tough. Had a right good taste. Not strong, at all. Had a kind of pine taste."

The Old Man paused. A smile played about the corners of his mouth. There was a twinkle in his eyes. The kind of a twinkle that belongs to a little boy, but rare in the eyes of a 98-year-old.

"Law me, what I wouldn't give to go gummin' and get a wad of pine chewin' gum," he said. "Best tastin' stuff in the world. But I don't reckon I could do much good at chewin' resin gum with store-bought teeth. They wasn't made for it. And pine resin gum is mighty tough.

"But when I was a boy, I chewed a lot. That I did. Most every'body chewed gum then. Same as they do now. Only it wasn't like the chewin' gum you buy. The kind we had was better than any storebought chewin' gum that was ever manufactured.

"Oh, the times we boys had goin' gummin'. It were a frolic. That it was. A springtime frolic. Spring was the only time you could go gummin'. You got the gum when the sap was risin' in the pines or spruce or birch.

"And that meant that we only had chewin' gum durin' the spring. Couldn't keep it the year-'round. Once it hardened up it was like a rock, only harder. Took a hammer to break it. That is unless you took a hunk and put it in boilin' water and softened it up and then it wasn't no good for chewin'.

"So we done our chewin' in the spring. And there was steady chewin', I'll tell you. It's a wonder we didn't wear out our teeth and our jaws.

"When gummin' time come along we'd go to the pine ridges and take our knives and cut holes in the trees. We'd do that some time durin' the week. That was so the sap would drip down into the hole and fill up come Sunday. We always went out of a Sunday to collect our chewin' gum.

"It would be thick and we'd take it out of the hole in the tree and chew it We'd chew it till we got tired and then we'd lay it up in the house and chew it again when we felt like it.

"A batch would last two or three days. It'd have a good taste for a long time. Took a heap of chewin' to get it so it didn't taste like nothin'. Then we'd go get us a new batch. It wasn't like the chewin' gum you get now. It didn't lose its taste in a minute or two and it lasted a heap longer.

"Most of the time we got our chewin' gum from pine resin. But spruce and birch was mighty good, too. Some folks liked spruce gum better. But I always was partial to pine gum. Somehow it had a sweeter taste.

"Birch chewin' gum was different. It wasn't like pine or spruce gum. We'd get out a heap of times and skin birch and make our chewin' gum from it. Birch chewin' gum didn't last like the other.

"What we'd do would be to chip off birch bark when the sap was runnin'. Inside the bark there's another layer of peeling. That was what we chewed. You'd take out that white inside peel. Scrape it out with your knife.

"For downright tastiness, there wasn't nothin' to beat birch. Only trouble was it didn't last long. The juice got away too fast. You know how good birch smells. Well, it tastes the same way when you chew it.

"Sweet gum made another mighty fine chewin' gum. But it was sort of bitter-tastin'. For them that didn't like pine gum and spruce gum, sweet gum was to be had hereabouts, too.

"Besides bein' used for chewin' gum, sweet gum resin was mighty good for treatin' sores and skin troubles.

"In my time, I've chewed 'em all. And for workin' the jaws and gettin' a taste, too, you can't beat pine or spruce gum.

"I don't reckon nobody ever bothers to get their own chewin' gum out of the woods any more. This storebought stuff has took the country. I chew storebought gum now and then. It's easy on my storebought teeth. But if I had my way, I wouldn't chew nothin' but pine resin chewin' gum. There's nothin' like it."

The Old Man paused. For a moment he looked off toward the far ridges where the pines stood like whispering sentinels.

"One of these days before too long," he said, "we'll have to go gummin'. It ain't right that you've never had any pine resin chewin' gum."

Alum-Root

Valley of Rubies

West's Mill

THE ROAD TO THE VALLEY OF RUBIES BEGINS HERE.
Many a man has followed its winding course in search of a quick fortune.

It leads into a rolling trough between the Nantahalas and the Cowees where the earth is crusted with rainbow crystals.

The Cherokees called the valley Cowee, meaning deer place, and the name has survived, albeit the deer have disappeared.

But it is really the Valley of Rubies.

There is nothing quite like it in all the land.

Its ruby-bearing gravels have been luring folks into the hills for almost 70 years.

Strangely enough, Hernando DeSoto missed it by a country mile or so back in 1540 on his gold-questing trek through the mountains.

Some folks reckon old Hernando was so hepped on gold that he couldn't recognize a ruby when he saw one, for he brushed aside the sun-red crystals in the Cherokee wigwams as so many pretty pebbles.

They didn't tease his imagination, and the Cherokee didn't bother to tell him about the Valley of Rubies.

But in the years since, a heap of folks has done a heap of digging in the valley.

Some of them have turned up rubies of as true color as any ever mined.

As a matter of fact, Dr. George Frederick Kunz of Tiffany's got mighty excited about the Cowee Valley rubies back in 1893.

Dr. Kunz made the first official report of rubies in Cowee Valley.

And it wasn't long until occasional good stones began to turn up in New York, usually at Tiffany's. Folks hereabouts sent them to be cut.

Dr. Kunz and William E. Hidden, a mining expert from Newark N. J., frequently visited the valley during the late '90's and the first decade of the 20th century.

Their enthusiasm for the future of the valley as a big ruby producer set the local folks to expecting big things.

Experts on mining in Burma's Mogok, the world's premier ruby field, visited the valley when the American Prospecting and Mining Company began operations on a fairly large scale.

This was in 1896, and these experts reported that the quality and percentage of Cowee rubies were equal to the Burma yield. But they added that American labor costs were too high and made mining here prohibitive.

One authority said that in color and brilliancy a great many stones taken from the valley were equal to the Burma rubies.

"If the percentage of the unflawed transparent material increases but little," he wrote, "this new field would be a well-matched rival to the Burma fields."

The early mining in the valley after Kunz's report was on a fairly large scale, albeit largely a hand operation. The percentage of marketable stones, while very consistent, was a shade too low to meet the costs. The field could not be made to pay.

And although there were rubies still to be had, efforts to make Cowee Valley a major ruby field were finally abandoned in 1914.

Since then some placer mining has been carried on from time to time only to be abandoned.

Now it is a place for folks to go and do a bit of digging in the hope of making a lucky find. Many do.

The original source of the Cowee Valley rubies never has been determined.

Mineralogists have tried and tried. At least two companies have tried to locate the source by expensive shafts, tunnels and core drilling.

The corundum crystals occur in the soil and in the exposed creek gravels.

But these sources have been long and well picked over.

The sure place to find them is in the gravel beds. These vary in thickness from two to 10 feet.

Local folks use a crude rocker for washing. The corundum crystals are picked out by hand.

The ruby color permeates the gravel beds. All the gravel has a sort of old rose tint.

For years collecting has been a side-line with many farmers.

Why, there's hardly a household in these parts that doesn't

have a small box of crystals sitting around.

When my mother was a girl and lived up the road at Iotla it was a sort of Sunday afternoon ritual for the children to go ruby-hunting.

To the expert collector, the corundum crystals of Cowee Valley offer a field day. Some 29 distinct forms of the corundum crystal have been found in the valley.

With the advent of the rock-hound fraternity in recent years the Cowee Valley has become a bee-hive of activity during the summer months.

Word has got around about the Valley of Rubies and folks are flocking in from all over.

The road into the valley that begins here is getting a good tramping.

Folks always have been sort of partial to rubies.

And even the myth-makers have had their way with this gem of the sun.

Some claim it was a ruby that lighted up Noah's Ark.

My great-grandmother, who lived just a whoop and a holler from here, always figured that a ruby was particularly lucky.

She lined her spring with hunks of stone imbedded with rose-tinted crystals.

Whether they brought luck or not, they sure made a pretty pattern about the spring and on a day when the sun filtered through the water the bottom of the spring was like a rose petal.

A while back I fetched one of the spring ruby-colored stones home.

"Why, when we were children," my grandfather recalled, "just about everybody had a yard full of ruby-stone. Sure made a pretty spring bed."

Missing Buckeye Causes Crisis

Sylva

THE OLD MAN WAS IN A WORRISOME MOOD. Now and then he turned his head to stare out the window at the rain that chatted monotonously in the gray afternoon.

In a way, the rain was responsible for the Old Man's mood. It reminded him of aches and pains and the miseries that come to a'body shut up all day.

This turn of mind had created a minor crisis in the household.

The crisis sprang up when the old man missed his buckeye.

And that was a calamity of the worst sort.

After all, everybody knew that a buckeye carried in the pocket—the left hip pocket, that is—warded off rheumatism.

And if ever a man needed a buckeye, it was now.

This was rheumatic weather, chill rain and fog, a time when a'body's blood gets thin and the miseries set in.

"Folks ought to let things alone that don't belong to 'em," the Old Man fussed. "That buckeye just didn't get up and walk off by itself. That woman that come to clean up probably throwed it out."

He felt through his pockets again for the hundredth time, shook his head, then muttered and punched at the fire with his stick.

"Why, I had it right here last night polishin' it up before I went to bed," he said. "Like I always do. Laid it and my knife and my pipe on my smokin' table when I started to turn in. When I come in this mornin' to put 'em in my pocket like I always do, my buckeye was gone."

The Old Man said he reckoned he'd just have to put up with the miseries until he could get word to his friend Oscar Lovedahl up at Caney Fork to fetch him another buckeye.

Did he really believe that carrying a buckeye warded off rheumatism?

He cocked an eye at me as if I had questioned the certainty of life and death.

"Of course, it does," he said. "Don't think I'd carry it if it didn't, do you? Ask any of the old folks. You don't have to take my word for it.

"Just like a lot of other things that you young ones don't put no store by. Seems like you think we've lost our senses because we hang on to the old things and don't lay 'em aside for the new. I ain't a'beratin' what's new. But when I've tried a thing and know it to work I'll stick by it.

"Why there's lots of the old things still being used. Home remedies we called 'em. I say if a thing works, then there ain't no need to give it up just because somebody's got somethin' else.

"Your daddy carried a buckeye. I seen it many a time. Course, I never could figure him out. He carried an Irish potato, too. You know, some folks say an Irish potato will keep off rheumatism. But I was always a buckeye man."

The talk broadened out and soon we were discussing other "home remedies," charms and cures that come under folk medicine, a field that has developed in the mountains through trial and error.

Most of the surviving practitioners of folk medicine are women.

And from the Blue Ridge to the Smokies there still lives the "granny woman" or midwife, the herb woman, and the old woman who has raised a large family to healthy maturity.

They are partial to herbs, leaves, barks, roots, seeds and fat meats for making teas, poultices, and ungents.

Some have a scientific foundation.

One good old folk cure for asthma is to swallow a handful of spider webs rolled into a ball.

This is not as far-fetched as it may sound, either.

For in 1882 a substance called arachnidin was isolated from spider webs which proved to be a remarkable febrifuge or medicine effective in reducing or removing fever.

But while there are many home remedies with a scientific foundation, there are many that are strange and are couched in mysticism.

Such as my grandfather's unshakable belief in the power of the buckeye.

There are old timers who will tell you that hanging a pair of pot hooks about the neck will stop nosebleed.

Still others are partial to taking a case knife, rubbing it under the nose and then sticking it in the ground.

Warts will disappear if you steal a neighbor's dishrag and wipe it across them.

Place a Bible under the pillow and you never will have nightmares.

Mare's milk is a good remedy for whooping cough.

When the baby has "hives," give it red alder tea.

A mole's foot tied about a child's neck will make teething easy.

Snake root will cure fever.

Smear the brow with crushed onions for headache.

A sty can be removed by running it over with the tip of a black cat's tail.

To cure cramps in the feet turn your shoes bottom side up before going to bed.

Chills can be driven away by boring a deep hole in the sunny side of an oak tree, blowing your breath in it, and plugging up the hole.

For boils, drink tea made from red alder instead of water for several days and the boils will entirely disappear.

A piece of nutmeg tied about the neck will prevent neuralgia.

There are some who believe that the leaves of the aspen, because they shake, are good for the palsy.

But it is the buckeye that my grandfather puts his faith in.

"Why," he said, "I never have been without a buckeye. Never had the rheumatism, either."

He turned his head again to stare out at the rain.

Then he rubbed his left leg.

"Got a twitch of a pain," he said. "It's this weather."

He was starting to mumble when my mother came hurrying into the room.

"Here's your buckeye," she said. "Found it in there on your dresser back of your bottle of liniment. Right where you left it."

The Old Man grinned and took it, rubbed it between his hands a moment, then put it in his pocket.

The scowl disappeared from his face. He reached over and got his pipe.

Outside the rain still came down and there still was a chill in the air.

But the Old Man had found his buckeye and the rain didn't bother him any more.

Now he was no longer worried about rheumatism and the miseries.

Grandma Smoked a Clay Pipe

Webster

REMEMBER WHEN GRANDMOTHERS WORE LOG-CABIN BONnets and smoked clay pipes?

Up until the turn of the century these were the symbols that distinguished many a grandmother. But like the one-horse shay and the flatirion, the tallow-dip and the ash-hopper, they have disappeared into the limbo of history's fashions and customs.

So has the typical old-fashioned grandmother who used to sit in the chimney corner and rule her son's and daughter's families with a gentle though unrelaxing hand.

She's been replaced by a peppy, enthusiastic individual who still likes to whoop it up occasionally and, unless she offers to disclose her secret, only a feller with a sixth sense would know she's a grandmother.

Many a modern grandmother finds her smoking pleasure in cigarets while her ancient counterpart was partial to clay pipes.

When my mother was a girl, grandmothers retired to a rocking chair, lit up their clay pipes, and made of their role of grandmother a recognizable one.

Back then folks agreed it was fit and proper for a grandmother, or a woman getting on in years, to take up pipe smoking.

It was a thing accepted without comment or censure, and never did create even a small ripple of the rowdy-dow that exploded when their daughters and grand-daughters took up cigarets.

Since time out of memory, there have been mountain women who smoked pipes. Chances are some of the old ones back in the hills still favor a pipe, albeit they are made of corncobs since nobody fashions clay pipes any more.

Both my great-grandmothers were pipe smokers, and both wore log-cabin bonnets. Yet, none of their daughters ever smoked a pipe.

"Your great-grandmother Wild smoked a clay pipe," my mother

recalled. "It was a small pipe, not much bigger than a good-sized thimble. There was an Indian who made them for her. She would get a half dozen at a time. One of mama's brothers made the stems for Grandma Wild. That was your Great-Uncle John. He made the stems out of cane and would go down to the creek or the river and cut cane. The stems were six inches to a foot long.

"I remember we children always argued about who was going to light grandma's pipe. All of us would beg to be the one to light it. When we went to visit her we would start out begging her to smoke so we could light her pipe. We lighted her pipe with candle-lighters. They were homemade. And she kept them in a candle-lighter holder that hung beside the fireplace. The holder was made out of a piece of cardboard and covered with a piece of flowered wall-paper. The candle-lighters were made out of pieces of paper that were twisted tight into a slim roll about the size of a pencil, although it was tapered. One end of it was bent. That was the end you lighted from the hearth and stuck to the pipe.

"Sometimes grandma would light up her pipe by sticking it into the fire and raking up a live coal on it. She would do that when we children were not about. She did it to save the candle-lighters because paper was hard to come by.

"I never remember seeing her once light her pipe with a match. Matches were scarce then and quite expensive, so folks didn't use them unless they had to. But there was always a fire in the fire-place. Kept it going winter and summer. Mama used to say that only lazy folks ever let their fire go out.

"Grandma Wild smoked homemade tobacco. It came in hanks, that is, in leaves. She would take the tobacco and put it in a bread-pan and put it in the oven to dry out. She would toast it."

This bit of intelligence on how my great-grandmother prepared her smoking tobacco caused me to wonder if perhaps one of the tobacco companies which now advertises that the golden weed used in its cigarets is toasted didn't come by the method from an old-time pipe-smoking grandmother.

At least, I can believe that maybe my great-grandmother was toasting tobacco long before somebody tipped off the advertising boys that toasted tobacco was something new.

"Well," said my mother, "when Grandma Wild had toasted her tobacco she then would crumble it up, rubbing a leaf between her hands, and put it in her pipe.

"Your Great-grandmother Hall, that was your Grandma Parris' mother, smoked a pipe, too. A lot of the old women hereabouts smoked pipes. Many's the time I've seen pipe-smoking done by women such as Aunt Jane Fullbright, the Swangum sisters, Aunt Viry and Aunt Betsy, who lived alone and did all their own work.

"Grandma Wild just had certain times she smoked her pipe. Never smoked it any time unless she was sitting around the fire. She would get up at five o'clock in the morning, and the first thing she would do after getting out of bed would be to go to the fire and light up her pipe.

"She'd sit there and smoke her pipe, then fix breakfast. After breakfast all the folks would get up from the table and sit around the fire and talk. She'd smoke her pipe again at that time.

"Most of the folks back then would do their family talking after breakfast. It was a time when the whole family would be together. Folks went to bed early back then, seven or eight o'clock of weekdays, and they got up early.

"There wasn't a lick of work done right after breakfast. Everybody sat around the fire and waited for it to get day-light, talking and smoking all the while. When it got daylight, the menfolks went off to work and the womenfolks did the dishes and the cleaning up."

Along with the clay pipe, the log-cabin bonnet was a symbol of a grandmother back in those days.

"A log-cabin bonnet?" said my mother. "You don't know what a log-cabin bonnet is? Well, it was a stitched bonnet that had splits in it. The headpiece was stitched and places was left so you could stick pieces of cardboard or pieces of oak splits in it to make it stand up. When you washed it you took out the splits. That's why they called it a log-cabin bonnet.

"Of course, there were other kind of bonnets. Like the poke bonnet. And there were fine bonnets made of silk and satin. Grandma's church or Sunday bonnet was a poke bonnet. It was made out of black silk. Mama made all of grandma's bonnets. I remember one she made out of black sateen. It was quilted."

My mother paused. "Just a minute," she said, and left the room. When she came back she had a bonnet in her hands.

"This was one of your grandma's bonnets. Don't know why I kept it, but I did. A few years ago when we had the Jackson County Centennial I wore it."

No, she said, she didn't have one of Grandma Wild's pipes.

"Grandma Wild died about 45 years ago," she said, "and I don't know what happened to her clay pipes. She smoked them right up until the time she broke her hip and passed away."

Only a poke bonnet is left to remind me that there was a time when log-cabin bonnets and clay pipes were symbols that distinguished many a grandmother.

Groun'-Hawg Meat's Good Eatin'

Stepps Gap

THERE'S NOTHING QUITE LIKE A MESS OF GROUN'-HAWG meat when it comes to choice mountain vittles.

Give mountain folks a druther between groun'-hawg meat and pork and they'll take groun'-hawg meat every time.

It's a dish to make the young-uns smile and the grown-ups drool.

"Why, there's nothin' like groun'-hawg for good eatin'," said Theodore Ray. "But you've got to know how to cook it. And you've got to know your groun'-hawgs."

Ray is something of a connoisseur when it comes to groun'-hawg. He's a mountain man. Born down at Pencacola. Married into the Big Tom Wilson clan. He's a bear-hunter, too. One of the best.

"There's a heap of groun'-hawgs this year," he said. "An uncommon amount. And they're mighty fat and sleek. The kind that makes good eatin'."

It was a dreary day. Rain and fog. The mists swirled about Mount Mitchell, towering over Stepps Gap and the Wilson diggings.

"They'll be burrowin' in for the winter before long," Ray said. "Right now's the time to get in your groun'-hawg huntin'. Time to load up your rifle-gun and call up your dogs and hunt 'em out."

Ray paused. "Just look," he said. He pointed out the window into the misty, gray morning. Pointed across the road. A groun'-hawg stood in the wet grass just off the road. Stood there like a little bear.

"They're all over the place," Ray said. "Been out since day They're stuffin' themselves for winter. Come the first cold snap or snow and they'll hole up for the winter.

"Now's the time to hunt 'em. Not too much time left. Way the weather's shapin' up they'll turn in between the fifteenth and the first of November. They hibernate like bear.

"Some folks—them that don't know—will eat groun'-hawg any time they can catch one. But this is the time to eat groun'-hawg. They're fat now. Not lean and stringy like in the spring and summer.

"Groun'-hawgs up here about Mitchell are mighty fat. Not like they are down in the valley. They're better eatin', too. I wouldn't get a nickel for a valley groun'-hawg. Too thin and stringy. Not as sweet-tastin', either.

"Most folks who turn up their nose at groun'-hawg meat never tasted any except valley groun'-hawgs. For real eatin' you've got to have a groun'-hawg that lives up high in the mountains. The higher the better.

"Some folks say the reason the valley groun'-hawgs don't taste as good as the ones up here is because they feed on angelica. Gives 'em a bitter taste.

"Groun'-hawgs on Mitchell feed on berries, ash nuts and this tender grass along the roads that the park folks cut. They come out and eat it after it's cut, stuffin' themselves. They thrive on it. They eat Balsam cone seeds, too.

"Anybody that's ever tasted a Mitchell groun'-hawg can tell the difference right off. The meat has a sweeter taste than valley groun'-hawg meat.

"But there's a lot in the cookin', too. Don't make no difference whether they're valley ground'-hawg or mountain groun'-hawg if they're not fixed right. Many a good groun'-hawg is ruined before it ever hits the pot.

"I wouldn't give you a nickel for all the groun'-hawgs in the country if they are not fixed right for cookin'. Now the first thing to do is to search out the brown spots under the skin at the forelegs. A heap of folks don't know that's the difference between good and bad groun'-hawg eatin'.

"Right there under both the forelegs are brown spots about the size of a quarter or less. If you don't see 'em when you remove the skin, then cut down through the fat and you'll find 'em. Cut 'em out. They're some sort of glands. If you leave the spots and cook 'em that way the meat'll taste awful.

"You remove the spots and cut up your groun'-hawg like you would a chicken. The old folks would set it under a water spout and let the water run over it all night. But it's just as good to set the groun'-hawg in salty brine over night. That takes out the wild taste. And groun'-hawg meat's pretty wild-tastin'.

"Once this has been done you place it in a kettle and cook it until it's barely tender. Then you drain it, salt and pepper it or put whatever you want on it. After this set it in a pan and put it in the stove and let it bake until it's nice and brown.

"And if that don't do it, then you don't like groun'-hawg. But if it's fixed like I tell you there's nothin' finer and you'll become mighty partial to groun'-hawg meat.

"Gettin' back to them brown spots. Can't talk too much about them. Cut 'em out or else you'll get a muddy, funny kind of taste when you start eatin' the meat.

"Another thing that helps, too, is to cut away most of the fat. Cut it off down to the lean, leaving just a sort of thin coverin'. That's where the good eatin' is. Most folks just leave on all the fat and souse themselves in grease before they get to the lean and tasty part.

"Groun'-hawgs, if you didn't know it, are not classed as a game animal. You can kill 'em any time and as many as you want. I usually kill off eight or ten a season for my own wants. Got so I put some away in the deep freeze. I kill 'em, dress 'em, cut 'em up into pieces, then fry 'em up and put 'em in the deep freeze."

Ray paused, looked out the window again. Looked into the gray morning. The groun'-hawg that had been there a moment before was gone.

"They don't like to get too far away from their holes," he said. "They eat a while and then disappear. Then they come back out and eat some more. Stay out until day-down. But soon they'll be holin' up for good."

Ray punched at the fire.

"Folks that know what groun'-hawg meat's really like wouldn't trade it for all the pork there is," he said. "It's mighty sweet and tasty eatin' when it's fixed right.

"Makes mighty good eatin' along about this time of year when it start's turnin' cold up here around Mitchell."

Ray paused. He grinned.

"There was a woman that stopped by here the other day," he said. "She was quite excited. Said she had seen a dozen woodchucks down the road a piece. Said that's what she thought they were. Asked me if that was right. I told her they were groun'-hawgs or whistlepigs. All one and the same, I told her. Asked her if she ever ate any groun'-hawg meat. Said she never had and didn't aim to. Well, everybody to their own choice."

But to Theodore Ray and many another mountain man there's nothing quite like a mess of groun'-hawg meat when it comes to choice mountain vittles.

Whittlin', Swappin', and Throwin'

Burningtown

THE OLD MAN REMEMBERS BEST THE DAYS AND TIMES WHEN folks sat around the country store and talked, or whittled, or swapped knives.

Such memories are inclined to favor the affinity he has for a good keen blade and his love for knife-swapping.

Perhaps this is because the Old Man has the reputation of being just about the knife-swappin'est man ever to strike up a trade in a land where knife-swappin' was born.

He counts his years two-less-than-a-hundred, and he's been swappin', tradin', and throwin' knives since he was twelve or thereabouts.

"I've done a heap of swappin' with knives in my time," said the Old Man. "Folks used to say there wasn't nobody that could beat me when it come to knife-swappin'. Seems like I just had a natural knack for it. Offhand, I don't recollect gettin' beat in a trade. 'Course, I don't aim to worry my mind none with tryin' to think back on the times I got skinned."

He grinned and his eyes twinkled. Like he was huging a secret and was just busting to tell it and knowing all the time that he wouldn't.

"Won't do for a'body to tell everything," he said. "Let's just say it stands to reason a'body that's done as much knife-swappin' as I've done is bound to come out short some times. Fact of matter, it helps a'body's reputation to let hisself get bested on purpose. Keeps folks interested in swappin'.

"Now, back when I was a boy, just about everybody swapped knives. Mostly it was old people and married men. They'd get to swappin' and tradin' and throwin' knives wherever a bunch gathered up. Mostly, it was down at the country store.

"There was always three or four fellers, sometimes more, around the store or at the mill where we took our corn to be ground. Seems like there was more knife-swappin' than anything else. Some times the swappin' and tradin' would go on all day. The grown folks and the old men swapped among themselves. It was rare for a boy to join in with 'em. He had to get an invite and that was hardly ever.

"So us boys got so we'd gather up at the store or the mill and have us a swappin' of our own. We'd have some hot and heavy swappin' and it got so the grown folks would put up their knives and gather around to watch us go at it. Then it got so they'd ask some of us if we didn't want to swap with them.

"A lot of parents wouldn't let their boys swap knives. Figured it wasn't proper for a'body to take up swappin' until they was grown or married. Reckon they figured, too, that us boys was too young to know how to swap without gettin' bad beat.

"But my father wasn't like some hereabouts. He always said a boy ought to take up knife-swappin' soon's he was big enough to reckon the value of a knife. Said it was the best way of learnin' a boy to watch out for hisself. He was right, too. There ain't nothin' like knife-swappin' or knife-tradin' to test a'body's wits.

"It ain't so much in just swappin' knife for knife. It's the boot you get. Takes a lot of talkin' to end up with boot. You've got to have a knife that catches a feller's eye right off and then sort of talk like you wouldn't part with it even with a dollar thrown in to boot. First thing you know, the feller's got such a hankerin' to own that knife that he starts offerin' this and that and then the whole kit and caboodle.

"Wasn't but a few times I ever swapped knives straight out. It didn't take me long to learn that the best knife-swappers was them that always ended up by gettin' boot. Many's the time I've swapped around all day and ended up with the same knife I started with and a dollar or more extra.

"Now, one of the best swappers I ever saw or heard tell of was your grandpa Rufus Parris. He was one of the old timers. He swapped all the time. Why, he'd go to town every day when he didn't have nothin' to do about the place and swap knives. You could usually find him around Dillsboro most any time swappin' knives. I never done much swappin' with him, since I wasn't there much. But the times we did get into a swappin' match it was right worrisome. He wouldn't budge an inch.

"I reckon what little swappin' that wasn't to my advantage was the swappin' I done with him. He always had a knife that looked like it cost a heap of money and set a'body hankerin' for it. It wasn't till you had the knife and got to really examinin' it that you knew you'd lost out in the trade.

"You know, I've always figured a'body ought to always carry at least three knives around with him. One for whittlin', one for swappin', and one for throwin'.

"Now, if you don't know what throwin' knives is, I'll tell you. It's another form of swappin'. Only you don't offer no boot and you trade sight unseen. A feller can shore get beat when it comes to throwin' knives. But there was a heap of fun to it. You'd have a triflin' thing of a knife for throwin'. Maybe it wouldn't even have a blade. Just the handle.

"When you met up with a feller and got into a throwin' bout, you'd reach in your pocket and get out your throwin' piece, all the time keepin' it shut up in your hand so he wouldn't see too much of it. About all you'd let him see was the jaws, just enough to let him see that it could be a knife.

"Then the two that was a throwin' would hold out their fists and put 'em in each other's left hand, still closed. One of the throwers would say 'Let go' and you'd open your hand and drop what you had in the other feller's."

The Old Man got his first knife when he was about four or five years old.

"My father brought it home to me one day," he recalled, "and said it was mine and I was to take good care of it. No, he wasn't afraid I'd cut myself with it. He let all the boys have a knife to carry no sooner than they was knee-high to a grasshopper.

"I kept that knife until I was about nine or ten years old. That's how I came by my first horse. I swapped it to my brother for a calf. Then I swapped the calf to a man in the neighborhood for a mare-horse. I kept the mare long enough to raise a colt. Traded the mare for a yoke of oxen. Traded her to my father. Then I made me a good ridin' horse out of the colt."

The Old Man paused. He shook his head, shook it slowly from side to side as a man will when a regret creeps into his thoughts.

"Folks don't follow knife-swappin' like they used to," he said. "It's hard to find anybody that wants to swap knives any more. Why, it's got so a knife-swapper's as rare as a June-bug in December. I ain't done no swappin' in more than a year now. Nobody wants to swap any more."

But there was a time when folks in the mountains made a habit of knife-swappin'.

It is the time the Old Man remembers best.

A long-ago when folks sat around the country store and talked, or whittled, or swapped knives.

Now, Talk About Freezin' Weather

Sylva

FOLKS COMPLAINING ABOUT THE BITTER COLD NOW GRIPPING the mountain region will get little sympathy from the Old Man.

"Why, this here is only a fairly middlin' cold spell," he said. "Talk about freezin' weather, now we had it back 60 to 80 years ago.

"I've seen it so cold the chickens' combs turned black and dropped off. Even the birds froze to death in their nests. All the rivers iced over so thick you could drive a wagon team across 'em. Tags of ice two and three foot long hung down from the eaves of the houses."

The Old Man paused to light his pipe and there was a twinkle in his blue eyes. He puffed it into life, then grinned at his grandson.

"Maybe you ain't believin' this, but it's a fact as pure as Scripture. Back then we had cold weather and it was a calamity, but folks never complained much. Why, we even had baptisms when we had to chop holes in the ice on the river to put folks under.

"But like I was tellin' you, we don't have cold spells like we used to. Not like when I was comin' up.

"I don't recollect no particular year when it was worse than another back then. Seems like all the winters were full of ice and snow. Can't put no dates to 'em but I can remember how it was and the winters just marched along full of freezin' cold up to 20 or 30 years ago when they got to gettin' warmer.

"When I was a boy over in Macon County I had the job of driving the wagon to the mill and I'd have to get out now and then to chop the ice out of the road so the horses could get through.

"Had ice shoes on my horses, too. What's that? Why they was shoes that had pieces in front about an inch thick that a horse could get a grip in the ice with so it wouldn't slip and fall.

"Why, I've seen many the time when a feller's shoes would

freeze to his stirrups. You know, saddle stirrups was wood in them days and if you got 'em wet or got your feet wet and it as cold as it was your feet would just freeze stuck to 'em. Sometimes you had to have somebody to prise your feet loose from the stirrups.

"After I got married and moved over to Webster we had some powerful freezin' weather. I remember there was times when it was so cold the chickens would just about freeze plumb to death. Their combs would turn all black and then drop off. Even their feet froze and dropped off. That is their toes would and they'd just have stumps sort of to walk around on.

"It wasn't uncommon for the river to freeze over. Many's the time there at Webster when I've seen the river froze over two and three foot thick.

"There was a ford about a mile up above where the bridge is now. Right there where your Great-Grandma Wild lived. Fellers haulin' logs to the sawmill at Dillsboro from up the river would come that way and they'd have to unload their wagons and roll the logs across the ice to the other side and then take their teams across and load 'em up again.

"Everything froze tight back then except the spring. And that spring never did freeze over. Don't know why it didn't. Even the milk froze and it would take her two or three days to thaw it out by the fire before she could churn.

"Folks that had to travel either went by wagon or buggy. And to keep your feet warm you'd heat three or four big rocks in the fireplace and wrap 'em up in a blanket and then put 'em at your feet in the wagon or buggy.

"We didn't have such things as hot water bottles and electric blankets back then. But we had a lot of smoothing irons, the kind you heated in the fire and done the ironin' of clothes with. Your Grandma would heat them irons and put 'em in the bed and that's how we kept our feet warm. Put 'em in all the children's beds, too. A smoothin' iron made a good bed-warmer."

He paused, gave my mother a sly, twinkling look.

"I'd rather have a smoothin' iron than that heatin' pad your mama puts in my bed. If I could find one I'd sure get it and use it.

"We had some big snows as well as ice. Not these little old flour-siftin' kind nowadays. Back then we'd have snow flakes as big as goose feathers. And it'd get three and four feet deep and just make everything all covered up. Why you wouldn't know where the roads was and the fences would all be covered over

"When I worked up at the Hog Rock mines it come such a big snow once that it busted in the roofs of the sheds where we dried the clay we mined. Had to knock off work for a whole week.

"Gettin' back to freezin' weather and the rivers icin' over, I want to tell you about the baptisin's.

"I remember one Baptisin' over in Macon County on Burningtown Creek, There'd been a revival meetin' and there was about 30 folks that had professed religion.

"Well, when they got ready to have the baptisin' the creek was all froze over. But that didn't stop 'em. They went right ahead with it. Some of the fellers got fence rails and broke holes in the ice and the preacher waded right out in there and started dippin' them folks.

"Of course, we had a fire built up there on the bank. The preacher was the one that almost froze to death, but he never give no complaint. He just stayed right there and put them folks under one after the other.

"It was so cold they couldn't make a sound when they come up. Somebody would grab 'em and steer 'em to the bank and put a blanket around 'em and lead 'em over to the fire. They made a sort of cover out of some planks and a quilt where they could get out of their wet clothes and into dry ones. It was a wonder some of 'em didn't die, but I never heard of it a hurtin' any of 'em too much. Leastwise, none of 'em died from it.

"One time they had a baptisin' over at Webster when they had to chop holes in the ice. Well, there was two brothers that was to be dipped. One of 'em was sort of off in the head and when he come out of the water his brother asked him if it was cold and he said no. The one waitin' to be dipped said it didn't do no good to get baptised if a feller was goin' to tell a lie that quick. He said, 'I ain't even been in yet and I'm freezin' to death'."

The Old Man chuckled, took a long puff on his pipe.

"Reckon folks' blood was thicker back in them days than it is now. Anyway, I've always been a Methodist."

Handle-Bar Mustache and Shavin' Mug

Sylva

THE HANDLE-BAR MUSTACHE, THE BROAD-BRIMMED BLACK hat, the big-bellied shaving mug and the celluloid collar belong to a vanishing world.

They have gone the way of jeans britches, hickory striped shirts and brogan shoes.

In the here and now, they are only a memory or a museum piece. Like the old-time country store with its pot-bellied stove, its rack of buggy whips, coal-oil lanterns, spool-thread chest, earthenware demijohns, and grimy checkerboards.

But time was when the handle-bar mustache and the broad-brimmed black hat were the mark of a mountain dandy.

They symbolized the sternness of manhood in the nineties.

The broad-brimmed black hat supplanted the broad-brimmed gray semi-Confederate which made its debut right after the end of the Civil War.

It had a six-inch crown and a three-and-a-half-inch brim. The quality and style was fairly staple. It sold for around a dollar and a half.

Most of them were doleful black. They gave to their wearers a sort of lantern-jawed appearance.

Like the famous split bonnets, the wide-brimmed high-crowned country-store hat became a symbol of a kind of simple but raw country dignity and respectability.

About the only one outside a museum nowadays is one my uncle wears. It's a prime favorite and he treats it well. It's become a part of his personality. Folks from afar recognize him by it.

But the handle-bar mustache he sported as a young man has long since disappeared.

Like the quart-sized mustache cup with its built-in china retaining walls.

A feller with a handle-bar mustache come hard by his coffee drinking unless he had a mustache cup.

Drinking coffee out of an ordinary cup was a chore.

He was forever getting his whiskers in the coffee.

For the fellers with the handle-bars it was a right welcome day when somebody invented the mustache cup and the merchants started stocking them.

The mustache cup sported china dashers. These dashers fought back the unruly ends of the handle-bar mustaches from the coffee.

They made it so a man didn't have to suck his whiskers. They kept the whiskers from dripping coffee on their shirt fronts.

The mustache cups were fancy. They were adorned with lurid sprays of flowers or lodge emblems. Most of them carried legends such as "Think of Me," "Father," "A Present," and "A Souvenir."

Companion piece to the mustache cup was the big-bellied shaving mug.

A shaving mug, with its heavy, round, looping handle, was as necessary as a straight razor.

The two went together like soap and water.

But unlike the mustache cups, potters were little influenced by the gaudy art of their day in the manufacture of these mugs.

Their primary concern was to make a receptacle that would hold a cake of soap with reasonable firmness.

Along with the advent of barber shops, most men became two-mug owners. They kept one mug at home, the other at the barber shop.

The barber shop was a sort of gathering place and the menfolks would drop by for a shave, a game of checkers or a yarn-spinning session.

The shaving mugs were lined up in a row on a shelf. Each bore the owner's name or an identifying symbol.

As a young man, my father owned a barber shop in Dillsboro. Dr. Charles Candler and Judge Joe Hooker kept their shaving mugs there. When he sold out there were 22 shaving mugs on the shelf. He fetched his own home, the one with his name in gold, and used it for more than forty years.

Back when he was barbering, a shave was ten cents and a haircut was fifteen. A shoeshine was a nickel. He stocked paper collars that came a dozen to a box and sold for three cents a piece. In time he handled celluloid collars that fetched from a dime to 20 cents.

Along with a shave, a shoeshine and a collar went a bottle of soda-water.

This was the era of the pique vest and the gold watch-chain.

The bigger the watch-chain the more affluent the man.

Until the late nineties the common everyday shoe was the formless brogan that retailed at prices from $1.50 to $2.50 a pair.

The brogan was companion to jeans britches and hickory striped shirts.

They went out with the advent of store-bought clothes.

A man could outfit himself from head to foot for $25. This included a coat, a pair of pants, a vest, a pair of shoes, a pair of socks, a shirt, a black necktie and a pair of gloves.

But those days are gone. They are only a memory. They belong to a vanishing world.

The vanishing world of the handle-bar mustache, the broad-brimmed black hat, the big-bellied shaving mug and the celluloid collar.

Hearts A 'Bustin' With Love

Always Money in Galaxin'

Old Fort

THE GALAX MARKET IS ONE OF THE MOST STABLE IN THE whole wide world.

Like diamonds and gold, it has bucked hard times and depressions and laughed at Wall Street and the men who gamble in man-made things.

For almost half a century many a mountain man has been using galax leaves for money.

Right now the market is booming—just as it does every year about this time—for galax has become synonymous with Christmas, and the round heart-shaped leaves of bronze and wine-red are fetching a pretty penny in the florist trade.

As a decoration in wreaths and sprays and nosegays, galax is one of the prettiest in the world and one of the rarest.

It is rare because it grows only in the mountains of North Carolina, Virginia and Georgia, and the choicest gathering grounds are in our own Blue Ridge, Smokies and Balsams.

And this means mountain folks, what with such other evergreens as balsam, spruce and hemlock, have got a livelihood to fall back on if the worst comes to the worst.

For galax leaves have taken the fancy of city florists.

Even during the depression, there was a steady market for them in the North where they are used for funeral wreaths.

As an industry confined to our mountains, gallackin'—that's what mountain folks call gathering the leaves—is comparatively new.

Some folks say that T. N. Woodruff up at Low Gap started it back in 1907 when he visited a florist friend in New York and took him a few bunches of galax leaves as a gift.

The florist recognized galax as a plant that could work for him the year round and immediately placed orders for all Woodruff would supply. That set Woodruff up into business and opened up a thriving trade for the mountain folks.

And it wasn't long until other folks grabbed onto the idea and began to hire mountain folks to scour the hills for galax.

A few years later, J. B. Haynes, who was living up on Buck Creek, some 15 or 20 miles northeast of here, got into the business.

Now some 45 years later, Haynes is one of the top gallackers in all the mountains, with a galax and evergreen "factory" here in Old Fort from which he ships out thousands of pounds of galax leaves and other evergreens week in and week out during the year.

"I reckon," he said today, which, incidentally, was his 79th birthday, "I'm one of the original galax pickers and buyers.

"When I started out up on Buck Creek I went into the woods and gallacked myself. Gallackin' is back-breakin' work, but a feller can count on it for an income even in hard times. Seems like there's always a market for galax leaves. And the price don't change much. It's pretty steady, although in good times a feller will get more than when hard money is scarce.

"Back when I went into the galax business I'd gather more than half of what I shipped out. Ain't done no gallackin' myself for nigh on to ten or fifteen years. Been in bad health, or else I'd be out in the woods myself a'gatherin' with the rest of the folks here in the mountains.

"You ask how much I sold back in them days, back 20 and 30 and 40 years ago. Well, I'll tell you. It was like this. I'd sell maybe three to five thousand pounds of galax. That's a heap of galax leaves. Now I sell more than 5,000 pounds a week and could sell more if I could get it."

He paused and shook his head, like a man who can't figure out why folks turn up their nose at a dollar bill lying in the street.

"It's gettin' harder and harder to find gallackers. All these big plants going up here in the mountains is gettin' folks to workin' on the inside and it's mighty hard to find folks that'll go out in the woods and pick galax.

"Reckon they know if they lose their job they can always go back to gallackin'. Course they make more money in the plants and they work inside. And that's a big temptation to a man that has to work outside in all sorts of weather, bendin' his back and gathering galax from the floor of the forest.

"Pay is better, too. But a feller don't never need to starve if he don't want to. Not here in the mountains, anyway. He can always get himself some money with a few galax leaves.

"Back when I started out in the galax business, folks got 25 cents for every thousand galax leaves they picked. Don't sound like much money now, but it was a lot in them days. A good gallacker could earn between two and three dollars a day, but he sure knew he'd done a day's work.

"Now," he said, "I pay gallackers a dollar a thousand leaves. Some of 'em can make as much as $10 or $12 a day. That ain't bad wages. If they was to work at it steady it'd be as much as they'd make in some of the places folks work on the inside, maybe more. Of course, it's a lot harder and a lot more tirin'. A feller's back gets mighty stiff and ackin' bendin' over day-long pickin' galax.

"But there's a lot of fellers that can't seem to get work and they just sit around and fret about not bein' able to find a job. All the time there's a job awaitin' for them if they'd only get up and get out into the woods and pick galax leaves.

"There's thousands and thousands of galax leaves a-growin' all over these mountains just waitin' to be picked and I'm just a-waitin' for folks to bring 'em in and get hard cash for 'em."

Haynes sells galax by the cases, the demand is so great. There's 10,000 leaves to a case.

"Back 15 to 20 years ago I'd sell about 20 cases," he said. "And I thought that was big business. And I reckon it was. Now I sell from a thousand to two thousand cases a year, and that's a heap of galax leaves."

A heap? Well, figuring 10,000 leaves to a case, it adds up to between 10 and 20 million leaves. And when you take into consideration there are places in Asheville, Burnsville and Low Gap that do a big business in galax and other evergreens you are not surprised that the evergreen business in Western North Carolina is a million-dollar-a-year industry.

"My gallackers," Haynes said, "gather galax pretty much the year round. They pick the old leaves first. They're good to summer. They die in the fall. Cold weather and sunshine causes them to turn from green to bronze. When they die they turn yellow.

"Back when galax first hit the market, I'd get orders for wine-red leaves in the summer from florists who didn't seem to know that red galax leaves have a season, too, just like berries. Took some time to straighten 'em out.

"Course I handle things other than galax. Folks got so they've learned about other evergreens we've got here in the mountains. And we do a big trade in dagger fern and hemlock and boxwood cuttings. I reckon we do almost as big a business in rhododendron at Christmastime as we do in galax.

"But there again I can't keep up with the market because there ain't enough pickers. If I had the pickers I could get rid of three or four hundred more cases than I do. What's that? How much is in a case? Well, there's fifty pounds of rhododendron leaves to a case.

"Now them dagger ferns is right purty. They're green in winter same as they are in summer. Even when it snows. The snow just rides them down to the ground and flattens 'em out, and when it melts you can pick 'em and they're just as purty as you please.

"No, I ain't sellin' much holly and mistletoe this year. This is a bad holly season. The cold spell last spring killed the holly in the bud and it ain't got berries.

"As for the mistletoe, I could sell all I could get. But it's hard to come by. It's well-bearin' this year, but hard to get. I tell my pickers to pass it up if they have to skin too high in the trees. That's too dangerous. Don't want none of my pickers gettin' hurt. So I tell 'em to just forget about it if it's too high in the trees.

"Mountain laurel is bringing a good price and is good on the market right now, too. I sell about 5,000 pounds a week and would sell more if I could get it. Like I say, pickers are scarce.

"But to get back to galax. It's the best there is for earnin' a man some spendin' money for the things he needs. Good times or bad times, galax will fetch money.

"Why, back in the old days when money was almost unknown in some parts of the hills, trade was carried on with galax leaves.

"When a feller needed a few store-bought supplies, he sent his folks to the woods to gather galax leaves and then took 'em to the store and traded 'em for cloth or whatever he needed.

"Times ain't changed much. A feller can still count on galax to fetch him money and the things he needs. It's just like money in a feller's pocket."

And that, J. B. Haynes will tell you, is why the galax market is the most stable in the world.

There's He-Holly and She-Holly
Sapphire

DARKNESS SPREAD DOWN FROM THE HILLS AND THE OLD woodsman watched the night chase the last shadows away.

In that magic moment of cold blue twilight, when earth and sky meld their colors, there was something about him that reminded you of the jovial, benevolent carrier of the Christmas message.

Perhaps it was the way he laughed, deep down and lusty and rolling, or maybe it was the white hair and white mustaches, the rosy tint of his round face, the shortness and the plumpness of him, the elfish twinkle of his blue eyes.

There was a feeling that if he had half a mind to he could whistle up his reindeer, and that the suit of blue denim he wore was really a garment of red, trimmed with ermine.

Something tugged at you, something seen and yet something not really seen, trying to pull you back there to the barn where the crude sled, with its handhewn runners, had been drawn with its load of hickory logs.

Was it really just a little old sled, like your grandfather used to bring wood from the hills long ago, or was it a handsome sleigh waiting to be piled high with the things many a boy and girl expected?

The old woodsman laid aside his ax and we moved into the cabin and took a chair before the fire.

On a table in the corner, like a parade out of Noah's Ark, a host of wood-carvings stood at attention. A fox, a bear, a rabbit, a horse, a turtle.

And there was an angel, carved from holly.

The feeling was still there. And you expected a host of little men in green with turned-up shoes to come marching out of the deep shadows.

The old woodsman stretched out his short legs, and the firelight danced on his face and on his white mustaches and his white hair.

"Christmas holly?" he said. "You wanted to know about Christmas holly and mistletoe? Well, there's a-plenty if a feller knows where to look for it. I reckon if I was a mind to I could steer you to just about the prettiest holly you ever laid your eyes on. Now, I ain't saying I won't. But I know where there's holly the likes that few eyes have ever seen.

"Trouble is," he said, that elfish twinkle in his eyes, "folks have got so they don't appreciate the things that grow in the woods, and I ain't about to see the pretty things destroyed."

He took the angel from the table.

"Carved it out of holly," he said. "White like it should be. Carved it here by the fire at nights when I had nothing else to do but sit and think back. And thinking back sometimes ain't good for a man.

"So I took my knife and I whittled it out. Just like you see it. Wings and all. Whittled it out to give to the boy here, maybe."

He turned to the boy who sat at his feet, eyes worshipping the man in the cane-bottomed chair.

The boy was twelve. He had come to live with the old man when he was small. And like the woodsman, he knew the name of every tree that grew in the woods. He knew, because the old woodsman had told him, where the holly was best and how a boy could get mistletoe.

The things that the woodsman carved with his pocketknife were wondrous things in the eyes of the boy who somehow talked as a child and lived as a man.

The boy did not expect things that he did not earn. And to him Christmas, which was coming on, would be a time when he and the old woodsman could rest before the fire and talk man-talk.

Somehow you knew that the old woodsman and the boy would see Christmas a little different from most folks. There would be no trees with glittering lights. There would be none of the things that most boys and girls could expect to find under the tree.

But, looking at the boy and the old woodsman, you knew that to them Christmas would be sort of special. That just being together would make it something that few folks ever feel.

"Me and the boy," said the old woodsman, "we know where there is more holly and more mistletoe, growing natural-like, than folks have ever seen.

"It's pretty growing out there in the hills. That's where it should stay. Like I say, folks don't appreciate it. They come in and tear limbs off the trees and go away and the tree becomes like a dwarf, all deformed and maybe die.

"I cut a little holly for my friends. And I use some of the wood to make a few things, like that angel. It's the prettiest wood in the world. And it's a blessing that it don't grow no bigger than it does, or else all the holly would have been destroyed long ago.

"For forty years I was an axman. I worked for men that cut trees all over. You might say I helped to fell the biggest trees there was in these parts. But I've got a feeling for trees now. Did you ever stop to think what the world would be like if there won't no trees? It'd be a sorry sight.

"Every year more and more folks come out from the cities and towns and gather holly. They rip it off the limbs. It'd be just as easy if they sawed 'em off with an ax. Tearing off the limbs leaves 'em open to disease and death."

For a moment he was silent, staring into the fire.

"Holly is prettiest a-growin' out in the woods," he said, finally. "When you run on a whole bunch of holly just a-growin' there like God meant for it to, why there's nothin' like it.

"Shore, I know. Folks have got so they got to have holly at Christmas. And as long as they can get to it easy-like they'll get it and make wreaths and use it for Christmas trees.

"If you notice, all the holly's about gone from along the highways. Been stripped by folks at Christmastime. But there's still a lot of it here in the mountains, way back where folks don't go.

"Seems to me like I've never seen the berries so red and full as they are now. Maybe it's because I'm gettin' old and they look sort of different. Some folks remember things they've seen years ago as different. Like they ain't what they once was. But I see things a-puttin' out like they never put out before. Maybe it's because I'm a gettin' on in years and I've got a sort of feelin' for everything that grows about me.

"Guess you didn't know there was he-holly and she-holly. Well, there is. Only she-holly has berries. You hear folks talk about years when there ain't no berries on the trees. They're folks that don't know nothin' about the woods. They just happened to see he-holly.

"Some years the she-holly don't bear as heavy as others. But you'll never find a she-holly without berries. They're bearin' heavy this year.

"You asked me about mistletoe. Well, there's a-plenty of it, too. Seems like there's more mistletoe than I can ever remember seein'.

"Now, mistletoe is something that a-body can get all he wants 'cause it seems to just keep a-growin' no matter how much you gather. Seems to me like every oak I look up into has got a passel of it growin'.

"There's plenty of berries on it this year, too. Reckon you know, mistletoe ain't easy to come by. Hardest thing in the world to get. Grows right in the top branches of oak. Some folks shoot it out with a gun. But they lose most of the berries if they ain't good shots. Now, if you've got a boy like the one here, he can skin up a tree and bring it down.

"Did you ever hear that mistletoe was good for the toothache? I never tried it but I've heard that it is. Some of the old timers said they learned it from the Indians. If you had a toothache, you got some mistletoe and chewed the berries and it stopped the pain right quick."

For a moment, the woodsman looked into the fire.

"Now, I can get you some holly," he said, "that is if you won't ask to go along with me to where I get it. It'll be full of berries, the reddest you ever saw, and the prettiest. Won't get much, but it'll be enough for your needs. Make a pretty thing for you."

The boy tugged at the old woodsman's knee.

"You'll let me go with you, won't you, Henry?" he said. "I want to get me a piece of pure holly and carve me an angel like the one you whittled out."

And Henry Alexander, the old woodsman with the white hair and the white mustaches, nodded his head and smiled at the boy.

In that moment you had the feeling that this was the house where the Christmas spirit was always a part of life.

And in the flickering firelight the shadows danced upon the face of a little man who reminded you of the jovial, benevolent carrier of the Christmas message.

Ghostly Choir of Roan Mountain

Roan Mountain

LONELY HERDSMEN KEEPING WATCH OVER THEIR CATTLE first heard the whispering tune of the ghostly choir here atop this mile-high plateau back in the 70's.

They listened with superstitious awe to the mysterious music and some said maybe it was the angels tuning up for Judgment Day.

The herdsmen fetched the story of the rare phenomenon into the valley and a legend began to grow.

Folks born with the wisdom of the ageless hills allowed a-body had no cause to be surprised at anything that happened on the Roan.

Why, since time out of memory, folks caught on the Roan during a thunderstorm had been seeing a circular rainbow that just might be God's Halo.

And down on the dark, balsam-covered slopes there were times when the fir trees made music for the Lord when He caused the wind to blow.

But on the Roan the wind was different, like it was the devil's wind, catching up the clouds and whirling them about the mountain.

It was a wind the like of which John Strother, a member of the boundary surveying commission back in 1799, had never known.

In his diary he wrote:

"There is no shrubbery growing on the tops of this mountain for several miles, and the wind has such power on top of this mountain that the ground is blowed in deep holes all over the northwest side."

He made no mention of hearing the humming of the ghostly choir.

But the herdsmen heard it and so did Colonel John Wilder

who, in 1878, built a summer resort hotel atop the Roan where his guests could sleep in Tennessee and have their meals in North Carolina without ever going out of the hotel.

The story of the humming music of the Roan was an old thing when Colonel Wilder came to the mountain.

He passed it on to his guests and to his friends over in Tennessee.

Until then nobody had bothered to offer a scientific reason for the phenomenon.

Some who heard it on an afternoon just before there was a thunderstorm in the valley or while one was passing over the mountain described it as a noise like the humming of thousands of bees.

A scientist named Henry E. Colton came over from Knoxville, heard the ghostly sound, and went away to publish a treatise on the phenomenon in his hometown newspaper.

"Several of the cattle tenders on the mountain and also General Wilder had spoken to us about what they called 'Mountain Music'," Colton wrote.

"One evening they said it was sounding loud, and Dr. D. P. Boynton of Knoxville, Hon. J. M. Thornburg, and myself accompanied General Wilder to the glen to hear it.

"The sound was very plain to the ear, and was not at all as described—like the humming of thousands of bees—but like the incessant, continuous and combined snap of two Leyden jars positively and negatively charged.

"I tried to account for it on the theory of bees or flies but the mountain people said it frequently occurred after the bees or flies had gone to their winter homes or before they came out.

"It was always loudest and most prolonged just after there would be a thunderstorm in either valley, or one passing over the mountain.

"I used every argument I could to persuade myself that it simply was a result of some common cause and to shake the faith of the country people in its mysterious origin but I only convinced myself that it was the result from two currents of air meeting each other in the suck between the two peaks where there was no obstruction of trees, one containing a greater, the other a less amount of electricity. . . ."

"Or," Colton wrote, "that the two currents coming together in the open high plateau on the high elevation, by their friction and being of different temperatures, generated electricity.

"The 'Mountain Music' was simply the snapping caused by this friction and this generation of electricity. Many have noted the peculiar snapping hum to be observed in great auroral displays, particularly those of September 1859 and February 1872."

Then he went on to explain that the air currents of the Western North Carolina mountains and the East Tennessee Valley form an aerial tide, ebbing and flowing.

"The heated air of the valley," he said "rises from eight in the morning until three or four in the afternoon, making a slight easterly wind, up and over the Roan Mountain.

"As night comes on the current turns back into the valley, almost invariably producing a very brisk gale by three or four o'clock in the morning, which in turn dies down to a calm by seven o'clock and commences to reverse itself by 9'clock."

Guests who stayed at the mile-high Cloudland Hotel said when the wind roared across the mountain it was like being on a ship at sea, with the structure seeming to rock and sway.

Despite Colton's theory, there were mountain folks who went right on believing that the origin of the humming sound came from the angels.

If you will take the road here and the time is right you will hear the ghostly tune.

Maybe you, too, will allow that it's the angels humming and that the circular rainbow in the sky really is God's Halo.

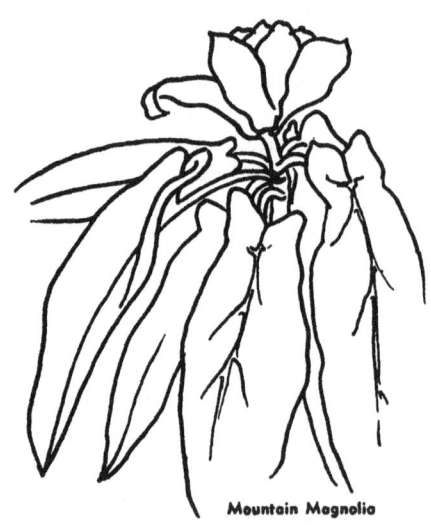

Mountain Magnolia

Of the Chimes and the Gift of Life

Sylva

IN OUR TOWN THE CHRISTMAS CHIMES GO SKIRLING ACROSS the winter night, and sometimes they give voice to an old, old carol.

The chimes are a memorial to a man who, on another Christmas long ago, brought the gift of life into a small cabin deep in the hidden hills.

And when they carol *The First Noel*, the one the shepherds sang, there's just a chance that someone is reminded of the story the doctor sometimes told in those rare and treasured moments of things recollected.

Of that Christmas long ago, only the stars and the spirit live on.

The baby—the one to whom they gave the strange name—has been forgotten and become lost in the tides of time and indifference.

And the others—the boy with a dream, the old granny woman, the young-old woman who came to her hour, and the father who blockaded—have all passed on.

But this is the way it happened. This is the way the boy remembered it years later when he spun out his last days as a beloved country doctor.

This is the way Asbury Nichols told it. . . .

He was barely 18 at the time, which was at the turn of the century. His brothers were doctors and his dream was to be a doctor, too. And he spent as much time with each as he could afford, watching and listening and reading medicine.

He lived on the western border of the state where the country was rugged and where the granny woman was usually preferred to a doctor. Or else a mother struggled through her hour the best she could.

It was the night before Christmas and in his brother's home there was tinsel and the spirit of Christmas although the brother was ailing with a cold that had tied him to the hearthfire for the past two days.

Snow had been falling since midafternoon and was beginning to pile in deep drifts. A north wind herded the whirling flakes and drove them against the window.

There was a knock on the door and young Asbury opened it to admit a little old lady whose head was bound with a shawl. He recognized her as "Granny Meg," a midwife in her sixties who was known throughout the countryside.

"I've come for the doctor," she said. "Hamm Waldrup's wife Biddy is laborin' somethin' awful. I've got the miseries in my hands and was afraid I couldn't catch the baby."

The older brother—the doctor—explained he was sick and couldn't go.

"But Asbury can go," he said. "He knows about as much as I do. Together you can see the woman through."

And a moment later, young Asbury and the old woman slipped out into the night and began trudging through the snow along the torturous miles to the cabin on Panther Creek.

The valley was gone, the trees, the rocks, the ground. The trees were only a gray blur against a grayer moving curtain. The lantern the boy carried was a faint star of ice-blue in the night.

Even in good weather the trail up Panther Creek was a torturous climb, rocky and steep, dwindling half-way up the four-mile stretch to the Waldrup cabin into a narrow footpath flanked by rhododendron and a little stream.

Now the trail was buried under knee-deep snow, a trail to be followed by instinct and the familiarity of much mountain travel.

At last they came to the cabin, perched precariously on the side of the mountain overlooking Panther Creek. The wind had died down and the snow was falling in great flakes.

The old woman rattled the door, then called, "It's me, Meg," and then pushed into the cabin with the boy at her heels.

"Never thought I'd get back," she said, untieing her shawl. To the woman lying on a bunk in the corner, she said: "You all right, Biddy?"

From the bed came a thin, tired voice. "As well as I've a right to be, I reckon. The pain ain't so bad just now. But it's still awful. I never recollect it bein' as bad as this with any of the others."

The boy stood silent, taking in the scene. There was only one room to the cabin, about ten by 12 feet. There were no beds, only bunks. A couple or three cane-bottomed straight chairs, a rustic table.

The woman lay on one of the bunks, the husband on another.

The man spoke up, never hinting that he was about to get up. "Strained my back," he said. "Got a cold, too. I've got the miseries bad."

The old granny woman spoke to the boy and said, "Take the bucket and get some water from the spring. We'll need lots of water." And all the while she stood before the fire rubbing her hands.

When the boy returned with the water, the old woman said: "It ain't enough I've got the miseries in my hands. Seems like they're froze, too. Ain't got no feelin' in 'em."

The boy remembered what he had read in his brothers' doctor books and what they had told him, but that all seemed strange now, and he was a bit scared. He wondered if he would do it right. Sometimes, he remembered his brothers had told him, you had to force the baby and sometimes you lost it.

The woman on the bunk cried out and the old granny woman nodded her head.

"I think her time is about come," she said. "You get over there and get ready to catch the baby. I'll tell you what do do."

The moans grew into screams and the woman's face was something awful to behold and the boy bit his lips and he felt hot and there was moisture on his forehead.

But he moved to the woman, drew back the covers, and swallowed the lumps that were big as his fist in his throat.

"Is your knife sharp?" the old granny woman asked him.

"It's sharp enough," he said.

To the man lying on the other bunk, the old woman said: "Where do you keep the hog-lard? In the cupboard?"

The man grunted, then said, "There on the bottom shelf, what there is."

The she asked, "You got any string?" and the man told her to look there on the mantel and she would find a little ball wound round a piece of paper.

There was a cry born of knifing pain, then a trembling whimper.

The boy and the old granny woman bent over the convulsing woman.

The two of them worked in silence, the boy suddenly strong with a new-found faith.

Finally, it was over, and the boy held the baby in his hands. And when it made no sound, he held it by the heels and gave it a whack that brought a tiny, thin cry, just like his brothers had told him to do.

Later, much later, he lowered the squalling baby to the bed, now wrapped in a piece of flannel torn from an old but clean nightgown. And he tucked the covers about it as it nestled in the arms of the mother.

The woman opened her eyes and tried to smile at him through the pinched skin of her young-old face.

The old granny woman said, "This makes the eighth or ninth one, don't it? Somehow, I can't recollect."

Across the room, the man on the other bunk spoke up.

"Nine," he said. "And I reckon this'll be the last 'un."

The old woman said, "I plumb forgot. What about the others? Where are they?"

"Sent most of 'em off to their granny's," he said. "The two youngest 'uns are up there in the loft, asleep or scared to death."

The man raised up, threw off the covers. He had on his pants and shirt and his socks. He put his feet onto the floor and slipped them into his shoes.

"Come with me, boy," he said. "Reckon you could do with a tetch of whisky."

The boy and the man went outside and back of the house to a little lean-to, where the man produced a jug and a tin cup and poured out a cupful which the boy drank.

Then they went back in to the fire.

"We was just talkin' about a name for the baby," the old woman said. "Biddy says she ain't thought none about it. What about you, Hamm?"

"I ain't give no thought to it, neither," he said. "Fact is, we done run out of names. Reckon there ain't no hurry. We'll get a name in time."

The old granny woman shook her head, "It's got to be done now. You got one, boy?" she said.

And the boy thought a minute, almost hesitant to speak the thing that had come to him, remembering as he suddenly did that this was a special night.

"I don't know," he said. "Maybe—maybe, I would call it Noel. Then folks would know he was born on Christmas."

"I think that's a pretty name," said the woman with the young-old face. "It soulds so gentle-like. Never heard it before. I like it."

For a moment she looked at her husband.

"If it's all right with you, Hamm, that's what it'll be."

"Call him anything you like," the man said. "A name's a name." And then, almost shyly, he added:

"Whatever you want."

So it was that the baby was named Noel.

And then the boy and the granny woman got into their coats, and the old woman opened the door and they went into the night.

The closing door shut from sight the bareness of the cabin where there was only a new-born baby with the name of Noel to remind the mother and the father and the other children that it was Christmas.

Overhead, the stars had come out and the boy looked up at them. Years later he would remember them as the brightest stars he had ever seen.

And now more than half a century later, only the stars and the spirit live on.

In our town the Christmas chimes go skirling across this winter night, a joyous voice tinkling the air of an old, old carol.

From the church tower where they ring it is only a few steps to the house where the beloved country doctor came to live and die, the one who brought the gift of life into a small cabin deep in the hidden hills that Christmas long ago.

And somehow, I have the feeling that he can hear the chimes as they float through the night, whispering *The First Nol*.

Holly

About the Author

JOHN PARRIS, SAYS EDWARD R. MURROW, IS TRUE TO HIS upbringing— "A Carolina mountain boy who went out and looked at the big world and then came back to the mystery and music of the mountains to write a column for *The Asheville Citizen*. To do what most reporters would like to do—to write of the people and places where his rootholds are."

He was born in Sylva, North Carolina, on November 23, 1914. At thirteen, he began working for his home town newspaper, the *Jackson County Journal*, and as correspondent for *The Asheville Citizen-Times*. In 1934 he joined the United Press, working in the Raleigh (N. C.) Bureau, two years later moved on to New York to become a by-lined feature writer. He came back to North Carolina for a year as roving correspondent for the *Winston-Salem Journal*, then rejoined United Press as cable editor and in 1941 was sent by UP to London where he covered the diplomatic run until 1944, taking time out from the homburg hat and striped trouser beat to cover the North African invasion. Shortly thereafter he joined the Associated Press in London, holding the post of diplomatic correspondent until 1946 when AP transferred him to New York to cover the United Nations. Finally, in 1947, he left the AP to return to Western North Carolina and devote his future to creative writing. In 1951 he became director of public relations of the Cherokee Historical Association which produces the outdoor Indian drama *Unto These Hills*.

In February, 1955, John undertook what Ed Murrow considers "just about the best assignment any reporter could wish for— roving the hills of Western North Carolina and writing a column called *Roaming the Mountains* for *The Asheville Citizen-Times*."

The best of his earlier columns were published in book form in late 1955 under the title *Roaming the Mountains*. He also is the author of *The Cherokee Story* and he co-authored *Springboard to Berlin* and *Deadline Delayed*.

Parris was married on August 17, 1946, to Dorothy Luxton Klenk, an artist-designer of New York and Topeka, Kansas. They now live in his home town of Sylva.

www.ingramcontent.com/pod-product-compliance
Lightning Source LLC
Chambersburg PA
CBHW032151080426
42735CB00008B/663